A
Radical Change
in Your
Approach to
Life

The Teachings of Joshua

A Radical Change in Your Approach to Life

By Gary Temple Bodley

To Lili, my love, without you I would miss the best part of life.

Other Titles by Gary Temple Bodley

The Teachings of Joshua

A Perception of Reality
Health, Wealth, and Love

Visit

theteachingsofjoshua.com

Contents

My Story

Just over a year ago, I surprisingly became the voice of a group of non-physical teachers known as "Joshua." During this remarkable period in my life, Joshua has written three exciting books that document their understanding of the mechanism of physical reality, the Law of Attraction, and the power of universal forces. They have also answered hundreds of fascinating questions from various people all over the world. As I sit and re-read every word they have written, through me, I am still stunned by their depth of clarity and their remarkable ability to convey their knowledge in practical terms. I am elated to be a part of it.

I am an unlikely channel. Although I have come to discover many other channels who are great teachers living today, I never imagined that I'd be one of them. It seemed an unlikely path for me to follow. Until very recently, I had almost zero awareness that channeling existed other than from watching John Edwards' show *Crossing Over*. But once I witnessed Esther Hicks channeling Abraham, I had no doubt that she was a true channel. I have since come to know many other channels such as Story Waters, Veronica Torres, Darryl Anka, and Jane Roberts who channeled Seth. These are all people who can speak the words that are being given to them. I cannot do that yet. I, like Neale Donald Walsch (author of *Conversations with God*), channel the Teachings of Joshua through writing.

I believe I was led to the higher vibration that allowed me to tap into the consciousness of Joshua. I also believe that anyone can do it. You can tap into the infinite intelligence inside you once you reach a certain level of consciousness. This book will teach you that process along with so much more.

For me, the process started with a deeply held belief that there was something more going on in the world. I could not explain it as a child, and as I grew older I became interested in learning about the philosophy of success. One of the first books in this genre I read was *Think and*

Grow Rich by Napoleon Hill. This was the first indication I had that one's thoughts play a part in one's reality. I went on to read all kinds of spiritual and motivational books by all sorts of authors. I read Deepak Chopra, Dr. Wayne Dyer, Tony Robbins, Eckhart Tolle, and many others. Each book was a step to a new level of awareness. My wife Lili and I watched documentaries such as *What the Bleep Do We Know!?* and *The Secret.* Eventually we were led to the audio CD *Ask and It Is Given* by Esther and Jerry Hicks.

I was led, step by step, to the teachings of Abraham. I have since learned that this is just how the universe works. You are presented with something that will alter your beliefs, and then you are presented with the next belief-altering step. Soon you find yourself at the point of manifestation of that which you truly want. Once it arrives, it's just the next logical step. After all that reading, I was prepared for Abraham.

Lili and I traveled to Asheville, NC in November of 2011 to attend our first Abraham Seminar. Our lives were transformed as a result of that weekend. We both decided to follow our passions and do what we wanted to do. At the time I had a small-business marketing firm that I did not enjoy, and Lili wasn't doing anything she enjoyed. Within a few weeks of that seminar, I closed my marketing company and started buying and renovating homes full-time. This had always been my passion since I bought my first investment house after graduating college some twenty-four years earlier. Yet, for some unknown reason, I did it as a hobby while I ran many other businesses.

Lili went on to do something even more life-changing. She opened a completely unique kind of furniture store called The Painted Ox. She would buy estate-quality furniture that was worn but had good bones, and completely re-imagine and re-design each piece. She opened a 4,000 square-foot store, hired painters and upholsterers, and has since become famous for her creations. All of this was achieved without any specific education or experience in this field. It was something she just wanted to do.

So, after becoming students of Abraham and attending many seminars, reading the books and listening to the bi-monthly CDs, Lili and I created our new lives based in joy and passion. We attracted many new friends who were also interested in this spiritual awakening and have found that many of our existing friends were also secretly fascinated by all of this. We found an old house in our dream neighborhood and took our time renovating it. It is now our home and is everything we had imagined. In fact, it will be featured as one of five homes in a new book about Palm Beach design.

After listening to Abraham for a while we understood that meditation could be an extremely helpful practice. However, neither of us had meditated before and we weren't sure if it would be enjoyable. Finally, we gave in and gave it a go. It turned out to be quite enjoyable.

We began meditating every morning to the guided meditations of Abraham as presented by Esther Hicks. At first, I struggled to get through the fifteen-minute exercises. In the beginning I could not last longer than five or six minutes at a time. All the while my thoughts were fluttering about as they normally do. However, I was soon able to complete the full fifteen minutes. Although my mind continued to wander, there were true moments of silence and calm.

I began to look forward to and enjoy each meditation. Lili and I would lie in bed each morning and play the meditations on her phone with our dog, Rocky, lying between us. After months of consistent meditation, I started to notice that many of my inner questions were answered immediately. I suspected it was just me answering my own questions, since the inner voice that was posing the queries was identical to the one providing the answers. I had assumed that if I was asking God, or Abraham, or my inner self a question, the entity answering the question would sound different. Eventually, I came to the realization that I was tapping into something larger than myself.

I began asking all kinds of questions and receiving answers that seemed to make a whole lot of sense. Instead of discounting the validity of the answers, as I would have done in the past, I chose to believe they came from somewhere or someone inside. It wasn't me answering my own questions; it was communication from another realm. In Abraham vernacular, I believed the communication was coming from "nonphysical." I was tapping into infinite intelligence, as Abraham calls it.

Okay, that's great. Infinite intelligence is now communicating with me. Abraham has always said it is available to everyone, but I thought I was the last one who could ever actually get to that vibration. I certainly wasn't going to tell anyone about it, but I was going to play with it.

If I lost my keys I would simply ask, "Where are my keys?" and the location would pop into my head. I made a habit of saying "Thank you" on each such occurrence. I always had tremendous difficulty remembering names, so much so that it was nearly a full-blown phobia. Suddenly, though, all I had to do was ask and the name would come to me. "Thank you again," I would say to whoever was giving me the answers.

Sometime in October 2013, I thought I would ask this entity its name. I immediately received the answer "Joshua." Believe me when I tell you that I was skeptical of whatever was happening to me. I was sure I was simply inventing the name.

As my meditations continued, I started inviting Joshua in to see what would happen. Soon, I felt a presence inside my body as I lay there meditating. It started slowly, first in my jaw and then in the right side of my head, then it moved into my entire body. The degree of this sensation varied during each meditation. One day it would be subtle and take a long time to progress, another day it would happen instantly and be obvious. It always started in my jaw and the right side of my head and expanded throughout my body from there.

On November 18, 2013, during a meditation, I heard Joshua clearly as they said, "Write, write, write!" I felt compelled to write like never before. Immediately after meditation that day I sat down at my computer and started typing. I can only type with three fingers, but the speed at which I was typing was amazing. It was so fast and furious. I could not look away from the keyboard. I just kept typing until I was exhausted. The first session lasted about an hour and when it was done, I printed out about four pages and shared them with Lili. We were stunned. It was obvious to both of us that this was not coming from me.

The next day after meditation I was urged to write again and in an hour another four pages came out. The transmission took off just as the previous writing was finished. It looked seamless, like it had been written in one session. Day after day I would write for an hour every morning after meditation and we saw a complete book being written. There was no outline, no re-writes, no editing other than typos and grammatical fixes. It was simply translation. It was as if someone was reading me the book and I was translating it onto the written page.

In eight weeks the book was completed. It was Joshua's first book, titled *A Perception of Reality* and it turned out to be nearly three hundred pages in length. This was no quick eBook; this was a significant manuscript. The day after that book was finished, a new book was started. This one was titled *Health, Wealth, & Love* and took exactly eight weeks to write in exactly the same manner. It is almost exactly the same length as well. Joshua's second book deals with more specifics surrounding the common desires of Health and Wellness, Money and Abundance, and Love and Relationships.

Once that book was finished in mid-March, 2014, I spent time having the first book edited and published. There was a lot to do in those days having to do with designing the cover, designing the interior layout, building the website, and promoting the book. Another enjoyable side effect of this relationship with Joshua was answering questions from people all over the world. As soon as people learned about Joshua, questions started pouring in.

At first, the questions came from Lili and some of our close friends. Then the questions started coming from people I had never met. I utilized the same method I used when writing the book. I meditated and then sat down at my computer and let Joshua answer the questions. While I was a bit nervous about the book-writing process (having some doubt as to what was happening), the information was obviously beneficial. But how would people respond to these questions? What would they think of the answers? You just need to read one to know the answer to that. They are brilliant. Each one gets to the vibrational heart of the question and provides an answer that is so clear it always resonates with the asker. These questions go on to help many other people as well.

I've included a few questions in the "Special Section" at the end of this book. I'm sure you'll find them fascinating. You can also read many other questions and answers at www.theteachingsofjoshua.com

Near the end of August 2014, I knew that a new book was coming. I even knew the title a few days in advance: *A Radical Change in Your Approach to Life*. I thought I knew what the book was about, since it was inspired by a question from someone who was dealing with chronic pain. Joshua's answer was for her to radically change her approach to life. It's fascinating that Joshua could be inspired by us, but that's just how it works. It turns out that we humans are on the leading edge of creation. We are the main attraction. Our lives are of great interest to those existing in the nonphysical realm.

However, as you will read, changing our approach to life is something quite different than you may think. It's totally different than what I thought it would be, but this information has the potential to be more transformative than anything that's ever been written before. That's how powerful it is!

In the beginning, very few people in my life knew about my experience with Joshua. I have gone from thinking all of this was very weird to accepting my role in the dissemination of this important information. I have decided to accept this information as the ultimate truth and live it as fully as I can. Those who will resonate with and understand this information will be drawn to it. I'm not going to preach Joshua to anyone who doesn't want to hear it, but for those few of us who are awakening to the reality behind reality, we are going to start living on a whole new level. There is so much more coming; I can just feel it and I'm exhilarated in anticipation. I hope you are too.

What you are now about to read came straight from Joshua.

Introduction

What if you were to wake up tomorrow morning with the complete and full knowledge of who you really are? What if you became the fullest and most profound manifestation of you? Your creation is you, and there is a peak point of creation. There is a version of you that is the absolute, real, and actual you. It is the you that has the power to deliberately create your reality. What if you became the ultimate version of you tomorrow?

Imagine for a moment that you knew who you really are. What would that mean? What would that look like? How would you be different? How would you behave? What would your life look like if you lived as if you knew who you really were? It would be a radical change in your approach to life.

There are two aspects of you: love and fear. You have a set of beliefs, of habits, and of routine, reactionary behaviors. Some of your actions stem from beliefs rooted in love, and some stem from beliefs rooted in fear. Take away the fear and what's left? Love. So the basis of your being is love. What does a life based on love with an absence of fear look like? How does one exist in this world expressing only love and no fear? Is this even possible?

When you were born into this world, you were born as a being comprised of love, expressing love, and feeling love. You loved your parents, your grandparents, your siblings, your pets, and your environment. You are a spiritual, vibrational being living in a physical world with a brand-new physical body. This body has certain aspects that enhance the physical experience you are taking on. One of the key aspects of this physical body is the survival instinct. This instinct creates the body's ability to experience fear. Fear in certain circumstances is a good thing. It keeps you away from cliffs and out of lions' mouths.

Fear is an aspect of reality that is necessary. Yet in your present life you no longer fear falling from heights or being chased by wild animals. You now fear bills, embarrassment, failure, and conditions outside of your control. These are fabricated, irrational fears. These are fears that have been concocted from undisciplined thought. It is your mind that is producing these elements of fear that have no real basis for existing in your life. If you find yourself arguing with this idea that your fears have no justification, you are simply providing evidence that your thoughts are undisciplined.

It is the thinking that causes a life of love or fear. Thinking without regard for the thought and the ramifications of those thoughts is what is creating chaos or stagnation in your life. Your thoughts control your perception of your life. Your thoughts form the basis of your reality. If you can't get your thoughts in line, you cannot create the life you truly desire. In these pages we will explore the means of creating the version of you that lives more in love and less in fear. The highest expression of your life is one of love. We will show you how to move in that direction.

It matters not what you have been living up to this point in time. You will learn to come to peace with everything that has happened in your past. You will learn to use that past as a springboard to your future. We will teach you methods that will create ease in your life and help you gain a new and more solid understanding of the mechanism of physical existence and how to create the life that you intended prior to your birth.

II.

Do you really know who you are? Can you even glimpse the magnificence that is you from where you now stand? Probably not, for this highest version of you is quite different from your personal ideals of what you think you could possibly be. From where you now stand, you lack the perspective to envision your own potential. Isn't that interesting? You can't see who you could become from where you are now. Your highest imagination of who you could be, what you could achieve, how you would behave, what you would be interested in, and how you would express yourself, are all completely and utterly hidden from you as you now stand. This is an interesting concept because it means you must go through a process of self-discovery.

If we were to show you a picture or a video of who you really are, you would not be able to recognize yourself. This is a good thing, because the ultimate version of you is so different from who you are now that it would seem alien to you. You might not even like what you saw. This is why you must embark on a journey, a long journey, of self-discovery. You must be led, step by step to slowly unraveling the mystery that is you.

We are not talking about going into your past and analyzing why things happened the way they did. We are talking about moving forward and uncovering the layers you have placed upon yourself so that you could shield yourself from the world. We will be stripping off those layers and exposing them. We will show you that the protection you thought you were gaining from these layers never did anything to protect you. These layers of fear only served to weigh you down and make your life more insulated.

As you created layers of fear and added them to your personality and your approach to life, you placed restrictions on how you experienced life. These layers of fear made you numb to life, which only added more layers. If you continue living life as you have been, you will continue to add more layers and become even more insulated from life. One day you'll find that your greatest joy in life is simply tuning life out. If you find yourself watching TV rather than doing what you really want to do, it is because you have added so many layers. The fear makes you believe that being less than who you really are is comfortable. This comfort you feel is a false comfort. We will show you this and you will begin to look at your life in a new way.

Comfort is the surrender to fear. Comfort is really not natural in physical experience. In order to become who you really are, you must confront your fears and experience discomfort. Therefore, comfort is your worst enemy. You should seek uncomfortable conditions and experiences. If you had no fear, these conditions and experiences would not seem uncomfortable; they would feel like challenge and exhilaration.

Exhilaration is the emotion felt when you overcome a fear. A roller coaster ride is not comfortable, yet the experience is exhilarating. But this is a simple example. Each of you experience fear in unique and personal ways. What is easy for one person may be extremely difficult for another. It is based on their fear surrounding the experience. If you can overcome the fear, you will find the experience exhilarating. If you allow the fear to overcome you, you will find the experience terrifying and extremely unpleasant.

The experience itself is neutral. It is neither terrifying nor exhilarating. It is just an experience. It's your ability to overcome or succumb to your fears that defines the experience. If you overcome your fears, you will feel positive emotion. If you succumb to your fears you will feel negative emotion. But it is always up to you. You always have power over any experience. You can choose what each experience brings to you. You can go through any experience and overcome any fear. You have the power - you just don't know it yet.

III.

Let's return to the idea of who you really are. Are you able to recognize that there is more to you than you understand? Can you know that you are older, wiser, stronger, more confident, more loving, more beautiful, more caring, and more courageous than the person you see when you look in the mirror? It is important for you to know that there is more to you than you are now able to understand. If you can grasp this truth, you can move toward that version of you that exists on another level. But you must first believe that there is more to you than you might know right now. We want to introduce you to the complete you that exists inside you and all around you. This you is the inner you.

Some call this part of yourself "the soul" or "your inner being" or one of many other names. We call the larger you your "inner self," and you must come to know your inner self in order for us to lead you through the steps to becoming who you really are. If you can believe that what we are saying is coming from a higher, broader, and wiser perspective and believe that what we tell you about your inner self is true, you can quickly move to an understanding of how to become the highest version of you. In order to move to the next level, you will have to come to know and then learn to communicate with your inner self.

So let us introduce you to your inner self. First of all, your inner self is you. There is no separation. The only difference is that while you are in your body and you're physically focused, your inner self is also nonphysically focused. Your inner self hears every one of your thoughts and feels every one of your emotions. Your inner self is with you every moment of the day. Your inner self knows what you want in the tiniest detail.

Your inner self also knows how to get you what you want. Your inner self can see the landscape that stretches out ahead of your path. It knows how to get you where you want to go. It knows what is needed for you to get what you really, truly want. Your inner self also knows who you really are. Your inner self is primarily focused on helping you become the highest version of you.

We will talk more about your inner self as we move along. For now, understand that you have a partner in all of this. You are not taking one step on your own. You have support, and more importantly, you have guidance. We will teach you how to understand the guidance and how to use it to navigate your journey to becoming who you really are.

This book is not about helping you win the lottery, for you have already won it. This book is not about helping you find love because you are already loved more than you can imagine. This book is not about helping you overcome some unwanted condition because the side effect of becoming who you really are will create conditions that are so far beyond anything you could imagine. This book is only about discovering who you really are and living a life based on love.

Chapter One

Love

You do not really understand the concept of love from where you now stand. Very few have experienced true love. You have felt good in the presence of your newborn child and you might say this is the highest expression of love. Yet when we talk of love, it is the absence of fear that is the major component. So when you look at your child or mate and you feel love, you also feel fear. You fear the loss of what you love.

This is perfectly natural and is really unavoidable given the way you live in your society. But if you could imagine love without fear, the feeling you experienced looking into your newborn baby's eyes would be quite different. It would be elevated. Becoming who you really are means living in love without the aspect of fear. Reducing fear enhances love. Eliminating fear allows only love.

The elimination of fear is strictly a concept used for the purposes of defining love. It is not possible to eliminate fear fully, just as it is not possible to eliminate anything fully. If a fearful thought exists anywhere, then fear exists at some level. However, as you reduce fear, you automatically allow more love. As we teach you ways to reduce the intensity and frequency of fearful thoughts, we will help you experience more love. It is the allowing of love that will enable you to discover who you really are.

Isn't it ironic that you all understand that love is something to be brought into your everyday experience of life, yet you are more fearful of it than anything else? You have been taught to fear love. You have learned to withhold love. You are very careful not to display too much love. In your society, it is not acceptable to fully express your love. You are a guarded people. You are taught to put up defenses and struggle to protect yourselves at all costs.

Since love is the basis of who you really are, you are designed to love freely and fully. It is right and good to express love. The only reason you would not express your love is fear. It's fear of rejection, fear of embarrassment, fear of loss, and many other equally irrational fears. You cannot lose when you truly love. You cannot be anything other than who you really are when you are showing love. When you act out of love, you are performing as the highest version of yourself.

II.

You have a learned behavior of resisting love. You are cautious when entering relationships. You are cautious when meeting new people. You like your small groups. You have learned to worry about what others think. You have been taught to behave in a certain manner in order to fit within your social groups. You have learned to disguise who you really are.

Love is freedom, and as you were designed to express love, you were always meant to be free. True freedom lies in being who you really are. When you limit or place restrictions on who you really are, you limit your freedom. When you are less than who you really are, you are imprisoned by your own restrictions. Since you yearn for total freedom, any restriction on who you really are causes inner tension and stress. You want freedom, but you also want to fit into your group. However, when you behave in a way that is different from who you really are, you become an inauthentic version of yourself and everyone else feels this deception in some way.

You might try your best to act in a way that you feel will please others in order to fit in and be a part of some social structure you deem worthy. But while you are acting in a way that is not true to who you really are, you are not even getting close to what you really want. You want love and acceptance from others, but you are not the one giving love, since you are acting in a way that defies who you are rather than in a way that defines who you are. This all stems from fear.

When you love more, you reduce fear. When you love fully, you all but eliminate fear. Imagine your life if you could love everyone you met with the same full and complete expression of total love. If you could love at this level, you would not care what anyone thinks of you. Loving at this level does not allow for thoughts of fear. You would not fear rejection, loss, embarrassment, or anything else. You would simply love.

If you lived in total love you would not be able to see the negatives in anything, since you would have no fear in you. You would not complain because you would love everything. You would not worry because there would be nothing to worry about. You could not get higher and you could not do better; you would just love.

We understand that this is a concept that stretches your imagination. We know that there are few examples of a life lived in pure love. But we use this as a tool to help you understand how adding love to your approach to life will help reduce your fears. There is no reason not to love. It is simply your own fears holding you apart from becoming who you really are. You can love more and once you do, you will radically change your approach to life.

III.

All love is self-love. It all starts and ends with the self. In order to love another, you must love yourself. In order for others to see your worthiness, you must feel worthy yourself. In order for you to appreciate others, you must learn to appreciate yourself. You will only ever be able to truly love another in an amount equal to your love for yourself. Loving yourself is the first step in radically changing your approach to life.

Self-appreciation defines who and what you can appreciate. If you appreciate the beauty of a sunset, you must appreciate your ability to see and understand nature's beauty. At some level you must understand that you are worthy of this beautiful sunset. If you do not feel awe at the sight of the sunset, you do not see yourself as worthy of that beauty.

There is no fear in the sight of a beautiful sunset. You do not worry that the sunset will fade away, never to return. You know it will come again another day and may be even more stunning. You do not fear that the sunset will reject you or that others will scoff at your appreciation of the sunset. In fact, you would think it odd if you could not appreciate the sunset. This is a form of love without fear.

When you look into your baby's eyes, you feel love and there is little fear. You do not worry that your baby will not love you because you can see that she does. You instinctively know your baby loves you unconditionally. Your only fears are for her safety and well-being. It's only later, as she grows, that you will allow fear to enter into the relationship and you'll start to modulate your love.

You see that pure love does not allow the presence of fear. But when fear is allowed to enter, love is reduced. Love and fear work on a sliding scale. The more love, the less fear; the more fear, the less love. You have control over your fears through your ability to choose your thoughts. The ability to deliberately choose loving thoughts over fearful thoughts will allow you to be who you really are.

You can see how this sliding scale works if you have ever fallen in love. At first, the love flows freely and you feel intense emotion, connection, and ecstasy. You love every aspect of the other person and they love you as well. You feel all is right, and in the beginning there is little fear. However, as soon as something happens to cause doubt, fear enters and you begin to restrict your love. As soon as your new love forgets to call you when promised or does not return a text quickly enough, your untrained mind allows fearful thoughts to rush in.

As these fearful thoughts enter your awareness, you automatically shut down love. It is as if you have no control over the situation. You just feel differently, you act differently, and your new love picks up on this very quickly. He now allows fear to enter his mind and also begins to limit his love for you. Once fear begins its rampage on your fragile emotional state, you must fight the negative momentum and consciously return to love. If not, you will end the relationship and fear will continue to linger and will be ready for your next encounter.

This is the most common form of behavior among most humans. New love is easily diminished by fear. Even the tiniest issue allows fear to barge into the relationship. It's as if you have prepared yourself for fear, not love. It's as if fear is more practiced than love. It's as if you chronically think more fearful thoughts than loving thoughts. Is this true of you?

Love and fear must be practiced in order to enter your thoughts. Which one do you practice more often: love or fear? Do you believe that fearful thoughts are natural and that loving thoughts are more difficult? The opposite should be true for you. It should feel natural and good to think thoughts of love and appreciation. It should not be an exercise or a struggle to think about love. It should feel strange and uncomfortable to entertain a fearful thought. You should find it unpleasant to worry or complain.

From our perspective it seems as if you enjoy fear. You talk about your fears, you complain about everything, and you rant and rave against what you do not want. You rarely talk about what you do want. You seldom speak of love. You are addicted to drama, gossip, and tragedy. You watch the news, you send out alarming emails, and you rally against this and that. Once in a while you'll look at a video of cute animals, but this is not primetime TV. You are mired in negativity for most of your adult life. Why is that?

You look at portrayals of love as cheesy or corny. You don't believe them to be realistic. Even when you're watching a chick flick or a rom-com, there is always drama in the storyline. Why can't you enjoy portrayals of true, undramatic love? Don't you think that's strange?

Your lack of allowing love stems from self-insecurity. The cure for self-insecurity is self- love. Self-love is self-appreciation. You must learn to love who you are now, in this moment, in order to become who you really are. You cannot love yourself only after you've become who you really are. This sounds like a catch-22 situation. How can you love who you are now when you are in the process of becoming who you really are? How can you love the imitation and the original at the same time? How can you love your inauthentic self when all you want to do is love your authentic self? This doesn't seem to make sense.

Oh, but it does make sense. It makes a great deal of sense. It is the most important aspect of becoming who you really are. The whole idea is to love more. You must love more to be able to transform into the highest version of you. You are not being who you really are because you have been limiting your love. Mostly, you have been limiting your love of self. In order to become who you really are, you must learn to love more and more and more. You start by loving who you are right now. You love the you that is reading these pages. You love you for all of the reasons you have found not to love yourself.

You must come to terms with who you are now in order to transform into a higher version of you. You must love the moment and the conditions that are present in your life. You have been loving conditionally your whole life. You love people when they're being good and you don't love those same people when they're being bad. You love yourself when you've done something right, and you don't love yourself when you've made a mistake.

Forget about that approach to life. It doesn't work. It's never worked for anyone. Your parents loved you when you behaved like a good child and they withheld their love when you behaved in some way that they saw as wrong or bad. Did this approach work for them? Did their style encourage you to love them unconditionally? What if they loved you no matter what you did or said? How would you feel about them now? It would be better, wouldn't it?

Unconditional love is talked about in your society as if it is the unattainable answer to all your problems. It is the answer to all problems, and it is attainable. In fact, it is natural. Animals do not love conditionally, so why should you? It is only your approach to life that makes this natural love seem difficult. This is why we're asking you to radically change your approach to life.

IV.

Unconditional love is to be your ideal. It is something to be reached for. It is the thought that we want to come to you first in any situation. If the love thought comes before the fear thought, your life will be magnificent.

Unconditional love is the ability to see the homeless man and the supermodel as equal. When you come to wanting to spend time with each of them equally, you have come to love unconditionally. If you're thinking that you could never come to this level of love, it is only because you have not been practicing love. You haven't been thinking about love. You haven't come to realize that love, the ability to really love, is a muscle that must be used otherwise it will lose its strength.

You believe that love comes naturally, and it does. But you live in a dualistic reality. You are constantly judging one thing after another. This thing is good and that thing is bad. This is right and that is wrong. This is up and that's down. This is smart and that's stupid. This is worthy of my love and that is not.

Unconditional love means loving everything equally. But you say it's not possible to love everything equally. Some things are just better than others. This is where you are getting off-course. Loving something is not a stamp of approval. It is simply love. You can love the wrong as much as you love the right. We are not asking you to forego preference. We are simply trying to separate love from preference.

You can love everything as it exists in the moment and still maintain your preferences. This is an advanced concept and we will talk about it later on in this book. But loving the situation regardless of the circumstances surrounding it allows you to live in freedom - freedom from fear.

Let's look at this subject from the perspective of preference. Let's say you are given a bowl of ice cream. In this circumstance, you are at a friend's house for dinner. You are given chocolate ice cream, but you prefer vanilla. There is no vanilla in the house and you accept the offering as it is. You love ice cream, and you love your friends and this dinner. You are able to love the chocolate ice cream in the present moment even though you prefer vanilla. You decide to love what is.

This can be accomplished in every situation through practice, intention, consciousness, and thought. You can love the conditions as they currently exist in the moment and still prefer something better. The something better you want does not preclude your love for the conditions in the moment. If you can grasp this concept, you can easily create the change you desire in the future.

Nothing is ever wrong in the present moment. It is simply your attention to what is wanted and the comparison to what is that makes you dislike the actuality of the present moment. Being able to appreciate the conditions of the moment even when it is not completely as you would want it to be allows you to create the future in a way that will please you more.

Your physical reality is designed to give you more of what you want and more of what you do not want. It is your attention and focus on whatever is at hand that brings more. Through the Law of Attraction, the universe brings more of what you are giving your attention to. If you want something to be different, you envision the thing the way you want it to be. You do not envision eliminating the thing you do not like. The more your attention is placed on annihilating what you don't like, the more of it will come to you.

Therefore, loving what is and giving your attention to what is wanted allows that to come true for you. It is a radical change to your habitual approach to life. When you complain about something that is unwanted, you bring more of it to you through your attention to it. A complaint is like a yellow marker: it highlights a subject. The spotlight of your attention lights up the subject so the universe can bring more of it into your experience.

When you decide to focus your love and appreciation on something, even if you would prefer something different, you are only able to see the good parts of the unwanted thing. When you decide to love the homeless man as you would love the supermodel, you see the positive aspects of the man. You see the soul that is in the homeless man as he attempts to navigate his reality as best he can. You see the courage that allows him to live as he does. You may even see freedom or expansion as he experiences something that you would not want for yourself. By loving what is, you automatically focus on the positive aspects and are able to withdraw your attention from the negative aspects. This allows the universe to bring you the positive aspects of your focus.

It is easy to love the supermodel because you are naturally drawn to beauty and you judge her to be radiant, beautiful, and graceful. However, you could just as easily focus on her negative qualities. You might believe her to be less intelligent, or weak, or shallow, or whatever. Do you see how you naturally see positive qualities in those things you love and negative qualities in those things you fear?

To radically change your approach to life, you will have to work on seeing the positive qualities in everything. This means you will learn how to love everything. Loving everything means that you must resist judgment and think about what you want. You must exercise your love muscle so that you are focused on things wanted rather than complaining about things unwanted.

V.

Unconditional love must become your new habit, thereby replacing your old habit of judgment. Habitual behaviors create stagnation. If it is your desire to move forward to the life you prefer, you must break old habits of thought. You have learned to judge and have forgotten to love. A radical change in your approach to life reverses this, and you now love before you judge. Can you imagine how your life would change with just this one simple change in behavior?

Imagine meeting someone for the first time. Your old habit would be to be polite and then judge every word that comes out of their mouth, all the while judging yourself for every word coming out of yours. Your new habit would be to love them for who they are and love yourself for who you are. You would not judge their words, but love their words. You would not judge your words, but love your words. Can you feel the energetic shift in this? Is it not obvious that you would have more fun, create more loving relationships, and feel better about yourself and all others?

Imagine going to a new restaurant and loving every aspect of it. Imagine loving the decor even though you might prefer something different. Imagine loving the server even though you've experienced better service. Imagine loving the menu even though you could imagine something else. Imagine loving what you were served even though you might have had something better elsewhere. Imagine loving the check and tipping big even though you've had less expensive meals elsewhere.

Do you see how your judgment can devalue any experience and how love can elevate that same experience? Do you see that it's your choice to focus on the positive or negative aspects of every situation? Do you see that it is your perception of the conditions or the event itself that makes it positive or negative? Do you understand that you have total control over what you choose to think about anything? Can you see how a radical change in your thinking will lead immediately to a radically improved life?

So we are asking you to love. Are you resisting this request? Do you feel that we are asking too much? Do you feel it's possible for you to move in the direction of love and away from judgment? Does fear enter your mind while you are considering our request?

Let us address your fears. You cannot love everything, for that would not be prudent. You cannot exist in your society loving everything. Some things are to be shunned out of the simple need to protect yourself. Is this what you are thinking? Are there just some things that you can never love?

You can never come to love a murderer because you believe that murder is wrong and murderers must be punished. Have you ever analyzed this belief? Let's single out some random murderer now facing the death sentence in one of your various prisons. You do not know anything about her, but she has been convicted and labeled a murderer. She is now facing execution. You might not believe that she should be executed, but at least she should be kept out of society and punished for her crimes. Most of you would agree with this and the thought of loving her is not within the realm of possibility.

Why not? Because she has done something wrong. How do you know? Because she was convicted. Is that the final say in the matter? Could there have been circumstances that were missed or unknown? Is there a possibility that the jury got the story wrong? Could she be innocent? Is there more to the story than you could ever know? Even if she did commit the murder, does it help you in any way to hate or despise her? What do you get out of hating someone?

If you looked at any situation where you judge something to be wrong and then withhold your love, you will find that fear is involved. You can't love something you fear. You must look at the subject rationally and if fear is involved you must identify the causes within you. Why do you allow fear in the subject? Is it real? It seldom is.

You fear murderers because you believe they could affect your life in some way. This really isn't true and you have little control over their actions anyway. Do you really think that the threat of prison or execution is going to do anything to modify the behavior of a murderer? It's a false sense of control. Murders happen outside of your ability to control them.

Okay, so maybe you can get to the point of not hating murderers, or criminals, or deviants, or homosexuals, or the homeless, or the ill, or the deformed, or the Republicans, or the Democrats, or the rich, or the poor, or the young, or the old, or the elite, or the ignorant, or the city people, or the country people, or whoever. It is all the same. But can you actually, really come to love them? If you want to radically change your approach to life, you must do so. Once you learn to love the damned, you will bless both them and yourself. Your life will open up and you'll be led to higher levels of experience. You will be moved to a greater and richer experience in this life. You will change and so will your life. You will move out of your comfort zone and that is a good thing because comfort is not natural in physical experience.

Chapter Two

Comfort

You live in a physical environment with great variations in climate. You live in an economic environment which has enormous variations from rich to poor. You live in an emotional environment which fluctuates between joy and sorrow. As you navigate your environments, you seek comfort. Your life may even be dedicated to becoming more and more comfortable. But this is a trap. The comfort you seek may rob you of your purpose for being here.

Your world is more comfortable than your society has ever experienced in its history. You live in lavish homes filled with luxurious furniture and fabrics. Your technology has made life easier. You travel in comfort and safety. You have so many options for ease. Your entertainment allows for the numbing of your minds. You can easily avoid all sorts of discomfort as you navigate your daily lives.

If you do not believe that you live a very comfortable life, just imagine the lifestyle of the average person in your town just a hundred years earlier. It was quite different indeed. Imagine their living conditions compared to yours. Imagine their homes, furnishings, and appliances. Did they have a refrigerator? Did they enjoy air conditioning or central heating? Imagine how they traveled. Did they own a car? Could they fly around the world as you can today?

Your society is driven to create higher and higher levels of comfort and this is a good thing. However, as you seek external comfort, you begin to desire comfort inside as well. The physical experience was not designed for you to seek comfort; it was designed for you to experience life. Sometimes these experiences are uncomfortable, but often there is a great reward for enduring a little discomfort.

Physical experience is a feeling experience. The only thing you are ever really doing is feeling. How you feel on the inside is the only thing that has any relevance. You do things because they are fun, and fun feels good. You like to fall in love because love feels good. You like new clothes because they make you feel good. You like to win because winning feels good. Anything you want is wanted because you think it will feel good.

You will make choices based on how you think you will feel as a result of the choice. Sometimes you do things that you believe are wrong because they feel better than doing the right thing. If you have ever shoplifted anything from a store as a child, you did it because it was exciting and excitement feels good. The good feeling of excitement was worth the risk of getting caught, which would result in a bad feeling. So, sometimes you are willing to gamble that the result of your actions will feel good even though there is the risk of feeling bad.

As an adult you will be less likely to shoplift for the feeling. The gamble is just not worth the risk. The level of excitement is less than the pain of embarrassment you would feel if caught. The disgrace would be an awful feeling.

You have learned to calculate the odds of feeling good in everything you do. You may not realize it, but every decision you make is made in the hopes of feeling better. If you are conscious of this fact, if you can understand that the feeling of anything is its reward, then you can deliberately make decisions based on what you want rather than what you think you will feel.

Since comfort feels good, you tend towards any decision that makes you feel more comfortable. You choose furniture, cars, modes of travel, lodging, and many other things based on how comfortable you think they will make you. This is easy to observe with anything physical such as furniture or homes. But you do the same thing with experiences. You choose experiences based on how comfortable they are.

It's one thing to choose your furniture based on comfort, but it's another thing to base your experiences on comfort. There are certain things you are here to do. Sometimes, you must go outside your comfort zone to experience what is necessary for your expansion. If you hide out in your comfortable dwelling safe from uncomfortable experiences, you'll miss the most important aspect of physical existence. You expand as a result of your experiences, and you're here to expand.

You are familiar with the term "comfort zone." You understand what it means to operate within that zone. But do you really understand what you're feeling when you step outside that comfort zone? All you're doing is facing emotions that you deem unpleasant. It is the fear of these emotions that keeps you trapped inside your comfort zone. But what is there really to fear?

II.

Physical life creates desire. You go through life developing preferences. Your experiences lead you to know what is wanted. As soon as you birth a desire, that desire is given to you. This means you are on a path to that desire and as long as you go with the flow of life, you will be delivered to that which you desire. But for you to have anything, you must become a vibrational match to it. You have to be ready for it. If you do not have whatever you desire in your life right now, it's only because you are not ready for it physically or vibrationally.

If you were a vibrational match to your desire, you would have that which you desired. Since you're not a match to it, it is still a dream. The way to become a match to your desire and to have it manifest in your life is for you to change from who you are now to the version of you that matches it. The thing you want does not change to match you; you change to become a match to it. It's a very simple system.

If you want something, anything, you must change to match it. Therefore, your feelings, beliefs, expectations, and thoughts will have to change. If the thing you want is big, you will have to radically change. If it's small, then you will only have to change a little. Your perception of a big thing compared to a small thing is the indicator of how much change is needed.

The trick is that there is nothing for you to do to make the change. The universe will change you. You just have to be willing and allow the change to happen. In order to do this, you will have to go outside your comfort zone. You will have to risk feeling bad in order to one day feel very good. You will have to endure a little discomfort in order to experience that which you truly want. The result of this will be your expansion.

To get anything you want, you'll have to change. In order to get something big, you must change into a higher version of you. You cannot change while living inside your comfort zone and you won't do anything consistently if it's uncomfortable. That's why most people don't change and why those people don't get what they want. In order to change, you must expand your comfort zone first.

The first step in expanding your comfort zone is analyzing what you believe to be uncomfortable. Let's talk about public speaking. This is a very common fear. Many people believe that public speaking is extremely uncomfortable. Why is this?

When you imagine someone on stage talking to a group, do you see any physical discomfort? Are they hotter or colder than the audience? Is it windier up there? No, the discomfort can only come from the inside. The only discomfort can be in the potential for embarrassment. But is embarrassment really something that can harm you? Or is the pain something you make up?

We understand the fear of public speaking, but we also see it as an irrational fear. It is irrational because you cannot die of embarrassment. Fear is meant to protect you from life-threatening situations. Fear of falling or being eaten is a rational fear. Fear of failure or embarrassment is not. So why are you entertaining these irrational fears? Why are you letting them hold you back?

Let's say that you were given the assignment to sing in front of a large group of your peers. Some of them you knew and some you did not. There are no instruments provided, no band to back you up, no other singers, just you and your voice. Everyone in the audience has paid to come and hear you sing. They all dressed up and were told of your amazing talents. They fill the theater and chatter in anticipation of your performance. You enter the stage to a standing ovation. The crowd quiets to hear every note and you open your mouth to sing.

What do you think would be the actual ramifications of this? Would they laugh? Would they heckle and boo? What would you feel? Why do you think you would feel this way? Why do you care what they think? Have you ever thought about this? Have you ever really analyzed why something like this would be so painful? Do you realize that the only real pain, the only way you could ever feel bad, is by making yourself feel bad? It's only ever you who punishes yourself on the inside.

Now let's say that you were offered $1,000 for your performance. Would you do it? What if it was $10,000 or $100,000 or $1,000,000? Would you do it then? Choose a number and that's your comfort zone. Reduce that number and you've just expanded your comfort zone. When you can come to perform a song in front of this group for just a dollar, you've expanded your comfort zone enough to manifest anything you desire.

The key to expanding your comfort zone is perspective. When you look at a fear and use a new perspective to understand that the fear is irrational, you can reduce the fear and expand your comfort zone. It is all in your mind. Perspective helps you see what you're doing to yourself. Change your perspective and you'll see discomfort as much less intimidating.

III.

Discomfort is a projection of one possible future reality. You are simply projecting fear into a future event. It often happens prior to the first time you do something. Once you've experienced the event and have made it through the other side unscathed, the discomfort dissipates. Prior to the event, you felt fear in your anticipation. You moved through the fear and did whatever it was you had to do. The discomfort you felt was only in the stages before the activity. Once you were doing the activity, the fear was gone and the discomfort you felt also disappeared.

You have experienced this many times in your life. You've worried about something you knew you were going to do and felt the fear. It was an uncomfortable feeling. But once you were in the middle of that thing, the fear and discomfort vanished and you realized that everything was fine. That's how it always is. You already know this. The fear is the worst part of anything. Once you've moved past the fear, you find the activity to be okay, even exhilarating.

Think of your first day at a new school. Prior to that day you were filled with dread. So many unpleasant thoughts filled your head. So many worries consumed your thoughts. You played the "what if" game with yourself. What if no one likes me? What if there are mean kids who tease me? What if I'm not smart enough? What if I can't make friends? What if this and what if that?

But once you made it through those first few days and you learned your way around the school and made some new friends, then everything was all right. In fact, you soon felt good again. You soon found your confidence. And when another new kid came to your school, you could observe them from a new, higher vantage point.

What you feared was the unknown. The unknown is neither positive nor negative; it's neutral. The unknown has no inherent qualities other than your projection of your own fears, which are always negative. If you did not project your fears into the unknown, you would not feel any discomfort in doing something new. So why are you chronically projecting fear? You could just as easily project confidence.

When facing any new situation, you have the choice to project fear or confidence. You could see the situation and imagine that the worst might happen or you could imagine that the best might happen. It is always up to you. You can look at it any way you like. You do not know what will happen, so why would you project fear? Why is that the normal reaction to any new situation? Let's look at an example.

Let's say you have been asked by your employer to give a presentation of your idea to a group of people. This is the first time you have ever given a presentation and you feel nervous. You dread public speaking and the thought of presenting your idea frightens you. However, you know that the idea is exciting and that if your presentation is successful, you'll be given the opportunity to create something new.

In the days before your presentation, you feel conflicted. You begin to play the "what if" game. What if they laugh at my idea? What if I forget what to say? What if I mess it all up and they decide I'm not the person to manage the project? Wouldn't that be terrible?

You make yourself so anxious about the presentation that you have thoughts of quitting. You approach your boss and ask if someone else can present the idea. You tell him you're not feeling well. He tells you that you must present the idea because it's your idea. No one else can present your idea but you. So you present your idea and it's a hit. Everyone loved your presentation and they give you the opportunity to move forward. You are elated and experience the feeling of success. You wonder what you were so worried about in the first place. The next time you're asked to present an idea, you will have no more fears or doubts.

This is most often the result when facing an irrational fear. The fear made you feel like it was a life-threatening situation. But once you moved through the fear, you realized there was never anything to worry about. This is due to the irrational nature of the fear. The reality of the fear, the reality that the situation was life-threatening, never existed. It was a fabrication of your untrained imagination. It had no basis in reality. Except for your own thoughts, which have the power to manifest what you're feeling and thinking about, the fears had no power of their own.

Irrational fears cause discomfort. Discomfort blocks action that is required to move you in the direction of what you desire. The belief that you should seek safety in comfort limits your ability to attain your desires. Learning to ease your fears will increase your tolerance for discomfort. You can reduce discomfort by reducing the effects of fear. By projecting confidence, you reduce fear. Confidence is the antidote for fear. Confidence reduces the level of discomfort associated with any event, action, or activity. You can project confidence just as easily as you now project fear.

IV.

Confidence is the ability to project positive thoughts in advance of any event. It's as simple as that. The thoughts you have do not need to be based in reality. When you were projecting negative, fearful thoughts onto an upcoming event, those thoughts were not based in reality. They were simply negative, fearful thoughts. Your "what if" statements had no basis in truth; they were simply projections of fears. You hoped they wouldn't come true. You prayed these negative thoughts would not actualize. When everything turned out okay, you felt relief.

You could just as easily project confident, positive thoughts onto the event. You could play the "what if" game in a positive way. What if everything goes well? What if they love my idea? What if I get to manage the project? Wouldn't that be great?

If you could project confidence, you would greatly reduce the discomfort associated with anything new. Your projection of confidence would reduce the fear. Confidence is simply your intention that everything will work out okay in the end. Is that not your intention? Don't you think it will work out okay in the end? Isn't a positive result more likely to occur than failure?

If your intention is for everything to work out okay in the end, then the projection of confidence, which coincides with your intention, causes you to align with your desires. This is a very powerful stance. You can overcome your fears and discomfort when you practice aligning your intentions with confidence.

The ability to choose confidence over worry is simply a matter of practice. If you allow your mind to operate on its own, you might gravitate toward fear. If you practice confident thoughts, you will automatically reduce the frequency of fearful thoughts. Only one thought can occupy your attention at a time. If you practice confident thoughts, the negative thoughts cannot occupy the same space.

By practicing confident thoughts you will be led and inspired to certain actions that will move you in the direction of your desire. You can see that any feeling of discomfort will limit your action and therefore reduce your ability to attain your desire. If you are worried, you will seek comfort and avoid action. If you are confident, you will be inspired to the proper action step.

Everything you want is attainable step by step. But if you stop in front of a step because you feel it's uncomfortable, you'll find yourself stuck right where you are. You will either have to find a way around that step, which will take you off your path, or you'll have to build up your confidence and just take the step that's in front of you.

We promise you that you can never be led to a step that you cannot handle. You will never be confronted with an action that is too many steps ahead as long as you are inspired to challenge the step you see in front of you. This step you see is simply the next logical step. Most of the time it will be easy. Most of the time you'll enjoy it and have fun. Sometimes you'll worry and maybe you'll even want to quit. But if you take the step that is right there, the step that you've been inspired to take that you realize is the next logical step, you'll handle it well and feel exhilaration in your success.

By practicing thoughts of confidence, achievement, success, clarity, and strength, you will reduce your tendencies toward fear and worry. You will ease the discomfort associated with any endeavor. How you think and how you feel really has an impact on your approach to life. You can look at people in your life and easily notice that if they just had a little more confidence, their life would improve. Don't you just want to help them gain a bit more confidence? Can you see that worry and fear are holding them back from being who they really are? Can you see the potential in others around you? We see that same potential in you.

All of you have so much more potential than you are giving yourselves credit for in this moment. You can become so much more. You can live more expansive lives. You can reach greater heights. You can be more confident. If you could see your lives from our wider, broader perspective, you would quickly gain all the confidence you needed to attain whatever it is you truly desire.

Do not be fooled by comfort. Do not tell yourself that living a small life is better than facing the fear of living big. Don't tell yourself that confidence is arrogance. It is not. Confidence is simply maintaining thoughts that align with your intentions. Do not fear failure, because you cannot fail. You are a constantly moving field of energy. You can't go backwards. You are always moving forward, even if it feels like you're stuck.

Entertain thoughts of success. Think bigger than you normally allow yourself to think. Start to exercise your imagination. Don't entertain negative thoughts. Use discipline when thinking. Think thoughts that feel good. When a fearful thought grabs your attention, replace it with a confident thought. Do this often and it will become your habit of thought. Think a confident thought enough times and it will become a belief. Once you've created a positive, confident belief, you will have altered the trajectory of your life in an extremely positive manner.

V.

Sometimes the next step involves doing something you do not want to do. You understand that the action step is necessary, yet you think it will not be enjoyable. You prefer something else. You start to look for alternatives. You see it as unwanted, but you have not analyzed what it is about this course of action that you do not like.

You may have come to believe that inspired action is pleasurable action. If you're meant to do it, then whatever you do must be fun. There is a flawed premise in this belief. First of all, you are here to expand joyously. When you see the word "joyous" you think it means "always happy." It does not. It means "with joy." You supply the joy in doing anything whether you think you'll like it or not. You are the one who decides whether you're going to take action with joy or whether you're going to take action with misery.

You may not necessarily like what you're doing. You might prefer something else. But you have the ability to do this thing you don't like doing with joy. You can appreciate the value of this next step and lean into it with joy. You can also despise this step and grudgingly work through it in anger, shame, or self-pity. It's your choice.

Sometimes there are obstacles in your path and in order to get where you want to go you must complete action steps you don't want to. But since everything itself is neutral, you must determine why it is that you feel that you don't like this next step. In the case of public speaking, it's easy to see that the fear is likely to be a result of insecurity about what others will think. But what about other, less obvious tasks you do not want to do. Why do you not want to tackle these things?

When Gary was in high school he wanted a car and his father loaned him the money to buy his first car which was a 1968 Mustang. He loved the car and wanted to pay his father back, so he got a job in a supermarket as a stock clerk. This was a job he absolutely hated. His tasks were to carry, clean, and build. He hated unloading the trucks, he could not stand mopping the floors, and he never enjoyed building the displays. To this day, he does not like to build, clean, or carry anything.

However, this was a necessary step in the path to so many of his desires. He wanted to earn a living with his mind and this experience gave him the motivation to go to and finish college. He did not want to earn a living doing anything physical. He also learned that he did not want to work by the hour or for anyone else. He wanted to be in control of his destiny and he learned that the lack of security in self-employment was worth the risk because he absolutely did not want to be told what to do.

He could have completed that step with joy. He could have appreciated how well he did his tasks. He could have seen that the action of unloading the trucks caused his muscles to grow. He could have made friends with the people he worked with. Had he acted out of joy, he could have made the experience enjoyable. Had he seen that this step was part of his path, he could have made the most of it.

At the time, however, he was not living consciously. He was in the process of awakening and this step allowed him to move toward that path.

But he saw it as a miserable step and always talked about that time as a dark, unhappy period in his life. Until now, that is. Now he can look back and appreciate how the universe lined up this manifestation event and how it positively affected the rest of his life.

You can do the things you don't want to do with joy and appreciation. You can see the action for what it is: the next step toward your desire. You can learn to love this part of your journey. For if you are able to change your perspective on the subject, your attitude will shift and your experience will lighten up. The radical change in your approach to life starts with the alteration of your current perspective on what's good or bad.

VI.

You can live a small, comfortable life or you can live an expansive and sometimes uncomfortable one. Guess which sort of life you intended to live prior to your birth? Yes, you've got it: the expansive life. An expansive life is uncomfortable at times because the very nature of expansion must take you out of your comfort zone. You are meant to live a happy life, you are meant to experience joy, but *you* were meant to bring the joy to everything you do. You have control over your thoughts and you can decide what you prefer to think. You can be happy or miserable; it's your choice. Aren't you happy you get to choose?

Expansion requires that you go through new and uncomfortable experiences. You are here to grow through the experiences of your life. You are not here to read romance novels, watch the news on TV, or sit around gossiping about the lives of others. You are not supposed to sit on the sidelines and watch the game; you're supposed to play in the game yourself.

So, what are you to do? In order to expand, where do you go now? How do you determine what it is you truly want? Who's going to tell you the next step? Are you to follow your bliss? Our answer is yes and no.

You are to follow your bliss, but you don't really understand what bliss means. You think bliss is ultimate happiness. It isn't quite that. For this example we want to define bliss as a state of enrapture. It is something that consumes you in the moment and fills you with joy. It is a state of being that blurs the space-time aspect of your reality. It is a state of being that blurs the beingness of your body to a point where you no longer desire food, sleep, or other normal bodily urges. It's a state of being that causes you to lose track of time.

So, this really boils down to two things: fun and interest. When you're having fun, you lose track of time. When you're having a lot of fun, you don't get tired or hungry. You just want to keep having fun. When you're having fun, you lessen your attention to the world around you. You don't care where you are or what strangers are thinking about you. This is bliss.

When you are passionately involved in an interest, you lose track of time. When you are working on something you're really into, you don't need to sleep and you often forget to eat. When you're fixated on your passion, you pull your attention away from the physical environment around you. This, too, is bliss.

When we say "follow your bliss," this is what we're talking about. Do what's fun. Find out what you're interested in and explore that. It may be uncomfortable at first, but soon you'll gain confidence because it's something you're interested in. Follow this path and you'll discover the means to your expansion.

Reduce the intensity of anything you find uncomfortable by changing your perspective on the subject. Enter it with confidence and you'll ease your worry. See it as the next, necessary step in your evolution. Realize that an expansive life is not a small, comfortable life. Be thankful you have the ability to choose your thoughts and you can choose to do everything joyfully.

Chapter Three

Energy

Physical reality is an energetic system. There are particles of energy all around you. These particles coalesce to create matter. Your thoughts are energy, your words are energy, and your actions are energy. You create manifestations through thoughts, words, and actions that use energy to form objects, conditions, and experiences. As you bring more energy to any thought, any conversation, and any action, you increase your powers of creation.

To radically change your approach to life you must come to understand how you operate in this energetic environment. Are you bringing energy to everything you do? Or, more likely, do you operate at lower levels of energy?

Energy moves at certain speeds. Low energy is slower, whereas high energy is faster. If you look at a substance like water, you can see that at lower energy levels, water takes the form of ice, and at higher energy levels, water takes the form of vapor. If you add energy to the ice, such as heat, the ice will transform into water and then into vapor. The addition of the energy creates the transformation. If you have been operating at lower energetic levels, you must add energy to every thought, word, and action in order to radically change your life.

Happiness is more energetic than sadness. Walking is more energetic than sitting. Smiling is more energetic than frowning. Passion is more energetic than apathy. Do you see how this system works? Can you understand how your current approach to life would be enhanced with the addition of energy? It is the energy in everything that forms creation in physical reality. You have the ability to reach for and attract more energy. It is a simple matter of focus.

Have you ever used a magnifying glass to burn a piece of paper? The magnifying glass focuses the energy of the sun into a concentrated beam of light that is many more times hotter and thus burns the paper. You have the ability to bring more energy into your life by the practice of focus. You can use the energy that is all around you to think more energetic thoughts. But it takes practice. The magnifying glass is designed to bring small objects into focus. You will have to practice this ability.

The first step is to practice bringing energy into your thoughts. What do we mean by this? The simplest explanation is for you to be aware of the current energetic level of your thoughts and then to replace those thoughts with higher-energy thoughts. This takes time and is not easy at first. It will take some concentration and a little effort. Your focus must be on the quality of thoughts you are thinking. Most of your thoughts are habitual. You obsess about the same things. When you purposely reach for high-energy thoughts, you radically change your habit of thought.

Let's say you obsessively worry about paying your rent. From the moment you put the check in the mail, you worry about making the next payment. It's a thirty-day-long habit of thought. You worry about what your landlord will think of you if you're late. You worry about the shame of being evicted. You worry about losing your job or about all the other bills you also have to pay. These are familiar thoughts, but they are low-energy thoughts. Your work is to bring energy to your approach to thought.

To radically change your approach to thought, you must create a standard for thought. You will no longer accept low-energy thoughts. Your standard has been raised. You now feel for high-energy thoughts. Now, from your higher level of energy, you attract thoughts that support this new stance. When a thought of worry enters your mind, you reach for a powerful thought. When you think "How will I manage to pay the rent?" you reach for more energetic thoughts: "I will pay the rent. I always pay the rent. I have no problems paying the rent or meeting any other obligations."

This is an example of a high-energy approach to thought. Oh, but we hear you say, "It isn't accurate; it isn't true. I always have trouble paying the rent. I always worry about the rent. I have been late many times. The rent is always a problem for me."

The rent is a problem for you because of your low-energy approach to thinking. Your rent is an issue in your life because you allow low-energy thoughts to consume you. You must realize by now that your thinking creates your reality. Therefore, in order to change your reality to one you prefer, start thinking a new truth. The truth now is this: "The energy I'm bringing to my approach to thought creates a new energy in my life. My life is the result of my thoughts. My low-energy life will be improved through the practice and standards of a whole new approach to thinking. I will no longer tolerate low-energy thoughts. That is no longer my truth. That was the past and this new approach will create my future as I want it to be."

II.

Your current approach to life is based on your current standard of thought. Your life, no matter how bad you think it is, is a result of your habit of low-energy thought. If you can add energy to your thoughts through the practice of focus, you will begin to see a real shift in the quality of your life. Your life will begin to improve. You will add energy to your thoughts, and in the process you will add energy to your life. The speed at which your life improves will be related to the amount of energy you bring to your habit of thought. If you practice often, your life will improve quickly and dramatically.

If your life is awesome, it will also improve further as you add energy to your thoughts. Your life, no matter how good you think it is, is a result of your habit of high-energy thought. However, you can even add more energy to your thoughts, and your life will continue to improve to even higher levels of awesomeness. There is no limit to how high you can go. Wherever you are now, no matter how well you're doing, you are still limited by the energetic level of your thought. Add even more energy to your thoughts and the quality of your life and your experience will improve even further.

When you add energy to your thoughts, you automatically add energy to your words and actions. However, due to social programming, you are not allowed to be too energetic in outward appearance. You have been taught to act a certain way in order to fit into your society. Some societies struggle with acceptable behavior more than others. Most of you were taught to control your natural exuberance for life. In order to radically change your approach to life, you must unlearn these constraints on your behavior.

Think of how you approached life as a child. If you had a difficult childhood, see if you can bring up an example of a happy childhood from someone you know. Maybe your own child or a relative lived a happy, carefree childhood. The way a happy child acts is the natural state of energetic behavior.

Generally, a child is full of joy, fun, and interest or curiosity, and he is loud in laughter and tears. Children are naturally confident and fearless. Children love and believe they are loved naturally. Unless told by their parents, they are not aware of what others think about them. That is the natural approach to life. This approach to life allows for everything they desire to come to them. It is only when they are taught to lower their energy that they allow the diminishment of their experience.

In order to radically change your approach to life, begin living as a happy child does. Do not worry about what others are thinking. Express your love. Express your passion. Be loud, fearless, and confident. Tempt failure by trying new things. Seek to find the joy that is inherent in all things and all people. Change your words to match your new approach to life.

Higher levels of existence demand that you focus on the energetic level of the words you speak and the subjects you choose to talk about. To radically change your approach to life you must increase the quality and energy of the words you use. The first step in creation is thought which is powerful. The second step in creation is your speech, which is even more powerful. It is important to understand that what you are stating with your words is what you are stating as your expression of self.

Imagine what happens energetically when you say, "I am bored." The statement "I am" is powerful and meaningful. It is your statement of self, and the universe has been designed to respond to it in a powerful way. In this case, the universe responds by removing clarity from your experience and giving you the confusion that allows you to continue to experience boredom. That is a low-energy statement that a conscious creator would not say out loud.

High-energy statements include any of the following: I am love. I am happy. I am prosperous. I am fun. I am free. I am intelligent. I am God. I am worthy.

Do you say these statements out loud often? If so, you are deliberately creating your experience from a stance of high-energy words and thoughts. If not, you are creating your experience from a stance that is of a lower energy. If not, it's because you don't believe these statements. If not, it's because you do not think yourself worthy of these statements. That is a low-energy approach to life.

From your perspective as a physical and individual being, your approach to life is most likely based on your experiences of life. If you were raised in a high-energy household with parents who were conscious creators, you adopted the high-energy approach to life. You had a head start in life. You were given the most precious gift of all. However, most of you were not so lucky to be born into a high-energy family. Most of you chose your low-energy families. Why did you do that?

You chose the time and place of your birth along with the energetic level of your family. Most of you who are on this path to reawakening and rediscovering who you really are need the clarifying benefits of living a childhood in a low-energy environment. This causes a slingshot effect that often creates a pathway to rediscovery. Your childhood made it more likely for you to reach this stage in your development. You are more advanced than most of humanity in coming to terms with your true self. You are evolving into a physical/spiritual being faster than most others on your planet. You need to understand now that the way you were taught to behave is not the way of a high-energy being.

From now on, your standard of speech and conversation must be raised. You will consider the energetic impact of your words and your topics of discussion. You will no longer feel good when gossiping. You will no longer tolerate the negative aspects of subjects that make you feel bad. You will no longer seek to reduce others with your words, even those who are not in your immediate presence. You will endeavor to speak your truth as you want it to be, not how you perceive it to be.

The truth is that you are love. You are a being based in love. Love is your nature. You are love, and you can no longer deny it. You can say "I am love" and mean it. You can express love to others, and you do not need to fear that they will not reciprocate because to be loved is the most natural thing in the world. If they rebuff your statement of love, you will understand that they were raised in a low-energy environment and that they remain at that level. You, however, are now living at a highly energetic level.

The truth is that you are worthy. You are a unique individual and no one like you has ever existed before or will ever exist again. Your uniqueness indicates that you are worthy. Without your unique contribution, the universe would not be the same. Therefore, you are absolutely as worthy as, but no more worthy than, any other being who has ever existed. It is time for you to live to your standard of absolute worthiness. It is time to adopt a stance of conscious confidence.

As your standards for speech are raised to a higher level, your life will automatically improve. When you focus on the words that come from your mouth, you will begin to experience a shift in the quality of your life that directly matches the shift in the quality of your words. As you change the topics you discuss from low-energy subjects to high-energy subjects, you automatically turn the course of your life toward a new, higher level.

It is not easy to change. That is why you cannot be timid. You must radically change in order for change to take hold. You must dismiss your limiting beliefs and habits of thought and speech. You must look for thoughts and words that reflect the new standards you now hold. You must accept that this next stage in your spiritual reawakening demands that you evolve to a higher level.

In order to change your behavior, you must change your thoughts and words. When you add energy to words and thoughts, you add energy to your actions. Action is the most powerful tool of creation. Inspired action creates inspired results. Uninspired action creates disastrous results. Never act before you're inspired to do so. Never act until you've raised your standards of thought and speech.

When you have begun to bring energy to your words and thoughts through the practice of focus, it is time to bring energy to your actions and behavior. All action is preceded by thought. You can think to move your arm and your arm moves. Much of your action is preceded by habitual, low-energy thought.

Look at the way you brush your teeth in the morning. This is an action of habit. Consider the way you wash your body in the shower. You most often use the same order every day. You wash one part first, move on to the next part, and finish up at the same spot. It's habitual therefore it's low energy. You may eat your breakfast the same way every day. You may watch the same programs each day of the week. You might shop at the grocery store the same way every time you go. It's habitual and it's low-energy.

When you consciously add energy to your actions, you automatically raise the quality of those actions. By adding energy to action, you create better results. What manifests as a result of high-energy action is in line with your true desires. Therefore, all action requires the addition of energy.

III.

There is high energy in love and there is high energy in fear. Imagine the letter "U" in a chart. At the top left point of the U, see the word "Love." This is the highest-energy positive emotion there is. At the bottom of the U, where it curves, see the word "Habitual." This is a low-energy thought, action, or pattern of speech that has been repeated over and over. At the top right point of the U, see the word "Fear." This is also a high-energy feeling.

For the purposes of illustration, we will describe love as a high-energy positive emotion and fear as a high-energy negative emotion. In reality, these terms are neither positive nor negative. Sometimes love can be negative and fear can be positive. Often, fear is necessary. But in the context of creating your life on purpose, we will discuss these terms relative to the creation of what is wanted rather than what is unwanted.

The energy of love is required to create wanted manifestations. The love energy is present in emotions such as love, appreciation, gratitude, interest, passion, joy, fun, happiness, exuberance, playfulness, empathy, etc. These are all highly energetic emotional states of being. These all have tremendous powers to create what is wanted. These feelings contain the energy necessary to fulfill your desires and to manifest your dreams into your reality.

The energy of fear creates unwanted manifestations, just as the energy of love creates wanted manifestations. The energy of fear is found in anger, despair, loneliness, frustration, revenge, hatred, etc. These are also very powerful states of being and have the energy necessary to bring unwanted experiences into your reality.

In order to radically change your approach to life, you must understand the impact of your emotional state of being in the moment. If you are in the state of appreciation, for instance, the object of your appreciation will grow larger. You will get more of the essence of your appreciation. That is what appreciation means. If you appreciate your family, your love for them will grow. If you appreciate your job, your job satisfaction will grow. If you appreciate your government for all the positive things it does to create a better life for you and those you love, your government will do more beneficial things.

However, if you allow yourself to linger in an emotional state of being based in fear, you will likely create scenarios that reflect this fear-based state which will manifest into your experience. If you declare your hatred of something, that thing will present itself to you in some fashion. You will then hate it even more. If you try to eradicate something you do not like out of anger, you will get more of it.

Hatred and appreciation are opposite sides of the same coin. Focus on either one and you'll bring more of it into your experience. If you appreciate the positive aspects of something, you will be given more reasons to appreciate that thing. If you hate something, you'll be given more excuses to hate that thing. The universe doesn't know whether you hate or appreciate something. It just gives you more of what you focus your attention on.

You are the one who decides if something is good or bad. If it's good and you focus your attention on it, you'll get more of it. If it's bad and you focus on it, you'll get more of it. The universe works in this manner because there are many people operating within the same system. Preference is an individual thing. Some people might look at a volcano and appreciate its beauty while others look at the same volcano and fear its destructive potential.

Do you see the perfection in this design? You get to choose what you like and then focus on that. However, you do not get to choose what another person should like or dislike. You do not get to remove all things you think are wrong from the experience of others. This includes your children.

You are meant to focus on what you like and to remove your focus from whatever it is you do not like. If you do not like chocolate ice cream, simply order whatever flavor you do like. Don't rally to have chocolate removed from the menu. There are others who get something from it even if you can't imagine it. Some people need to experience certain things even if you think it's wrong, and even if you think they are wrong.

IV.

Part of the radical change in your approach to life will come from your understanding of how the energy present all around you helps form your version of reality. Imagine a reality show you've recently watched on TV. Some of the contestants have a very high level of energy. They are alive. They are in motion. They speak loudly and quickly. Other contestants seem flat and lacking in energy. Maybe they are shy or reserved. You can sense that the producers have tried to ramp up their energy levels because their energy is carried through the television. It is obvious to viewers that some people have energy and others do not.

If you watch the energy of the contestants closely, you can see the difference between the people who are energetic because of their confidence and those who have energy based in fear. The next time you view a reality program, watch closely and observe how the contestants act. Those who are confident have high energy levels and those who are fearful also have high energy levels. Both groups are wide awake and focused. However, those focused in confidence have the energy of love, while the others who are focused in doubt and worry have the energy of fear. The winner will always be the one whose energy came from a place of confidence. The winner spent more time focused on thoughts of confidence and fun. The losers all spent more time focused on fear-based thoughts.

Base your stance on love and you will gain real confidence. View the universe as supportive and you will start to believe there is nothing to fear. Appreciate where you are now and bring that energy into everything you do. Think of the energy in the words, thoughts, and actions that emanate from your being. Bring in the love energy and remove your focus from anything that may attract the fear energy. Your conscious awareness will dictate your new approach to life.

You may not have understood the energy that surrounds you. You may not have realized the benefit of love energy and the limitation of fear energy. However, you have come to understand this aspect of physical reality in a clearer way than ever before. Now you simply have to remember what you have learned. You just have to pay attention to what you're thinking, saying, and doing in each moment. Do not fall back into old habits. Create new habits.

Look again at our graph which resembles the letter "U." At the top left point of the U, we have the word "Love." Love-based actions are all actions that come from a place of love, appreciation, joy, fun, happiness, excitement, exhilaration, passion, interest, etc. Any time you are doing something that is based in love, you are moving toward your desires. You are in the process of manifesting what is wanted.

At the bottom of the curve is the word "Habitual." This is unconscious action. Habitual action involves no deliberate thought and therefore lacks the power to create anything new. Habitual action is preceded by habitual thought. This type of action keeps you stuck in the same place, living the same life, over and over in each new moment.

At the right tip of the U, we see the word "Fear." Fear-based action is also full of creative energy. Action taken out of fear has the potential to manifest unwanted outcomes. Fear-based action is preceded by thoughts of fear, anger, hatred, jealousy, injustice, revenge, greed, worry, etc. These fear-based actions have the power to create something new, but it will not be something pleasurable.

If action is not inspired from love, it is not action worth taking. Since action is the most highly energetic step in creation, you must understand where the thought is coming from. Is it a love-based thought, a habitual thought, or a fear-based thought? Before acting, think about the inspiration. Why are you doing what you're about to do? What will be the ramifications of this action? Where will this action ultimately lead you?

If you are happy in your relationship and are inspired to buy your mate a gift, you can easily recognize that this inspiration to act is based in love. Only positive things will come from this action. If you are worried about the condition of your relationship and are inspired to send a hurtful text, you can see that this action is inspired by fear. It is likely that this action will create an unwanted condition or experience.

Inaction can also be based in love or in fear. If you choose not to do something because doing it would not be good for you or another, this is inaction based in love. If you choose not to do something because you're worried about your ability, the potential for failure, or what other people will think, then this inaction is based in fear.

Inaction based in love is not engaging in an activity that has the potential to do you harm or to harm another. It takes courage not to do something you are urged by others to do. When others expect you to take uninspired action, it takes fearlessness to say no. Action taken that does not serve you has the creative ability to lead you away from what you truly want. Succumbing to peer pressure, for instance, is taking uninspired action.

Inaction based in fear has the same effect. If you do not take action because you are afraid of the action itself, you will not be able to go where you say you want to go. If you do not attempt something you want to do because you fear failure or rejection, then the fear-based thought has prevented the universe from delivering to you that which you truly you want.

To change your approach to life, start thinking about what you're thinking, what you're saying, and what you're doing. Are your thoughts based in love? Are they based in fear? Or are they just habitual? Now that you know about the energy that surrounds all thoughts, words, and actions, you can consciously choose high-energy, love-based thoughts, words, and actions. This one simple understanding can radically change the quality of your life forever.

Chapter Four

The Present Moment

The concept of the present moment is very difficult for physical beings to understand. How do you capture a moment? It is fleeting. It is here and then it's gone. The moment is found somewhere between the past and the future. Once it comes, it becomes the past. How do physical beings understand something as ethereal as the present moment?

We can talk about the present moment in two ways. You can think of it as a photograph or as a short scene in a film. Let's look at both examples.

The moment you are in right now, while reading this book, in this chair, in this room, is a special moment. Mentally take a picture of yourself, wherever you are, whatever you're doing in this moment. Now pretend that you are looking at a glossy 8" x 10" full-color photograph of the moment you just took with your mental camera. What do you see?

Do you see yourself there in the center of the picture? Do you see your surroundings? What is the first thing that comes to mind? Do you notice that everything is all right? Everything in that photograph is fine the way it is. Everything is as it should be. If not, it would be a different photo. Can you appreciate the photo for what it is? Can you see the beauty of the picture or are you picking out the flaws?

You must come to understand that the moment is right the way it is. You must come to appreciate what is good in the picture. You must see everything as okay *and* improving.

This is such a key step in radically changing your approach to life that we want to stress it again. This moment in time is your creation. You have set up the scene through every thought you have ever had in your life. This photo-moment is the summation of your creative abilities. It is just you, sitting there, reading a book. Do you realize that if you had lived another way, if you had made different choices, if anything in your past had occurred differently, then this photo would literally never exist?

This photo, this moment, is your creation. You could create nothing grander than this moment. It is not possible to change the moment in the moment. An incredible amount of unseen momentum and energy has brought you to this moment. You think you're just here, that it's just a random moment like any other moment. It just happened and it's no big deal. The next moment will not be that much different, and there are so many moments.

That is why it is so hard for you to understand the concept of the present moment. To you it means nothing. There are occasional big moments in life, such as the birth of a child, a school graduation, a wedding, a death, New Year's Eve, Christmas, the last day of school, the first day of school, a retirement party, etc. Then there are all the moments in between that you discard as non-moments - all the meals, all the showers, all the conversations, all the contemplations, all the worrying, all the little arguments, all the frustrations, all the smiles to strangers, and all the laughter. These moments you consider small.

What if we were to tell you that all moments are equal? None of them are big and none of them are small. It all depends on your judgment. If you had no judgment regarding the moment, you would see each moment in a new light. If you believed that each moment was as valuable, as important as the next, your life would radically change.

Each moment affects the next moment and works to shape your future. How you act or react in this moment creates the reality of your next moment. Imagine your life as a huge steam locomotive barreling down the track. There is a lot of momentum, and it's not easy to change course. Trains must change direction over long stretches of track. Up ahead you're laying the track. Each piece of track you lay is a moment in time.

As the train rolls over a track, in each moment, you can see that it is a different piece of track. The view from this track is slightly different than the view from the last track. But with each new moment, you're in a new place. As you lay new track, you have the ability to move in a slightly new direction. Because the momentum of the train limits how much you can change, you make gradual course changes. We call this change "radical."

This is the reason it is difficult for you or anyone you know to change. There is momentum that has been built up over time. The older you are, the more momentum has been created. But since you are always laying new track, you can always change direction. You only have to be conscious about the track you are laying in the moment.

You cannot lay track in the future or the past. You can only lay track in the now. You create your future, the direction of your life, from the track you lay in this moment. You can move the track a little to the left, a little to the right, or keep it going straight. It's up to you.

Another way to change the direction of the train is for the train to jump the tracks altogether and land on a whole new track. This type of change is never pleasant and often the train crashes in the process. You have seen many examples of this yourself, where people attract serious life-threatening diseases or experiences and change the course of their life. Something so frightening has occurred that they are able to rethink their approach to life, and they jump the tracks to a new approach to life. It's painful but effective.

In our examination of a radical change in your approach to life, we seek to show you how to make little changes in the moment that will allow your momentum to carry you where you want to go in a painless, easy, and enjoyable manner.

The moment carries the momentum. This means that the only way to change the momentum is to change within each moment. The moment is the only way you can change the momentum. Moments cause momentum. Momentum causes you to miss the moment.

Let's go back now and look at that photo you took of the moment. Let's examine what you see. You see yourself in a room sitting on a chair or lying in bed reading a book. You see yourself in the center of the picture. You see yourself with someone else in the room or not. You see yourself with a pet or not. You see a lovely furnished room or not. You see the good that is there or not. You are happy with the scene or not.

When you look at that photo and feel good about what you see, you lay the track in the direction of where you want to go. If you look at that photo and feel bad, you lay the track so that it will take you where you do not want to go.

If you appreciate what you see in the photo, you're building a solid track toward what is wanted. If you see all kinds of things that are wrong with the photo, you are laying a solid track toward more of the same. Things will not improve until you come to understand that everything in the photo is fine the way it is. We wanted to use the word "perfect" rather than "fine," for that is the truth. But we feel your resistance to that word because you feel that nothing can be perfect, that everything could be better; and this is what is ultimately keeping you stuck where you are.

The dichotomy is this. Everything in the moment *is* perfect and *has* the potential to get better. However, it can't get better if the *what is* in the moment is seen as less than good or less than perfect. If it is, it's perfect. Get used to this word in a new way. The *what is* can be no other way than what it is. The picture, in that moment, cannot be changed. It cannot be airbrushed or touched up. It is what it is, and therefore, by definition, it is perfect.

Perfection is what is. That is the ultimate truth. And what is can get better and when it comes in the next moment it is perfect again. Even if you judge one moment to be better than the next, each moment is perfect in and of itself,. Perfection means you would not change a thing. It is perfect. Since you cannot change anything in the moment, we call that perfection. If you wouldn't change it, it's perfect. If you can't change it, it's also perfect. Since you're unable to change anything in the moment, the moment must be perfect.

If you find yourself arguing with this concept, you are not doing yourself any favors. It is imperative that you understand that each moment is 1) perfect, and 2) cannot ever be changed. It does not serve you to wish for things to be better in this moment, for then you are simply placing your attention on the negative aspects of the moment. If instead you saw that the moment was perfect and eagerly awaited the next moment for the improvement you desired, you would move the course of your life to a radically new and improved place.

II.

Another way to look at the moment is to see it as a scene in a film. The moment is now a short film rather than a still photograph. You are doing something in the moment. You could be making breakfast, jogging, or having a nice telephone conversation. One moment changes to the next when something happens in the moment to cause your feelings to shift or the scene to change. The moment ends when you finish your shower, and a new moment begins. The moment ends when you've finished making breakfast, and a new moment starts when you eat your breakfast. The moment ends in your telephone conversation when you hear something you don't like, and a new moment begins as your feelings change.

In that conversation, the person you're speaking with says something that causes you to go from one feeling to another feeling. What they said makes you change the way you feel. You have a reaction to what was said. That is a physical, chemical, emotional reaction. Your reaction radically changes the next moment.

How you react to the moment causes the track you are laying to shift to another course. In your reaction, you change the track to match how you feel about what has happened. There are no positive or negative reactions, for these are simply judgments. There are only reactions that align with what you want, who you really are, and where you say you want to go or not.

Reactions for most humans are unconscious and automatic. You do not think about the ramifications of your reactions. If you could even out your reactionary responses, you would live a much smoother life. Reactions to events are the bumps in the track. React more softly to these events and you will smooth out your ride. Become consciously aware of your reactions and you'll react in a way that aligns with what it is that you truly want. If you were aware of the way your reactions shape your future reality, you would become masters of the art of reaction. You would take things much more lightly.

Just as in the moment that we represented as a still photograph, where everything in that moment is perfect, everything in the moment that is the short scene is also perfect. Again, if you would not change a thing because it couldn't be any better, you would call that thing perfect. However, if you could not change a thing because the thing could not be changed, we would call that thing perfect.

It is for your benefit to define something that cannot be changed as perfect. If you cannot make something better, then it is perfect the way it is. *What is* is perfect because it could not be any other way. The moment is always perfect because it could not be any other way. You cannot change the moment. If it is, then *what is* is perfect. If you see the moment as flawed, you are arguing with *what is*. That is what keeps you feeling stuck.

In order to radically change your approach to life, you must come to understand that the moment has occurred and cannot be altered in any way. What you have lived your entire life has brought you to this moment. There is nothing you can do about it once the moment has arrived. You cannot change the moment or ask for a different moment. You just have to accept the moment exactly as it is.

There are two ways to experience any moment. You can wish that it was different in some way. You can look at all the flaws within the moment. You can pick out aspects you would change. You can complain about the moment. You can wonder how this moment came to you. You can allow the moment to cause negative emotions, and you can react negatively to the moment.

Or you could love the moment no matter what. You could understand that it is here, and that there's nothing you can do about the moment in the moment. You could look for the positive aspects of the moment. You could soften your judgment about the moment. You could appreciate that *what is* was created by you. This moment is your creation, and you can learn a lot from it. You can grow and expand in the moment. But the most important thing about this moment is how you react to it.

It is possible for every moment to be better than it is. We will accept that from your perspective, you could analyze each and every moment and figure out how to improve it. You are beings who have a magnificent ability to define preferences. This is all part of being physically focused. However, once you've realized that momentum has caused the moment to arrive and there's nothing you can do to change the moment, you must come to love it with all your heart.

If you fight against the moment, you are waging a losing battle with what is. Nothing can change what is. You can only have an effect on what will be. What is already is and cannot change. Once it has arrived it is fixed in time and space. More importantly, *what is* is your creation. To find flaws in your creation is not to appreciate your own powers of creation.

It is perfectly natural for you to be disappointed with the moment if you believe the moment just happened and you're a victim of someone else's creation. However, this victim mentality does not serve you. You give away your power when you claim to be the victim of fate or some other force you have no control over.

Since you are coming to understand that you create your reality, you are now able to see your powers of creation for what they are. However, if you believe you create your own reality and you judge your creation as flawed, you sink back into victimhood. Now you are the victim of your own creation, which makes it even worse.

What we want you to see is the next level of beingness. We want you to know that you create your own reality and that your creation, in the moment, is perfect, because that is the truth. From your perspective, you may have developed the habit of focusing on the flaws in the moment or the problems with what you have created. We want you now to understand that you are an evolving being. You are getting better all the time. You are improving your powers of creation in every moment. But your perspective is limited. If you can come to know that each moment that has been created by you is perfect, you can begin to consciously and deliberately create what is wanted.

The way the universe works is that you are given what you ask for. You ask with your feelings and your thoughts. If you feel that something is wrong and you think about the problem, the universe will respond with more of what's wrong and with even bigger versions of the problem. That's the mechanism of The Law of Attraction, and it is a perfect system. It works for everyone all the time, whether they know it or not. It's like gravity, but it's even more consistent.

So, imagine now working within the system. Think about how you could make this mechanism of physical reality work for you. How would you view each moment? What would you think about?

If you wanted to radically change your approach to life, you would stop complaining about things that could be better in the moment and start appreciating whatever is good about each moment. You would remove your attention from anything you judge to be negative in the moment, and you would look for whatever positive aspects you could find in the moment. Your habit of complaining would change to a habit of appreciation. Let's analyze how this works within the framework of these universal laws.

If the universe is designed to give you whatever it is that your attention is focused on, and you have the ability to place you attention on things wanted and unwanted alike, where would you choose to focus? Would you look at what you perceive as negative in the belief that your focus on the negative aspects would cause those things to disappear, or would you focus on what you consider to be positive in the knowledge that what you focus on brings more of that into your experience?

The universe brings you more of whatever you are focused on. You have the freedom to discern whether something is preferable or not. Your judgment is the only thing that matters. If you judge that something is good and that it is what you want, the universe will not question your judgment. It will give you more of it. If you judge that something is bad and you remove your attention from it, then the universe will remove it from your experience. Doesn't this all make so much sense to you now? Do you see the perfection in the design?

You could have a preference for chocolate ice cream and think it's a wonderful thing. Another person could hate chocolate ice cream and think it's horrible. That's the beauty of this environment. One person can pursue what they like, and another can pursue the opposite, and everyone can live happily pursuing different things with no one getting in anyone else's way. If you all liked the same things, you would have a very limited experience. Since everyone can like what they want, the experience of life is unlimited.

Since this system cannot be improved, we call it perfect. Since this system of physical reality and the laws that go with it cannot be changed, we call it all perfect.

The moment is what the moment is, and it can never be changed, no matter how much you love or hate it. However, your reaction to the moment will create the next moment and many moments after that. Momentum is created in the moment, which creates the next moment. How you feel about the present moment tells the universe what you want to feel in future moments. You order your future from your present.

If you look at the moment and see what you do not like, the universe brings you that. This is how you get stuck in life. This is how the rut is sustained. This is what makes change difficult. To radically change your life, you must look for what you like in the moment. This is as easy as appreciating what is.

III.

It is easy to appreciate the moment when you consider it to be a good moment. In these moments, you must extract as many good feelings as you can. You must linger on these moments. You must feel as good as possible and relish the moment. This will signal to the universe that you want more of these moments.

However, when you judge a moment to be bad, you must also look for what is wanted in the moment. We will call what is wanted "positive" and that which you do not want "negative." When you look for the positive aspects of a moment, you are offsetting some of what you judge to be negative. The better you are at looking for positive aspects in these unpleasant moments, the more you will tune yourself to what you prefer.

This is the key to creating a life that is comprised mostly of what you want. This is the method by which you can constantly improve the experience you are living. You may choose to focus on any aspect of any situation. However, your future is shaped by the focus of your attention. How do you want that future to unfold?

It might be a habit of yours to rant about injustice in the world. But would you still want to express these thoughts if you knew that you bring to your future what you focus on in your present? It's something to think about isn't it? Sometimes it's fun to gossip about the problems of others, but what are you really doing? What if you knew that everything you said would come back into your experience at a later date? What would you talk about then?

There are three components of creation: thought, words, and action. If you know how this system works, what are you now going to think about, talk about, and act on? This is food for thought.

Momentum has led you to these pages, so we know you're on the right track. You want to create a wonderful life and to feel good. You have a habit of being a certain way in this physical reality. You like to think the same thoughts, talk about the same things, and do the same activities. If you can break these habits and replace them with a more deliberate approach to life, you will start to build a track that will take you where you really want to go.

To radically change your approach to life, you will start accepting each moment as it is. You cannot change anything in the moment, for as soon as the moment has occurred it becomes the past and a new moment presents itself. If something cannot be changed, it must be thought of as perfect. When you cry out in frustration because the moment is not to your liking, you seek to change that which cannot be changed. This is not only a worthless use of your energy, but it also sends a signal to the universe to bring you more of the same.

If you can gain the posture of neutrality in those moments you judge to be less than ideal, you'll create a standard by which all future moments have the potential to improve. If you can see the moment for what it is and release your negative judgment of it, you will become a neutral observer.

This ability to analyze the moment and understand why it causes you to feel bad will help improve future moments. Let us explain this further.

For our example, you find yourself in a hurry. Something has caused you to fall behind on your schedule and now you're running late for a meeting. You feel anxious in this moment. You fear the ramifications of your tardiness. You believe yourself to be punctual, and to you this is a fine quality. To be late would tarnish your valued reputation.

On your way to your appointment, you find yourself trapped behind two slow-moving cars taking up both lanes on a two-lane road. There is no easy way around them, and you're forced to succumb to their pace. You find yourself becoming angry. It is at this point that you decide to decipher the scene. You choose to analyze this moment consciously. Your emotion has indicated that you are judging *what is* to be wrong.

You feel the emotion of anger well up inside you. It really doesn't matter what the emotion is; if you don't feel good, it's a negative emotion. It could be sadness, regret, pity, apathy, worry, doubt, etc. It just feels bad. In this case, it's anger, because you want the drivers in front of you to do something they are not doing. You want the moment to be different than it is.

Now, before you became a conscious being and realized that every moment is created by you and you must take responsibility for your creation, you would blame the drivers in front of you for causing you to be late. However, you know better now. You now understand why they are there and how they got there. You understand that it was you who put them there. This moment is your creation and you're going to take responsibility for it.

There is a lot to talk about in this scene, but we will not spend too much time on the story that led to these two drivers blocking your path. Let's simply look at the two ways you could view this moment. The unconscious creator would not be in this moment at all. The unconscious mind would be focused on the future. The unfocused mind would play scenarios over and over that would show the negative impact of the tardiness. The mind would play images of the worst possible outcomes. And this would create more anger and anxiety.

The conscious mind, however, would see this moment for what it is. It is perfect. There is no other way to view what is. The two cars are blocking the road for a reason. The reason is always spiritual growth. Spiritual growth can only occur in a conscious mind. Only someone who is in the process of reawakening can understand the potential for growth in every moment.

If you are in this moment and can find the growth factor within it, then the moment has a purpose. Since all moments are purposeful, your ability to see its true purpose means you have reached a certain level in your spiritual growth. You understand that the cars blocking your path are there specifically to alert you to an aspect that must be changed in order for you to continue your growth. There is only one reason they are there; they're there for you.

An unconscious mind would consider this unusual moment to be random and would curse it for what it was doing to them. The unconscious mind would feel like a victim of fate. "How can these two cars block my path and cause me to be late? Why is this happening to me?"

A conscious mind would assume that there is something embedded in this moment. The negative emotion would signal that there is something to learn here. The conscious mind would begin to analyze the situation. It would look for the lesson. It would begin to do this automatically whenever negative emotion arose within.

You are a conscious thinker. What do you think the placement of these two slow-moving cars blocking your path means to you? What is this moment trying to tell you? It is telling you that your belief that you must be punctual is not serving you. It is telling you that you are not being in the moment, but are being in the future. If you are being in the future, and that future looks unpleasant, then you are creating what is not wanted. It is fine to be in the future as long as what you are imagining (creating) is something wonderful. However, when you find yourself out of the moment, worried about what might occur, you are creating what you do not want. You are laying track in a direction away from where you want to go.

The message from the universe in this example helps you grow spiritually. It is for your benefit, even though it may seem as if things are not going your way. You could easily view the moment as a problem to be solved. You could take a risk and drive in the oncoming lane in order to pass the two cars and arrive at your appointment on time. Or you could drive into a truck and make a swift transition to the nonphysical. Either way, you will have lost the message in the moment.

If you feel negative emotion, the moment has a lesson. If you solve the moment, you lose the lesson. If you view the moment as a challenge, you overcome the moment and miss the message. The universe will offer you the same message over and over and over again. The message will get louder and louder. The moment will become stronger and more pronounced. You will have to fight harder and harder to miss the message. One day the message will cause so much pain that you will have to receive it. It will be unavoidable.

Our example of the two cars blocking your path and causing you to be late to your appointment was a subtle message from the universe. There was some negative emotion involved, but the pain was slight. If you got the message, you moved to a new level, and new messages will be delivered. If you didn't get this lesson, then stronger versions of the same message will be sent.

The next time you find yourself running behind schedule and late to a meeting you might encounter a moment where a policeman gives you a speeding ticket and makes you really late to your appointment. If that doesn't work, you might find yourself in a car accident. If that doesn't work, something bigger will have to get in your way until you realize that your beliefs about promptness are not serving where you say you want to go.

This is simply the mechanism of the universe, and it cannot be any other way. Therefore, it is perfect. What cannot be changed must be considered perfect.

IV.

There is always something to be observed in the moment. In every moment, there is the life you have led that has created the moment. Every single moment in your life is your creation. It is the result of your thoughts and beliefs over a very long period of time. Moments are products of momentum. In this physical reality there are the two aspects of time and space. It is a space-time reality.

What you think now will manifest itself in some other time or place. It does not become physical instantly (thank God). Your mind is undisciplined, and your thoughts fluctuate from what is wanted to what is unwanted every other second. If you instantly manifested every thought, you would spin into oblivion in a matter of moments. Time slows the manifestation process to a controllable level.

Yet you still create that which you do not want. The aspects of time and space make manifesting what you prefer a very simple task. What you do not prefer is manifested with surprising frequency. Why do you think this is? Why, in an environment designed to help you create what is wanted, would you create so many unwanted experiences? We have two answers for you.

Our first answer has to do with your clarity of thought, which we will discuss in detail later on. Our second answer, which has to do with the present moment, is a matter of your perspective. When something happens that you do not prefer, you believe you have created an unwanted condition. Yet this unwanted condition is necessary to your spiritual growth. Both wanted conditions and unwanted conditions further your expansion. You deem the wanted experiences as positive and the unwanted experiences as negative. You are proud of your creative abilities when something wanted occurs, yet you damn those same abilities when you judge that something negative has happened.

If you are a spiritually enlightened being, you do not consider yourself more worthy just because you are a punctual individual. This is a characteristic of an ego-centered mind. You only believe this to be a virtue because you have been told by others that it is good to be on time and bad to be late. Yet there is no natural law that asks this of you. In fact, this belief is limiting, and for you to get where you say you want to go, you must alter this belief.

The universe will work within many moments to help you see that this belief does not serve who you really are. You have asked to become who you really are. You have asked to peek beneath the veil. You have asked to look behind the curtain. If you are reading this book, you are on a spiritual journey of reawakening and becoming who you really are. You cannot go back. You know too much. You have asked for it, and now the universe is delivering it to you.

Resistance to the present moment is resisting who you really are. When you fight against, argue, or complain about what is, you resist the modifications to your belief system that must take place for you to allow yourself the growth you seek. The universe is doing its job. Are you resisting or going with the flow?

So you experience a moment where you are trapped behind two slow-moving cars. You understand you created this moment, but you judge it to be unwanted. Therefore, you believe you've created that which you do not prefer. You think you've created an unwanted condition. If you were a timely person, you would create an open path to your destination. Now you can see that this is a flawed premise. There is a much higher purpose involved here.

If you are in the early stages of awakening you might have difficulty experiencing the Law of Attraction as you have learned about it. It does not seem to be working in the way you thought it would. Some things are going your way, and other things seem to be working against you. This is the most common belief among those new to this journey.

The universe is answering your call to reach a higher level of being-ness. Your petty desires based on egotistical preferences are not the concern of the universe. You have asked to become more, and the universe is responding to what you are asking for, which in this case is the highest version of you. All things that come to you now are for your growth, even if it seems wrong or bad from your perspective. You are now being asked to reach for a much higher perspective. We will attempt to explain how this is achieved.

Chapter Five

The Higher Perspective

Physical reality seems like an individual experience. You feel like an isolated individual living in your body. You believe there is no one else with you inside your body. But this is not true. You are not alone. You are one with your inner self.

Your inner self is the part of you that is still focused in the nonphysical realm. From this vantage point, your inner self sees everything. It sees your past, your present, and, based on your current trajectory, your potential future. Your inner self knows you and everything you want. It knows what you're thinking, who you're being, and where you want to go. Your inner self is here to help you navigate this reality and lead you wherever you say you want to go.

From your individual perspective, on the ground, in the present moment, you have a very limited perspective. You see the world and your place within that world in a very finite way. You have beliefs that narrow your perspective even further. Your inner self can see a much wider, broader view of your life. You see a small portion of what's really going on, while your inner self sees the full picture.

In order to radically change your approach to life, you will begin to view the world and your place in that world from the same perspective as your inner self. You must learn to see more than what's right in front of you. You will need to practice this larger perspective. Right now, your inner self can see your world through your eyes. You must start to see your world through the eyes of your inner self.

II.

Imagine you are living in a valley. You have lived in this valley your entire life. There are huge mountains that surround your little village. You have not dared to brave these mountains to see what's on the other side and you can only imagine what's out there. When travelers come to your village and tell stories of the world outside, you will view the world through their perspective. If they tell dark, fearful stories of the world outside, you will cling to the security of your little village. If they tell wondrous tales of the outside world, you may long for adventure and wish to see these things for yourself. But until you brave those mountains on your own, you'll never know the true story.

Your reality is limited to the beliefs you hold. The world around you is formed strictly to conform to your set of beliefs. Until you start to venture out on your own, you will be constrained by what you believe, whether the beliefs support what you want or not. Almost all of your beliefs were formed from the tall tales of others. Like the travelers to your village, you formed beliefs about the world based on what others told you. You did not form very many of your beliefs from your own personal experiences.

The beliefs that came to you through the influences of others fall into two categories: limiting beliefs and beneficial beliefs. Limiting beliefs hold you apart from what you want, while beneficial beliefs allow you to move in the direction of what is wanted. In order to become the highest version of you, you will reduce the intensity of limiting beliefs and raise the intensity of beneficial beliefs.

Limiting beliefs are always born out of fear. You are afraid of something and you form a belief about it. All limiting beliefs are based on some irrational fear. Once you are able to consciously analyze a limiting belief to discover the fear it's based on, you will reduce its intensity. When you see that a belief does not support you because there is no evidence to support the belief, you can then work to reduce its impact on your life.

The fear that you are not good at something is a limiting belief. The fear this belief is based on is the fear of failure. Since we now know that fear of failure is an irrational fear (because it is not life-threatening), we can truly know that it is a limiting belief. We lower the intensity of the limiting belief by showing that it is a false assumption and that there is no real evidence to support it.

Let's say you believe you're bad at math. Whenever someone asks you a question involving a mathematical problem, you feel negative emotion. This is your first sign that you have encountered a limiting belief. In this case, the belief is that you're not good at math. Because this belief is present, you will have difficulty answering the question. Fear has made itself present and you have lost the ability to answer the question.

If you felt confident in your mathematical abilities, you would be able to answer the question easily. It is not a matter of education, or even of having an aptitude for math; it is simply a matter of belief. If you believe you're good at math, you'll have confidence when facing the question. If you believe you lack mathematical aptitude, you'll encounter doubt when facing the question. The only difference is confidence over doubt. You are the same person.

The belief that you're good at math is a beneficial belief. Any belief that supports you is beneficial. This belief has arisen within you because people have told you that you were good at math. That's it. The more you believed it, the more evidence supported your belief. This is a fundamental law of the universe. It is the Law of Attraction. What you believe is always supported by physical manifestations of evidence. It matters not the subject, but only what you believe.

If you believe you're a poor math student, you'll be given evidence to support your limiting belief. You'll encounter situations that prove you're not good at this subject. You will start to believe that you have a mental block when it comes to math. When even the simplest math problem is given to you, your brain will shut down. The belief that you have a mental block will show itself in your reality time and time again. If you reverse this belief, you will learn that you are good at math.

How does one normally overcome a limiting belief? Through study and practice. If you believe you're no good at math but you want to become good at it, you'll likely decide to study math and practice what you learn.

This is not an easy thing to do. Many people who grow up with the belief that they just aren't mathematically inclined will simply make it through life avoiding anything related to math. You would have to have a keen desire to go back to school and learn the subject all over again.

The person facing this new challenge will have to reduce the intensity of their limiting belief and raise the intensity of an opposing belief. The poor math student will have to realize that he or she is actually good at math. How do you imagine this is accomplished? Let's take a look.

Something has caused a great desire for this person to suddenly want to learn math. He may have stumbled on a passion that requires a new understanding of math in order to explore this passion further. He has always believed he just didn't get math. But now he needs to understand it in order to do what he really wants to do. He knows he cannot follow his passion without gaining confidence in his mathematical abilities. So he decides to "learn" about math.

We want to tell you that there is nothing to learn. You simply think that learning is the only way to know something. While there is truth to that statement, what you really need to do is move from doubt to confidence. It is the vibrational stance that will allow you to know what you need to know. It is your belief system that will allow you to learn whatever you want to learn. So what our student is really doing is moving from fear to love and from doubt to confidence.

We understand this is a very difficult concept for you to believe. But it is a true concept, and if you believe it, it will be highly beneficial to you. Your thoughts are accessed by your vibrational stance, not created by your mind. You do not manufacture ideas, you attract them. You do not learn anything, you allow the information to flow or not to flow. Your stance of confidence turns the knowledge flow on and your stance of doubt restricts the flow of knowledge. Obviously, it is your belief in education that creates either a confident or a doubtful stance.

In order to radically change your approach to life, you must start adopting a confident stance in everything you do. You no longer have the luxury of entertaining doubt. You have come too far. You are on a journey of self-discovery. If you maintain your doubtful stance, you will endure pain and suffering. You will be pulled in the direction of who you really are while clinging to the limited version of who you are now. You have a stance of fear that does not serve you.

Unconscious minds think that living in fear is normal. They are accustomed to the pain of life. They do not expect too much and are not disappointed. But conscious minds understand more of what is going on around them. They know more about the mechanism of physical reality and they are moving toward who they really are. They are reawakening in this highly energetic time. They are evolving to an entirely new level. When conscious minds cling to fear-based beliefs, they feel the pain fully and completely. It is not easy for a conscious mind to resist its own evolution.

When you cling to beliefs that do not serve you, you will feel negative emotion more intensely. It is easier for you to want to give up or to fall back into self-pity or victimhood. This work might seem difficult. You might become overwhelmed or frustrated. Everything you've been taught is being turned on its head. Most of what you've learned does not serve you as you become who you really are. You will have to relearn a whole new approach to life.

Fortunately, your inner self is here to guide you. But you must be able to hear and understand that guidance. You must come to know that you are guided by your emotions. How you react to those emotions determines the direction of your life. If you react negatively to what you feel in the moment, you move away from who you really are. If you react positively to your emotions, you move toward the highest version of you. If you are able to be neutral in a situation you once would have considered negative and you understand the lesson in the moment, you move toward your true desires.

Donning the perspective of your inner self will allow you to see more of what is really happening. It will allow you to react to situations and conditions in a way that serves you. It will allow you to identify and reduce the intensity of limiting beliefs. It will help you gain the stance of confidence. It will guide you through life and keep you on your path toward the manifestation of what is wanted.

A negative reaction to what is happening in the moment is your sign that you do not see the situation in the same way your inner self sees it. You have judged the conditions that appear in the moment to be wrong, while your inner self sees the conditions as right. Why is this? It's simply a matter of perspective.

Your inner self can see the event from a wider, wiser perspective. You see the event through your perspective. The difference, then, is just the perspective. If you can modify your perspective to align with your inner self's perspective, you'll free yourself from your overly active judgment.

If you're running late to work and the stoplight turns red, you react negatively and wish that the light was green. You feel frustration and maybe a little anger. You might wonder why this is happening to you when you're running behind schedule. You might even feel a little like a victim, believing that things are happening to you rather than for you.

There are only two real emotions: love and fear. You either react positively to something (love) or negatively to something (fear). The basis of you is love. The basis of your inner self (who is also you) is love. You allow fear to enter when you judge something to be wrong. Your inner self is unconditional love. Your inner self knows that everything is happening for a reason, even if you don't. Your inner self sees that everything is always working out for you, even if you won't. Your inner self can see that what's happening is perfect, even if you see it as flawed.

When you align with your inner self, you feel positive emotion (love). When you disagree with your inner self, you feel negative emotion (fear). So every time you feel negative emotion, it's because you aren't aligned with your inner self. When you're aligned, you feel good, but when you're not in alignment, you feel bad. In order to gain the same perspective as your inner self, in order to be in alignment with what you want, you must simply feel good more often.

It is one thing to sit in your chair and just feel good. You probably feel good right now. When you are focused on what you want, what you enjoy, what you like, you feel good. Your inner self is focused on those things as well.

When you jump ahead and think thoughts of the future that are worrisome, you feel bad. You've just gone somewhere you're inner self would never go. You've allowed fear to enter your mind and your inner self has not. A worrisome thought, no matter how small, is a fearful thought and it does not serve you. Your inner self guides you away from these thoughts by using the negative feeling you are receiving. This is your guidance system in action.

The worse you feel, the more strongly your inner self wants you to move your attention away from the subject. If you feel awful, if you have a very strong emotional reaction to something, you see it in a way that really does not serve you. Your perspective is completely different from the perspective of your inner self. As soon as you can alter your perspective to match that of your inner self, you'll feel relief. As you soothe yourself by thinking in a way that brings you more in alignment with the higher perspective, you'll quickly start to feel better.

Feeling good is the key here. Can you understand that? Your work is always to help yourself to feel better in the moment. As soon as you notice the emergence of negative emotion, you must soothe yourself by thinking thoughts that align with the higher perspective.

Physical reality is really a feeling reality. It is only what you feel that matters. If you feel good, you are navigating your reality in a way that serves you. Feeling good brings you closer to where you want to go. Feeling bad takes you in another direction. You must always strive to feel good and then to feel better and better and better.

You have become accustomed to feeling bad. It does not bother you as much as it should. You have learned to live with it. Many of you believe that it is a normal part of being alive. You think you should feel good some of the time and that it's natural to feel bad some of the time. You even think it's strange for people to feel too good too much of the time. You suppose they have a mental condition or are on some sort of drug.

Yet feeling good all of the time is your nature. Feeling really good is your birthright. Feeling joy is how we gauge success in this reality. To be truly successful is to feel joy.

Humans strive for the feeling of accomplishment. This only feels good because you're trying to justify your worthiness to yourself and others. It is a good feeling and it's commendable, but it takes you on a false path. Since you are already worthy, as worthy as any other person but no more worthy than any other, you don't need to justify yourself. You have not come here to waste energy proving your own worthiness, because once you've proved your worthiness and felt the satisfaction associated with it, you'll be left feeling empty and searching for more ways to prove yourself to others.

You came here to experience. That is the reason for this physical reality. You are meant to feel joy, be happy, and expand through experience. You can and have experienced many things. However, what you now really want to experience is the highest version of you. If you are reading this book, then you are yearning to become who you really are.

IV.

Becoming who you really are is not simply knowing yourself. While that is certainly a key component of the process, it is not the end of the process. You must come to know who you are and then become the highest version of that entity while here on earth. You must come to know who you are, that you're worthy, that you're based in love, and then you'll discover the highest version of you. It is a process of self-discovery, then self-awareness, then self-creation, then self-actualization.

We will talk more about this process as we move along. But you are now starting to see that there is more to you than you realize. There is more we want you to become than you can imagine. There is a higher version of you that you are unfamiliar with. There is so much more to you, but you must remove the layers of fear you have wrapped around yourself. We are going to work together to peel away those layers to reveal the highest version of you.

You have come to believe that certain aspects of physical life within your society are to be admired and pursued. You believe it is good to have a college education. You believe it is right to be patriotic. You think it is admirable to be employed, own a home, raise a family, pay taxes, obey laws, vote, watch sports, have friends, celebrate holidays, and participate in all other aspects of your society. We agree. These are all wonderful aspects of physical life. Yet they are intoxicating if you do not stand back and see what is happening.

There is nothing wrong with enjoying the trappings of your wonderful society. It is so much fun to participate in all the activities. It is a joy to be with friends and family. But it is also easy to fall into becoming someone who conforms to society rather than someone who strives to become who they really are.

You cannot be anyone less than who you really are. You cannot admire another and then believe that you are less worthy than this person. You cannot look with pity upon another and think you must be more worthy or more fortunate than them. You cannot allow the magnificent facade of your society to fool you into believing that you have been assigned a certain role to play or a specific class to belong to. You cannot allow yourself to believe that you have limitations when you compare yourself to others. You are a limitless being living in a universe that has the potential to allow you to do, have, and be anything you want. You just have to want it, understand how it all works, and then believe you can get there.

You cannot allow yourself to be fooled by the illusion of reality. You are not one of many. You are not a tiny individual in an infinite universe. You are the center of your universe. Everything you see has been constructed for your expansion. This is your playground and all the others are simply your playmates. You are not the best or the worst, you are simply the only one who really matters in your universe.

You are love, so now you must love. All love is self-love. All love is aligning with the higher perspective of your inner self. All love starts with you. You are the center of your universe. You start with self-love and self-appreciation and it will spread out from there. Love is alignment with the higher perspective. Love is the good feeling. Feel good and you've allowed love. Feel bad and you've allowed fear.

V.

We are not saying it's wrong to feel fear and right to feel love. We are simply pointing out that the design of this physical reality is meant to move you more towards love and less towards fear. The duality of love and fear was created as a device to help you move more towards love because love feels good. It was not meant for you to feel love and fear equally. It was assumed that you would naturally move toward love, since love feels better. It was thought that humans would want to feel good rather than bad. But humans were given free will and desire. Humans are able to contemplate their actions and allowed to create methods to achieve those desires. Humans were also given a survival instinct.

The survival instinct allows for the proper use of fear. Since survival is innately and naturally desired, fear is used to achieve that desire. Fear of heights prevents death by gravity. Fear of being eaten prevents death by lion. Fear as part of the desire to survive is extremely helpful. In a wild and rough environment, you might experience fear in large doses. You might even get accustomed to the feeling of fear.

You have evolved to become a species that has overcome much of what is considered dangerous in your environment. In this society, you have little to fear with regard to your survival instinct. So now you have come to fear smaller things that are not life-threatening. This is just how it is and it's unavoidable. This is why you must wake up to the trappings of your more-evolved society.

All fear that is not life-threatening is irrational. It is time to rationally contemplate what you're afraid of. If you feel negative emotion in any situation, it is due to some fearful (negative) thought. Now you must analyze it. Why do you feel negative emotion? What concerns you? Is it rational?

Is it worth the unpleasant feeling? Can you soothe yourself? Can you look at it from the higher perspective? Can you find relief?

This is your work. In order to become the highest version of you, you must reach for the higher perspective to soothe yourself and feel relief. To become who you really are, you must make this process a habit. You can no longer live a random-feeling life by reacting unconsciously to every little event. You must now form a habit of no reaction. You must become neutral when faced with situations that have the potential to cause a negative reaction. You must reach for the higher perspective quickly and naturally.

Your future is determined by your reaction to the present. It is time to react deliberately to create the future you prefer. This is a small but radical change in your approach to life, but it is one with immense power and it is a crucial skill needed to become who you really are.

Chapter Six

The Truth of Who You Really Are

You probably consider yourself an honest person. You probably like the qualities of honesty and truth. But in order to radically change your approach to life, you must become who you really are by completely altering your understanding of the truth of you.

The truth of you is the truth of who you really are. It is not the current version that sits reading this book. The you who you now display to the world is a chameleon. You behave (be) one way with this person and you behave (be) another way with that person. Which is the real you? You act confident in this situation and you act fearful in that situation. Are you confident or fearful? The truth of you is who you really are, regardless of the person you're with or the situation you're in.

Truth is transparency. In truth, there is nothing to hide. In truth, there is only unconditional love. All love is self-love and therefore your truth is the unconditional love of self.

You can probably imagine what must be done to become who you really are. You must strip away the layers that hide who you really are. You must abandon your insecurities, for they do not protect you. Why are you insecure about anything? Because you think that shying away from that which you fear is safe. It protects you from potential pain and suffering. But don't you see that you suffer in your insecurity? Choosing to lie about some aspect of yourself does not serve you and it keeps you apart from who you really are.

What is the secret you keep about yourself? Why do you hold this secret? What are you really afraid of? You are afraid of what others may think. You worry about losing love and respect. You fear the loss of something you really don't possess. You cannot hold onto this lie and live freely as you were meant to live. The only way to become who you really are is through the absolute truth of you.

The fact that you are not currently living as the highest version of you indicates that you are not living your truth. You are hiding out to some degree. There are parts of you that you are proud of and in those areas you show confidence. Maybe you believe yourself to be good at some aspect of your life. Maybe you were told you are attractive, or tall, or athletic, or intelligent. Maybe you can cook or have good taste or are funny. In these areas, you are able to live your truth.

However, there are also areas in which you do not believe you are good. In certain areas, you judge yourself to be less than. Maybe you're not that smart. Maybe you feel lazy compared to others. Maybe you lack the abundance you see around you. You find fault with certain aspects of who you are. You compare yourself to others in these areas and consider them to be so much better than you. You accept that there are some areas where you feel good about yourself and other areas where you just don't have it. You resign to the belief that it will always be this way. This is how you get stuck.

The truth is that you are immensely talented in every single area. It's just that some aspects of life are more interesting than others. You do not need to judge how you compare to others. Simply see how you compare to you. Are you growing? Is the present you evolving? Are you getting better? Are you coming to understand who you really are? Is the present you closer to who you really are than the past you? If so, you're on the right track.

II.

In this physical reality you can be, do, and have anything you want. What do you really, truthfully want? This is an important question. If you do not know what you truly want, then how will you get it? This is the first step toward living your truth.

If you are currently living life without knowing what you want, you are simply hiding from life and not living your truth. You are living a lie. If you are just going through life without interests and passions, then you are not living as you intended prior to your birth. You are meant to live with joy, following your interests and passions and experiencing expansion in the process.

If you cannot think of what you want, then you cannot be living your truth. You have wanted things in your life, but you've learned to set aside these desires because you felt unworthy of them. That is the truth behind your inability to think of something you really want. You believe that you cannot get what you want, so you don't even try. You give up before you start. You squelch the idea before it even gets off the ground.

Most of the things you want are to ease some condition you don't want. You want something so it can take you out of your present condition. You want this thing because you do not like what you have now and you believe that getting this new thing will erase this bad thing. You want money because you hate being broke. You want a partner because you hate feeling lonely. You want a new job because you hate your current job. You want a leaner body because you don't like your fat body.

The truth of who you are can be found in the real and honest reason you want something. In this system of physical reality, you can have anything you want. But the desire must be based in the truth of why you want it. The universe does not understand the word "not." It has no perception of negative or positive. It gives you what you ask for. If you want abundance to ease the feeling of lack, what you are saying is "I do not want lack." The universe cannot see or understand the word "not," so it gives you what you want, which is lack. It hears you say "I *do* want lack."

You cannot say "I do not want to be lonely," because the universe will hear your words as "I *do* want to be lonely." You cannot ease sickness by saying "I want to be healthy," because what you're really saying is "I do not want to be sick," which the universe hears as "I *do* want to be sick."

The universe does not listen to your words; it picks up your vibration. It only understands the signal you are sending. You can only send a signal that is purely positive. There is nothing negative in your signal. You are not able to emit the "not" in your vibration. You cannot lie in your vibration. You can only send what you really feel. Therefore, the universe only responds to the truth of how you are being as you send your vibration. You can lie to people, but you cannot lie to the universe. In order for this system to work for you, you have to be the truth of who you really are rather than the smaller, limited truth of who you're being right now.

This is the key to getting what you really want out of this life. It is the ability to project what you truly want through a vibration that is in complete alignment with who you really are. You can't fake your way to what you want. The truth of who you're being is always exposed to the universe. If you're not being who you really are, you're going to continue to get some of what you want and some of what you don't want. You're going to continue to live as you've been living without much progress.

If you can be honest about how you're being in this time of your life, you can begin to strip away the layers to unwrap the real you. There is really nothing to hide. As you become more honest about what you feel and what you really want, you'll experience vulnerability and some discomfort. You think the world around you will react one way to who you really are, but you'll be surprised how well the real you will be received by those around you.

Some may not be ready for the metamorphosis you will undertake. Others will be delighted. There will be a shift in your reality as you move rapidly to becoming the highest version of you. Some people will not be able to deal with the new you, as they have their own insecurities to work through. But many more people will gravitate to the new you. As you become who you really are by living and expressing your truth, you will raise your vibrational frequency. You will begin to attract others into your life who also vibrate at your new, higher frequency.

There is great freedom and joy in living your truth. There is frustration, anger, and depression in living outside of your truth. Illness and unwanted conditions often exist when one is resisting the truth that must be expressed. By becoming who you really are and by living your truth, you begin to express the essence of your inner self. You begin the path to ascension.

III.

There is no spiritual imperative at work here. It is simply truth. Either you will live your truth and become who you really are, or you will live outside of that truth as someone you are not. You are either on a path of spiritual growth and expansion or you are resisting that journey. You are either living in fear or moving toward love. This is the mechanism of physical reality.

You are here to joyfully expand. You come to this physical reality to experience joyous expansion. You do not come to make money, to prove your worthiness, to be the best in some competition, to become well-known, admired or famous, or to achieve any of those things you think are accomplishments. They are not the goals you seek. They are the side effects of your spiritual journey to become who you really are by living the truth of who you are.

You have little memory of the nonphysical realm or the mechanism of physical reality. You are influenced by others to become grounded in physical reality. Your senses reveal a textural environment that seems so real. It appears to be all that is. You might even come to believe that this environment is all you will ever know. From that context, you might even believe you have only one life and that you must make the most of it by doing something that proves your worthiness.

However, this physical environment is simply a vibrational illusion. It's just a fabricated playground. Your senses allow you to play the game vividly. You can do anything you want in this environment, but there is no rush. There is no end to life and you can't do anything wrong. There's nothing for you to prove because you are already worthy. All you wanted to do before you were born into this world is to live the highest expression of who you really are. You only wanted to live in truth.

Truth is a scary concept. There is a lot of fear around this idea. If you live in your truth, others may not like what is revealed. You have been living something you're not for a very long time. All of you have been putting on a show to some extent. Everyone wants others to see them in the best light possible. Everyone is afraid of showing who they really are. Everyone fears rejection.

So what is true for you? This is the most important question you will ever ask yourself. Who are you really? What do you really, truly want? What is it that truly inspires you? Why are you not living your truth now and in every moment? What are you hiding?

The paradox is that when you learn to live your truth you will also learn to love yourself. You will become the person you always wanted and knew was there. Down deep there is a part of you that wants to break free from the shackles that bind you to conform to what you think those around you want to see. You act in a way that you think others will approve of in order to gain their love. However, it is a conditional love and it is resistant in nature.

As you reveal who you really are, you will develop self-appreciation. Your first truth is that you are love and you must come to love self. Only from the love of self can you become who you really are. Without the ability to appreciate yourself, you will not truly appreciate others. Until you can come to love yourself, you cannot truly love another. You are the essence of love. If you are not living that truth, you are resisting it. Resistance causes inner conflict and stress on the body.

Living your truth frees you from resistance. As you journey towards becoming who you really are, you reduce inner conflict and stress on the body. Your conditions ease. Fear dissipates. You begin to feel lighter. You allow more joy.

IV.

What is truth? How do you know what is true for you? How can you determine if you're living your truth or not? Let's see if we can analyze it.

The physical world you see all around you was specifically designed for you. You are a nonphysical, spiritual, vibrational being experiencing a physical existence. You are an eternal, worthy, and unique being and you wanted to come forth into this physical, space-time reality to joyously expand. You wanted to experience this reality and move your experience to someplace new. You wanted expansion. You wanted to experience more than what has come before.

From this perspective, can you understand how much more there is to life? Imagine that you are an eternal being existing in a nonphysical realm. In that realm you flow as one with all that is. You do not experience time, so you exist in the moment for eternity. You can observe anything and everything you like. You can move and flow in any direction you like. You are in a constant state of bliss experiencing, whatever you want, whenever you want. But you cannot know what it's like to be physical unless you come here.

So you enter a life and you experience physicality. To you, a single physical life is but a brief, intense experience. You enter physicality and you leave it only to enter and leave again and again. In order for this physical experience to have meaning, you must forget where you came from and what happened in other lifetimes.

You have no agenda to fulfill in any lifetime, but you do seek new experiences. It is always the new that you seek, for you have experienced much in other lifetimes. You set intentions prior to each life and those intentions set a trajectory for this life. Your intentions are mainly general in nature. You intend to experience joy, happiness, freedom, love, well-being, passion, interest, fun, etc. But there are also one or more specific intentions.

You might also intend to explore abundance, science, teaching, discovery, etc. You certainly wanted to push the envelope of what is possible in this reality. You wanted to move things forward. You wanted to move thought forward.

You came to this life with the understanding that you would live life as intended if you lived your truth. As long as you were on your true path, your life would unfold as intended. However, you also knew that if you were influenced away from your true path, you would not live your truth. Not living your truth means not living as you had intended.

This all leads us to one conclusion: the truth for you is what you would live if you were not influenced by others. If you were allowed to live fully as who you are, your life would unfold as you intended. You would accomplish what you wanted to accomplish prior to your birth. All of your intentions would manifest into your reality. You would live in joy, freedom, and happiness while pursuing your specific passions and interests. You would live on earth in the physical realm as you existed in the nonphysical realm (on Earth as it is in Heaven). You would live in bliss.

If you are not living in bliss, you are not living your truth. It's as simple as that. To live your truth means to live in bliss. Bliss is the state of living as you intended. To live your truth you must follow your bliss without giving in to the influences that might lead you away from your true path. Your true path is toward what interests you without interference from those around you who would seek to guide you away from those interests.

You must come to understand and believe in two key aspects of yourself: 1) You are worthy. No one has ever existed who was more worthy than you and no one will ever exist who is more worthy than you are right now. You are as worthy, but no more worthy, than anyone who has ever or will ever exist in this physical reality. 2) You are a unique being. You are unique in all the world. There has never been another quite like you and there will never be another like you, ever.

You are truly unique and absolutely worthy. Therefore, you must follow your own true path. You cannot allow yourself to be placed on a path that is not your true path. You cannot allow yourself to be swayed from your path by others. They have their path and you have yours. They have their truth and you have yours. All people are unique and all paths are unique, so following another's path cannot lead you to become who you really are. It can only lead you to becoming who you are not.

The first question you must ask yourself is "What do I really want?" Only when you focus on what's wanted can you start to move in the direction of your true path. The next question to ask yourself is "Why do I want this?" Until you come to understand the reason you want what you want, you'll never know if the desire is a true desire. What do you want and why do you want it? If you want something because having it will make you feel worthy, it's not a true desire. If you want something because it will make you stand out and feel unique, it's not a true desire. You are already worthy and unique, so there is no need to prove it.

You may not know what you really want at this moment in time, or you may not know how to verbalize it. It might seem strange if you were to write it down. It might not seem plausible, feasible, or even possible. If others learned of your desire, they might laugh at it. At this point in your reawakening, you do not really understand the greatness of who you really are. But the journey of self-discovery is always initiated with a few small steps. You cannot see the destination or even very much of the road ahead, but it is a joyful one and it always starts in the same place. Look for something, anything, that interests you and go in that direction.

V.

The Truth of who you really are is also found in the truth of your approach to life. There is an approach to life that you are most likely living at this time and throughout your adult life that does not match who you really are. Your goals, for instance, might be based on a belief that comes from the influence of your society and not from who you truly are.

The desire for wealth or prominence is largely a projection of what your society deems favorable. The car you drive, the clothes you wear, the money you spend, is all a result of the influence of your society and it keeps you apart from who you really are. You think you need to make money to belong to your group. You believe that you must have formal education to belong to the group you deem worthy. Yet these trappings of your society do much to hold you apart from who you really are.

There is joy to be had in wealth and in owning things if you are aligned with wealth and the possession of things. However, more often the attainment of wealth and things brings suffering because the sacrifice made to attain the wealth was too great. If wealth is your goal, then you must be who you are not in order to attain your goal. This is a great sacrifice. What you really want is to become who you really are and to follow your true path. You just don't realize this yet. You just don't quite get it.

We are not saying that we want you to shun wealth. On the contrary, we want you to embrace the abundance that comes from being who you really are. Be who you are first and the side effect will be everything you really want.

When you believe you have to be a certain way to attain a goal, you cannot be who you really are and that will lead to dissatisfaction, inner conflict, and suffering. When you walk on the path to becoming who you really are, you encounter joy, bliss, and eagerness for more. By living your truth, you live a life of allowing, and thus all you really want is delivered to you.

Would you rather be someone you are not and be wealthy or be who you really are and live a life of bliss? If you would rather be wealthy than live in bliss (and many of you would), it's because you have no idea what it's like to live a life becoming who you really are. You have lived in denial of your true self for so long that to live as who you really are would be uncomfortable. But what if we were to tell you that living your truth would mean an end to your suffering? Living your truth reduces the amount of fear in your life. You no longer do things just to hang onto what you've got. You allow everything to flow knowing that things are always working out for you as you move along your true path to uncovering your true self.

We want to express to you that there is no other way to live. Living any other way is a less appealing way to live. Only on the path to self-discovery can you live in bliss. Only by doing and being what is right for you allows you to live in freedom and joy.

Suppressing who you are for the sake of some other goal will only lead to frustration, anger, and regret. It is time that you lived your truth. It is right for you to live the life you intended. It is good to be you.

VI.

This world was created for one thing: joyous expansion. You expand when you live and experience life. The expansion you seek comes from experiences that are authentic. Authentic experiences come from being who you really are. Inauthentic experiences come as a result of being who you are not.

Your experiences are deeper and more meaningful when you are living your truth. Your experiences are shallow and less meaningful when you are living by some other standard.

Some people were born into this society with pronounced differences that were intended prior to their birth. These differences made it difficult for them to be who they were not. It made it very difficult for them to live anything other than who they were. Society wanted conformity, yet to conform was to mask who they really were and it was extremely painful. So most of them decided they would not conform and they began to live their truth.

Those born with a preference for the same sex cannot easily deny who they really are. Society demands that all conform to its rules, yet these people would not yield to society. So, over time, they began to live their truth and society changed its rules to conform to them. In less than a century, your society will move from intolerance to acceptance, all because they decided to live their truth.

If you were born with a preference for the same sex, you learned at a young age who you really were. You knew that you had to make a decision. You either became who you really were or you submitted to the pressures of your society. If you lived your truth, your life would be free and you could find joy and love. If you lived as society would want you to live, you would have had to endure pain and suffering. It is not easy to deny who you really are.

Being born into a heterosexual society is not easy if you're homosexual. However, you come to know who you really are at a very young age. You also learn what it's like to hide your truth and what it's like to live your truth. It is an easy distinction to understand.

Most of you are born "normal." For you, there is no obvious sign of who you are and who you are not. You can easily fool yourself into living a life that conforms to society's goals and believing you are living your own dreams. Yet if you are following the path of another, you are not on the road to becoming who you really are. If you are doing something because your parents, teachers, or peers believe it is right for you, you might not be living out your true dreams.

If you are not doing what you really want to do, if your life is not the way you really want it to be, or if you are not involved in something you're passionate about, you might not be living your truth. If you're doing something because you think it gives you security, it probably doesn't. If you're doing it because it's giving you the lifestyle you want, it really isn't. If you're not on your true path, then you're on another path. If you're not being who you really are, then you're not living as you intended.

That's okay. Everything you have done in your life has brought you to this point. If you weren't on your way to becoming who you really are, you would never have found this book. If you were not interested in self-discovery, you would have not made it this far into the book. The Law of Attraction has brought you to these pages and to those teachings that have come before, and it will bring you to those teachings that will follow. You are on the path to becoming who you really are. You are beginning to live your truth.

It is now time to make a distinction between man's laws and natural laws. It is now time to see the difference between what society wants for you and what you want for you. It is now time to understand whether your decisions are love-based or fear-based.

Why do you have the job you have right now? Why do you spend your time in this profession? Why do you own the car in your driveway or the house you live in? Why do you live in the town you live in? Why are you with your mate, or why do you not have a mate?

For some of you, everything is right and you are already living your truth. For others, you are well on your way to becoming who you really are and all you need is a little fine tuning. For most of you, you are still consumed by the false values of your society and you are mesmerized by what you believe is good and proper.

There are man's rules and there are natural laws. If you can understand what is natural and what has been fabricated by fearful men, you can learn to move toward what is natural and ignore what has been created by society.

You can certainly see that fame is a creation of your society. Naturally, there would be no need or desire to be famous, because there is no value in fame. If you are worthy, then there is no need to prove your worthiness to others. Those with fame experience limitations to their freedom even when it comes with great wealth. You believe that wealth equates with freedom, yet these famous and wealthy celebrities desire the freedom anonymity brings. How ironic.

What other desires does your society hold as ideal that are not necessary? Status is a man-made ideal. In a natural society where all members are equal, which is absolutely true, there is no need for status. In your Western society, where all members have the opportunity to create their dream, why is it necessary to show your status with cars, homes, clothes, and jewelry?

We are simply saying that your pursuit of these false desires will lead to dissatisfaction. Time spent being other than who you really are is time away from joy and satisfaction. Learn to discern whether the goal you seek is in line with who you really are or whether it is one of the many trappings of your society. Your society is rapidly changing and evolving. What was once considered admirable is becoming obsolete. When you decide to become who you really are, you will lose interest in being who society thinks you should be.

VII.

Living the truth of who you really are is living consciously. Being a deliberate, conscious creator means that you understand the mechanism of physical reality and the laws that hold that reality together and that you operate within those laws. You create what is wanted from love, not fear. You understand how the system works and you make decisions from within the framework of the higher perspective.

Living your truth allows you to free yourself from the restrictions that once held you stuck in habit and repetitive thought. You now understand that you are a limitless being able to experience whatever you choose. You are no longer plagued by self-doubt or insecurity. You understand your own undeniable worthiness. You realize your own potential.

From this new and higher perspective you can glimpse your potential. You can see beyond the narrow confines of your previous life. You can dream again and know that the essence of those dreams will be fulfilled. You can place your faith in your own powers to create what is wanted. You do not need to see the result. Instead, you understand that the universe will support your desires and you live in the knowledge that you will be taken care of.

You become patient. You do not react to what you would once have judged to be wrong. You are creating a new habit of understanding that you cannot see the road ahead from where you stand. You start to trust that it is all unfolding perfectly. The setbacks are now seen as clarifying moments and events that are shaping you so that you'll be in alignment with what you want when it arrives.

As you start to live the truth of who you are, you'll remove your attention from what is not wanted. This means you will no longer think thoughts of worry about future conditions, no longer talk about things you do not like, and no longer do things that do not serve who you really are.

So think about how you will be when you are living your truth. Your thoughts will be very different. You will think thoughts that feel good.

You will not worry or fear the unknown. You will not dwell on unpleasant subjects. You will not judge your conditions, you will not judge yourself, and you will not judge the people around you. You will think thoughts of love rather than fear. This is a radical departure from how your mind has operated for most of your life. This change in your habit of thought will not happen overnight, but a shift will take place, and that change in momentum from negative thought to positive thought will radically change your life. You will change and your life will change.

This change will be so profound that you cannot even imagine the ramifications from where you now stand. It seems like too much of a change. It might even be frightening because everything will be different. But don't worry, we promise you that you will enjoy the change as it happens. It will be a satisfying ride.

Living your truth means you will speak in a radically new way. You will no longer talk about the problem or complain about anything or anyone. Complaining is expressing fear. Now you will only talk of what is wanted with love and appreciation. This too is a radical departure from how you've been speaking most of your life. If you're not complaining, judging, or talking about all the bad things in the world, what will there be left to talk about? At first, you will simply talk less. This is not a bad thing, for most of your speech has been unconscious. Deliberate creators choose their words very carefully, for they know the power of the spoken word.

The truth of who you really are will be displayed through your actions as well. You will no longer do the things that hold you back. You will break your habits of unconscious action. You will no longer allow fear to control your actions or your inaction. You will be inspired through love rather than uninspired through fear. You will start to follow your passions without excuses being made and without the constraint of fear. You will do whatever it is that you find blissful. You will allow yourself to be consumed by what you love.

You will not be afraid that doing what you love will not allow you to support yourself. You are supported by the universe and if you're following your passion fearlessly, the universe will find a way to support you financially to the extent to which you allow it to. If you worry about money, then the universe can only provide you with more reasons to worry. If you trust that everything is unfolding in order to support what is wanted, then you'll be inspired to action that allows money to flow to you. It is a simple matter of faith.

Now you find yourself living your truth and living consciously. But you are still immersed in a world where most are not living the highest versions of who they really are. Those around you are still reacting negatively and unconsciously to the present conditions. How does a conscious creator live peacefully among the unconscious?

Chapter Seven

Life as a Conscious Creator

There are only two ways to live a physical life: as a creator or as a victim. Most of humanity believes they have little control over what occurs in their lives. This is a victim's mentality. To believe that things simply happen to you without your control is to believe you are powerless. It is difficult to live a life filled with joy when you believe you have no effect on your own life.

However, you have come to realize that the mechanism of physical reality is designed to yield to you as a creator. You have the powers of creation at your disposal, as does everyone else, whether they know it or not. How you use those powers determines whether you will believe yourself to be a creator or a victim.

Everyone is a creator and their life is their creation. Since most people living unconsciously believe that things simply happen out of their control, they do not realize that they are actually creating their reality through their habit of thought and their unconscious approach to life. If we were to tell them that they have been creating their reality all along, they would scoff and say, "This must not be true, for if I have been creating my reality, I would not have created this and this and this. My reality would have been much better."

This is the main reason most people do not believe that they have the ability to create in their own reality. They presume that they would leave out the bad and only experience the good. But since they focus on the unwanted, on the bad, on the negative side of most things, they end up experiencing that which they say they do not like.

It is much easier to live an unconscious life and believe that luck or fate controls one's destiny. You can live without taking personal responsibility for what occurs. You can approach life with an attitude of apathy, believing that whatever happens simply happens and that it's all out of your control. But this is not the approach to life you intended prior to your birth.

Since you now understand more about the laws of the universe and the mechanism of physical reality, you can live as the conscious creator you really are. You can understand how life operates and see things from the higher perspective. You can react to occurrences in the way that supports what you truly want. You can continue on the path to becoming who you really are.

The highest version of you is who you really are. Your purpose in this life is to become this highest version. To do so, you will have to adopt a radically new approach to life. You will have to live fully conscious. This is not an easy task given your habitual pattern of thought. You've lived your life for a very long time in the old, unconscious manner. Now that you are reawakening to a completely new approach to life, you will have to shed most of your old ways.

II.

As a conscious creator, you understand how the world operates. You know what is really going on here. You know you are an eternal being and that there is no death. You know that you receive more of what you place your attention on. You know that your thoughts, words, and actions create your reality. You understand the difference between beneficial beliefs and limiting beliefs. You know that how you feel in the moment is the only thing that matters in this feeling experience of physical reality. You understand that everything is vibrational and you attract what you are a match to vibrationally. You realize that you are a worthy and unique being and that no one is more or less worthy than you. When you know all this, life for you is just different.

You have been interacting with your family and friends for a long time. You have been complaining along with them. You have been fighting injustice along with them. You have been wallowing in their misery with them. You have been watching the news, condemning your politicians, talking about everything that is wrong, and living an unconscious life right along with all of them. Now you have reawakened. Everything is different.

As a conscious creator, you no longer talk about that which is unwanted. If it is unwanted, you do not give it your attention, for you now know better. When a friend complains about some aspect of everyday life, what are you to do? You are to change the subject or leave the room. It's as simple as that. You no longer participate in conversations that revolve around negative subjects.

When one of your parents talks about another in your family, you move the conversation to the positive aspects of that person. When they try to disparage this person, you point out a positive aspect. When they say something derogatory, you work to align with the positive aspects of this person. You are not fighting against the opinion of the parent, you are simply trying to move the conversation in the direction of what is wanted. You are not sticking up for this person, you are simply focusing on the positive aspects. You are not trying to make your parent wrong, you are just highlighting positive aspects so that these wanted traits come into your own personal experience. You are not trying to improve the experience of your parent by being positive, for that is not possible; you are simply trying to improve your own experience.

Living as a conscious creator is a selfish approach to life. Everything you do is to make your life experience better. You are not trying to improve the experience of others by focusing on the positive aspects; you are improving your experience. Since you cannot create in the experience of another, you must realize that everything you are doing in your new approach to life is for the benefit of your experience alone. This may be a difficult concept for you to understand.

You cannot create in the reality of another even if you think you can. All you can do is influence others from your place of alignment with whatever it is you personally desire. If this stance positively affects another, that's wonderful. If not, there's nothing more you can do. A conscious creator is a selfish creator. Everything you do is for your own improvement because you cannot bring another up to your vibration.

Everyone else must be left to discover their own path to conscious living, to their own truth, and to the highest version of who they really are. You cannot do anything that will affect their path other than being an example yourself. You must focus on your own work and allow them to raise their own vibration themselves. They have a path to follow and your guidance will lead them to your path, not theirs.

It is very difficult for a conscious creator not to teach. You believe that you have found the answer to happiness and bliss. You have only found your answer. You have not found the answer for anyone else. This is a very important concept to understand. You cannot create in the reality of another, but you can and do influence the lives of others.

You believe that your influence is a good thing and so do most other people. Most unconscious thinkers believe that they know what's best. Your unconscious parents certainly tried to move your life to what they thought was best. Yet they likely knew little of the laws of the universe or the mechanism of physical reality. They poked and prodded you toward so many different beliefs and fears based on their own beliefs and fears. Yet they did not understand that you were here to experience your life in your own way.

Now that you are a conscious creator, you think you know more than others - and you do. However, you do not know what they need. You cannot see how they are going to get where they will go. Your perspective is narrow. You believe your guidance will help, but you do not have an understanding of what they must go through to get to where they have intended to go.

Believe it or not, you have an inner guidance system that works perfectly for you. Everyone else has their own inner guidance system as well. You are being guided by your inner self and it is your inner self that has brought you to this point in your life. If you are becoming a conscious creator, it's because your inner self has brought you to this point, step by step, over many long years. Your inner self has known all along how to get you to this point. If you think you have been influenced by others in reaching this point, it's because it only seems that way to you. What has actually happened is that your inner self and the universe have worked together to place you in situations that would help you could grow into the person you now see when you look in the mirror.

Everyone else has an inner self bringing them along at the pace they are ready for. If they are introduced to a book or a teacher, it is because their inner self has lined it up for them at the right time. If they were to receive the book or the teachings at the wrong time, through pressure from another, the teachings would not be understood. They were not at the right vibration to understand the teachings. This leads to frustration on the part of both the student and the teacher. The negative thought delays progress.

For you to be a teacher, the student must come to you when they are ready. Your desire to help another along their path does not make it appropriate for you to push them in the direction you feel is to their benefit. When a student believes he should learn something but cannot, the student believes he has been betrayed by himself or by the teacher.

Everyone must be a vibrational match to what they are ready to receive. You have been vibrationally modified over time so that you are ready to understand some of the material presented in this book. If you are reading this book and have understood some or much of what we have come to say, then you are simply a vibrational match to the information. You are ready for whatever you receive.

There is some information in this book that you are ready for. As you are ready, you'll understand it and you might even start to test it out in your own life. But there is also some material that you are not a match to. This information will not be absorbed. You will not even notice that you're not getting certain information contained in the book. It's not that you should understand everything, it's just that you can only absorb what you are vibrationally ready to absorb. You can only learn something if you're vibrationally up to speed with the information.

Vibrational readiness is a gradual process. You are being led, step by step, to a higher vibration. Each time you reach a new level, new information will come to you and you will be ready to absorb it. Until you've reached that vibrational level, the information cannot come to you. You may have read a book several years ago and when you reread it now, from your present vibration, there will be a vast trove of information in that book that will now be revealed to you. You will find it odd that you can't remember that information from the first time you read the book. It's because you've reached a new level and you're now open to new information.

Everyone else is living life, consciously or not, at their own vibrational level. You cannot see where they are. You cannot know how their vibration will be raised. You cannot raise their vibration for them. Any attempt to do so might fail. It is not your place to raise another's vibration. You must allow them to follow their own path and let their inner self assist them at the pace that is right for them.

III.

Imagine what it looks like to live life as a conscious creator. You understand the laws of the universe and the mechanism of physical reality. You know exactly why you're here, what life means to you, and how to create the life you prefer. You are in a state of fascination, appreciating all the diverse aspects of this unique physical experience. You are becoming the highest version of who you really are.

Imagine living fully conscious and aware in every moment. Imagine a life without fear, without judgment, and without concern for what others may be thinking about you. Imagine that powerful approach to life. Imagine what that kind of life would look like.

Living fully conscious is quite different from how you have approached life up to this point. It is far different from how almost everyone else lives life. It is an evolved style of life with tremendous potential for creation. Let's take a closer look.

If you were to live fully conscious, the first thing you would drop from your current way of life is irrational fear. Since you understand the laws of the universe, you know that what you put forth will be returned to you. If you live without fear, you live with confidence in these universal laws. You know that if you follow your passions, you will be supported. If you can maintain your focus on what is wanted, you will receive that which is the essence of your true desire. You will live fully trusting in the laws of the universe and you will allow everything you want to come to you at precisely the right time.

Irrational fear takes you out of the present moment and places you in the future (worry) or the past (regret). Conscious living removes the fear so that you live in the moment. You now realize that there is nothing to worry about because the future has not yet arrived and there's nothing to regret because the past has unfolded perfectly to bring you to where you are now. Therefore, living consciously is living in the moment.

When life is lived in the moment, life is lived as it was meant to be. Experience is what life is really about. Physical reality is an experiential reality. You are here to experience many things. You are here to be moved by these experiences to new experiences. You are not here to do the same things over and over. You intended to expand through experience. Living consciously allows you to experience new things without fear.

Fear is what keeps you from new experiences. You are afraid of failure or embarrassment. When living consciously, you drop irrational fear and realize that you cannot control what others think because their thoughts are dependent on their own level of consciousness. If they are not living fully conscious lives, they are plagued by irrational fear which clouds their ability to process information. Therefore, what they think of you is flawed to the degree of their own fear-based thought process.

Since this is an experiential reality, failure is not possible. The experience is the goal, not the outcome. From your limited perspective, you can only assume that a certain outcome is preferable. Yet it is the experience that is needed to move you to where you truly want to go. Every experience, whether you deem it successful or a failure, is simply an experience containing a lesson. We don't like to use the word "lesson," for it implies that there is something for you to learn. Rather, the lesson simply moves your vibration to the next step in your readiness to receive what you truly want as long as you allow it to.

Imagine you're an actor and you go on an audition for a part. You go on many auditions, most of which result in rejection. You can look at the rejection in two ways. The most common way rejection is viewed from the perspective of the unconscious creator is as failure. If you were success-ful, you would have received the part. Since you did not get the part, you must have failed. When your friends ask you about the audition, they all hope you received the part. When you tell them you were rejected, they all feel "bad" for you. This is the automatic and unconscious reaction to the process of creation.

If you are an actor and your passion is acting, you have one true desire. In this case we will say that your true desire is to follow your passion for acting by taking roles that allow you to express yourself through your craft. You want to earn your living as an actor and perform roles you feel express who you really are. You are a conscious creator and you audition for a role; let's look at how you now approach the audition process.

Your stance prior to the audition is completely different. You have no fear. You do not worry about the future or regret what happened in the past. You are confident in this moment that the universe will yield to you that which you truly want. You now enter the audition from a neutral stance. The neutrality is the key to this situation.

Why would you be neutral upon entering the audition? Because you are not attached to the result, only to the process. The audition process is the platform that will allow the universe to deliver to you that which you truly want. You do not know if this part you're auditioning for will lead you to the fullest manifestation of what you truly desire. You cannot see how the path will unfold. But the universe, from its higher, broader perspective, can see the road ahead.

You audition for the part not knowing whether it will lead to what you want or not. There is no way you can tell. It may look right, but you can't know if it's really right. If you want it so much because you think it's the only (or the shortest) path to what you want, you'll be very disappointed if you don't get it. But you might be even more disappointed if you do get it. Can you see the difference here?

The conscious creator allows the universe to create the path to what is truly wanted. He doesn't interfere with the plan; he simply takes part in the process. He is not attached to the result; he is neutral to the result. He knows that everything is always working out for him. So the conscious creator performs his best at the audition, as he has freed himself from the fear of rejection. He offers the performance he wants to give rather than tailoring his performance to suit what he thinks the casting directors will want to see. He can now allow himself to be authentic in his performance, which allows him to show the finest version of himself.

The practical application of living consciously is that you can be the finest version of your authentic self. You have no fear of the future, of the past, of what others think, or of failure. You can be in the moment in a state of neutrality with regard to the outcome. Either way, you'll now judge the outcome to be good. If you get the part, good. If you don't get the part, good.

The next thing you'll release when you become a conscious creator is judgment. Judgment is fear-based. Typically, you judge one aspect good and its counterpart bad. This is a dualistic view of life and an unconscious one. In duality, something must be good and the other thing must be bad. If something is up, the other is down. If one is right, the other is wrong. Everything is defined in duality through your judgment of it and this is an unconscious approach to life.

It is unconscious because the judgment is made habitually and automatically. You are not thinking about what you are judging; you are simply judging automatically. "That's good," you say automatically when you agree. "That's bad," you say habitually when you disagree or judge something to be wrong.

Imagine living without judgment. You see a homeless person pushing a shopping cart with all her belongings. Imagine not judging that as bad. Imagine being interested in or even fascinated with what you are seeing. As a conscious thinker, you no longer instantly feel pity. You don't feel bad and look away. Instead, you now attract thoughts of a deeper nature.

You understand that every individual is here for an experience and that is hers. You do not jump habitually to a feeling of guilt, nor do you feel the need to help her. You simply contemplate the experience that she is going through. You do not need to imagine yourself in that experience; you simply observe from a neutral stance.

Imagine seeing a young mother in the grocery store with her two young children. You see the children laughing or crying or running around with the mother hopelessly trying to control them. You do not judge the mother for her inability or unwillingness to quiet her children as you once would have. You do not judge the children for their behavior, which you might once have considered improper. You simply observe in delight from a stance of neutrality. Imagine your improved sense of well-being from this judgment-free approach to life.

The third thing you leave behind when living consciously is concern for what others may be thinking about you. You are living in a wonderful time of reawakening, yet most of those who inhabit your world are not living consciously. They are thinking thoughts that have been influenced by other unconscious thinkers. They have been living habitually without consideration for their beliefs, words, or actions. They can only view their world from a very limited perspective.

Imagine yourself living in ancient times surrounded by people who believed all sorts of things that no longer apply in your modern world. Imagine being around people who thought the world was flat or that the earth was the center of the universe and the sun and the rest of the stars revolved around it. They would think you were crazy for offering an idea that opposed their beliefs, even though, from your modern perspective, you know a different truth.

These people lived their whole lives believing that the world was flat and the sun revolved around the earth. They were so attached to their view of life that it would not be possible for you to change their minds. And so you would soon give up trying and allow them to believe whatever they chose to believe. Yet you would not be influenced by their beliefs. You would not suddenly start to believe that the world was flat. They could not influence you any longer because your perspective came from a higher level of understanding. If they ridiculed your beliefs, your knowing, you would not take offense because you would realize that their perspective was simply limited.

There is a mass consciousness in your society and people believe certain things to be true. In the future, as society gains its beliefs from a broader perspective, it will come to realize that new ideas are true. The beliefs of your society will evolve and the perspective will change.

Less than a century ago, most people in your society believed there was a fundamental difference between races. The color of one's skin was considered an important indicator of their level of intelligence and was even thought to have evolutionary implications. This was the mass belief of an entire society and it was a very limiting belief. Today, the mass beliefs of your society have evolved to a new, higher perspective where the color of one's skin makes no difference. You know this now, but it was contrary to the beliefs of the average person less than a century ago.

You can see implications of mass belief in all sorts of subjects. Sexual orientation, women's equality, animal rights, class distinctions, etc. Perspective always moves from more limited to broader. Beliefs always move from fear to love as a society evolves. Yet, you personally are becoming more evolved than most of those in your society.

Through your personal reawakening, you are evolving at a much faster pace than the rest of your society. You are becoming conscious while they are remaining mostly unconscious. You are coming to understand new truths and a new approach to life while they are living a habitual way of life. You are analyzing your beliefs while they cling to their beliefs. You are releasing fear and stepping into love while they hold onto their irrational fears.

In the future, your society will give up certain limiting beliefs. Your ideas about death will change and you will allow people to choose the time and manner of their death with dignity. You will understand that there is no death and will ease the pain associated with it. You will come to believe that we are all immortal and that death is simply the transition to another state of being.

You will change your views about intelligence and realize that we are all intelligent beings with the same access to whatever type of knowledge we personally need when we need it. Your education system will be radically different in the future, as you will no longer seek to teach but rather you will support learning at the individual level. You will no longer judge one person's intelligence to be superior to another's. You will see that all are equally capable of learning based on one's interest and development.

You will no longer come to think that one member of society is more valuable than another. You will begin to break down borders and live as a united world, rather than many factions of the same people separated by borders. You will no longer feel fortunate for being born rich or inadequate for being born poor. Wealth and power will lose their luster as you begin to understand that experience, expansion, and joy are the only meaningful aspects of life.

You will come to understand that there is consciousness in all living things and energy in everything, and you will know that it all works together to create this playground in which you live. You will think about your environment and the impact your actions have. You will not do anything that would cause harm to another, for you will know that you are all one. To do something to harm another or your environment would be the same as doing something that would harm you.

Your society's perspective will become broader in the near future, but today it remains very limited. Your perspective is already broader. You know things that most others do not. You now see your world in a whole new way. As your approach to life radically changes, you must remember that you are on the leading edge of this new perspective. There are others with you, but most remain behind. As a conscious thinker, you must remember that the opinions of unconscious thinkers are simply habits of thought that come from a limited perspective.

As you take a new approach to life, you do so without concern for what those living the old approach will think about you. You are a different thinker. You know more. Your higher perspective has opened up new neural pathways in your brain. You are now open to new possibilities of thought. You have reached a new, higher vibrational stance. You can see over the heads of others. You can see what they cannot. You can also understand and empathize with them for not being able to keep up with you. You are no longer attached to what they think about you, for they are unable to see who you really are.

IV.

Empathy is a very important quality for a conscious thinker to possess. You have been living your whole life believing that everyone thinks the same thing about how the world operates. You might not have considered what others believe, but now from your new perspective, you can see that most of their beliefs come packaged for them and delivered by society. They have not analyzed their beliefs. They do not understand that their beliefs might be flawed or limiting.

Most people you know believe that things just happen. They believe in luck, coincidence and randomness. They retain a victim's mentality. They do not believe in the laws of the universe, nor do they have any idea how the mechanism of physical reality operates. Most people go through life getting some of what they want and some of what they do not want. Most are living at a lower vibrational level.

You are living at a higher vibration and therefore the thoughts you attract are different from the thoughts most others attract. While you are receiving newer and higher-level thoughts and you are expanding as an evolving being, they are mostly still thinking the same thoughts they've always thought. But they can sense a change in you. They can see how you are becoming different. You are now challenging their approach to life and they feel different.

Some of these people are also in the early stages of awakening. There have been many books and documentaries that are gaining mass appeal. They are bringing many people to a new level of consciousness. A lot of people are getting sparks of consciousness and some people are moving to higher levels. This is especially true of younger people who already have a higher vibrational frequency. But everyone is at a different level of awakening.

A conscious thinker is well aware of his or her own level of consciousness and understands that everyone else is on their own journey. Some have just made the first step and others are well on their way. Yet no one wants to be prodded and asked to walk at another speed. They are all walking as fast as they are comfortable walking along their path. If they come seeking more insight, then serve their interests as best you can. However, you cannot help another on their path by bludgeoning them with your perspective. You must empathize with their current place on their journey.

This is one of the most difficult aspects of conscious living. You want everyone else to be up to speed with you. You want all your friends and family to join you in your clarity. You are enthralled with this new level of consciousness and you want everyone to experience what you have learned. But it is simply not possible. You cannot help anyone rise above their level of understanding until they are ready. Attempting to do so will only cause frustration and resentment.

Remember that you and everyone else are vibrational beings. Things come to you based on the vibration you emit. At your current vibrational speed, you have access to certain thoughts. Thoughts and ideas are revealed, shall we say, when you reach certain vibrational levels. If you're not at the right vibration, you cannot access those thoughts. If you're not on the proper channel at the proper time, you cannot watch that particular show.

You may be at one vibration while everyone else you know is at a different vibration. Let's say that you are with a group of people, all of whom have read the books and watched the videos. You are all familiar with the teachers and the higher perspective. Yet you are all vibrating at different frequencies. You are all vibrating at a certain level so that you can enjoy talking about certain subjects. But when you, from your higher frequency, want to talk about the higher-level ideas you've been thinking about, no one else can follow you.

Even in this group of very conscious thinkers, you find yourself alone at your own level. In these times, you must have empathy with the others, who are not yet where you stand. You cannot preach or try to explain because they cannot, by design, understand where you are. You are at a new level and are ready to discuss new ideas, but these are ideas that they have no access to. They will not even hear your words. Maybe one day they will reach your level, but you will already be on to a new level. It will always be this way.

Now imagine those in your life who are not even beginning to awaken. They are still stuck in habitual, unconscious thinking. What are you to do with these people? You can only empathize with them. You can only be a beacon to them. You can't try to bring them up. You must love them for who and where they are. You do not need to drop to their level; simply and consciously understand how the system works and allow them to be as they are.

V.

Life as a conscious creator is vastly different from your old approach to life. As you awaken to the reality of physical reality, you leave behind many of the beliefs that grounded you in unconsciousness. One of the staples of unconscious living is competition. To a conscious creator, competition no longer has the same meaning.

Since you are creating your own reality as you prefer it from the stance of your new understanding of the mechanism of physical reality, you now realize that competition is an illusion, as is everything else. You are creating your reality. No one else can create in your reality. You have nothing to prove, nothing to lose, and really, nothing to gain. Hence, there is no competition.

You cannot strive to be better than someone else, for you are both equally worthy. By your judgment of success or failure you demonstrate your belief in lack rather than in worthiness. If you are already worthy, as worthy as any who have ever or will ever live, then winning a competition does not justify or prove your worthiness. If all others are equally worthy, then beating them does not disprove their worthiness either.

All competition stems from lack and fear. You feel good in winning and bad in losing. Yet this is a false sense of satisfaction. You are not here to win at the expense of others or to lose to others. You are here to come to know your own individual greatness and to explore that.

We will say that competition in fun can be pleasing and enjoyable. Competition can also encourage learning and bring you to a new level of understanding about yourself and other universal forces. But it is the competition that you seek to prove your worthiness that is not necessary. You are good, you are worthy, and comparison to others will not prove or disprove your worthiness.

Another aspect of life that falls away when you begin to live consciously is the aspect of time. There is nothing you need to do and there is no hurry. Time is an illusion, for you are an eternal being. There is no need to rush. Patience really is a virtue. Conscious thinkers live moment to moment and one moment is not necessarily better or worse than the next. Each moment is valuable and interesting in and of itself.

When you become a conscious creator, you slow down. Your vibration may speed up and you might get things done faster than ever before, but you are now less concerned about time itself. Deadlines lose their meaning. You become more interested in what really matters and less interested in the lack-based beliefs of your society. Those who have run out of time do so because they view it as a precious and scarce commodity. They see the lack of time, not the abundance of it.

Time is so abundant; like money, it does not truly exist. It is simply an agreement you have made among yourselves. Your perception of time is different from another's perception. You see an hour as either shorter or longer than others do. Some hours go by quickly, such as when you're having a good time, and other hours move at a snail's pace, such as when you're bored. Time to you moves quickly, but time to a baby does not even exist.

As a conscious creator, you now realize that you are an eternal being and that time is simply a construct of this version of reality. You understand that the aging process is simply a mechanism that allows your perspective to be altered over time. You no longer think that anything needs to be done because you now know that you have all the time in the universe. Instead, you savor the moment and in the moment time freezes.

Time is one of the most difficult aspects of physical reality to ignore. You have been living under a clock your entire life. You count the seconds, minutes, hours, days, weeks, months, years, decades, centuries, and millennia. Time is a very real thing for you. You have a finite experience within this body. In this life, death gives time its value. Yet when you understand fully how this reality operates in conjunction with nonphysical reality, you would not change a thing. Therefore, the aspect of time in this reality is quite perfect indeed.

As a conscious thinker, you now put time in its proper perspective. You now know it as simply one aspect that defines this reality. You see it for that which it is and nothing more. You now ease your relationship with time and come to understand the abundance of it rather than the lack of it.

When you change your perspective on time just a little bit, from lack to abundance, you radically change your approach to life. Seeing that you have loads of time rather than a shortage of time means you operate from an entirely new paradigm. Seeing the abundance of time is beneficial to what you want to do in this life experience. Seeing the lack of time limits what you can do in this life experience. It is simply a matter of perspective, but the ramifications of this alteration of perspective are enormous.

When you relax your dependence on time, you change how you operate in this reality in a fundamental way. If you are no longer in a hurry to get things done, you align with the forces of the universe that will give you the leverage needed to do things right. When time is no longer a factor, you have time to think about what is wanted. The thinking is the doing; the action is only the next logical step. When you act before you think, you know what happens. Action without time to think creates unreliable results. When you give yourself time, things work out as intended.

We are also going to say that conscious creators lose interest in the pursuit of wealth and the possession of material objects. These are artifacts of unconscious creators. We fear that stating this obvious fact will leave many of you with a bad taste in your mouth. Most of you have been on some sort of quest for wealth and possessions your entire lives. The pursuit of your desires may even have sparked an interest in learning about the laws of the universe and the principles of physical manifestation. You wanted to learn this stuff so you could use it to get rich. We understand that and we will say that abundance is the side effect of conscious living. However, we will go on to say that you will gain even more satisfaction and joy from the next level above abundance. You will learn to see your newfound wealth for what it really is: a security blanket.

Conscious creators soon lose the need for security, as anything based in lack is soon dropped. You don't need piles of money in the bank because the universe is constantly bringing you all that you ask for and your stance as a conscious creator allows it to come. The only difference between you as an unconscious creator and you as a conscious creator is that you now allow all the things you want to flow to you effortlessly and naturally. Unconscious creators are given all that they want as well; it's just that they block it from manifesting into their reality. Conscious creators allow, while unconscious people put up blocks in the form of fear, doubt, worry, and disbelief.

Would you rather have a million dollars in the bank or the ability to live and experience life fully as the highest version of you? You would not want the money if you knew the joy and abundance that living consciously provides. To live without fear is to receive all that you really want from life. Money cannot release you from fear, nor can it keep you secure. You must move past that. Money and possessions are not the panaceas they seem. There is so much beyond that and once you begin living conscious-ly, you will come to understand that there is much more you truly want out of life.

You will have abundance, you will have all the money you want, but your perspective on the subject will change. You will no longer struggle for money. You will ease into money and you will allow it to flow easily out and allow more to come in. You will not care so much about your possessions, as you will scale back the having and allow possessions to come and go. You will give more and more and then give away much of what you receive. You will focus on the abundance, not the scarcity, and you will see it as an exchange of energy rather than as mundane physical currency in your bank account.

There are many exciting changes coming as you accept a conscious approach to life. The key in all of this is learning to have trust in the process.

Chapter Eight

The Process to Consciousness

Anyone can travel the journey to becoming who they really are, to living a conscious physical experience, and to living from the higher perspective by following a simple, gradual process. This is the process to conscious living.

Where you are now is somewhere between unconsciousness and full consciousness. You can never be completely unconscious, nor can you ever be completely conscious. Consciousness is a sliding scale. As you evolve to live more consciously, you expand and as you expand, you reach higher levels of vibration and higher degrees of consciousness. But once you've expanded, you never go back. You cannot contract. Therefore, each new level of consciousness opens you up to more expansion. You are never finished. There is no end to expansion.

In this life experience, you have expanded and gained higher levels of consciousness. You are more conscious now than you have ever been before. You have reached a new, higher level of consciousness than in any other past life experience. You are more now than you were. You might have built empires in past lives, or even in this one, yet you are more awake than you've ever been. Where you stand now is more evolved than any past version of you. This is true of everyone.

You could have been healthier earlier in your life. You might have been more financially successful in another part of your life. You may have had more friends or deeper relationships in other times in your life. But you have never been more conscious than you are right now. Once you've reached a certain level, there is no going back.

So where you stand right now is the perfect starting place for even further expansion. You have lived your life and it has unfolded perfectly to bring you to the starting point on this new, higher platform for your expanding consciousness. You are ready to begin the process to consciousness.

The first step in this process to consciousness is one you have already taken. You must have the desire to become aware of the mechanism of physical reality and the laws of the universe. You must want to know the highest version of who you really are. You must want to know more. You have this desire and you have been led to this material and other information that has stirred something inside you. Everyone who begins the process of consciousness wants to gain insights into the real story of physical reality. They know that there must be something more, so they become seekers of truth.

The process is always started with the question "Is there more than what I see?" Many of those who begin this process have been seeking the truth of their experience. They have looked at religion and found it contradictory. They have looked at what society finds virtuous and have found it empty. They have lived as proper citizens and have realized that there must be more, and they have all felt that something is urging them from the inside.

When you begin your quest for knowledge, you might start in one of many different areas. Maybe you read a book that talks of spirituality in a new way and you follow that for a while. You might desire wealth and pick up a book like *Think And Grow Rich*, and this starts you on your journey. Maybe you become a vegan because you believe it's wrong to exploit animals and this starts you on your path of self-discovery. Maybe you're introduced to Abraham and you watch Esther on YouTube. It really doesn't matter how you get here; once you're here you realize that there is more to physical reality and this begins the process to consciousness.

Early in the process to consciousness, you are excited to find that you are not held by the whims of fate. You are exhilarated in your newfound freedom. You feel strong positive emotion at the thought that you create your own reality. For the first time, you see the physical world with a new sense of clarity. You are looking at reality from a new perspective and once you have done this, your entire world shifts.

You are now living more consciously and it is extremely fascinating and different. In these early stages, you have one foot in the new world of consciousness and another foot in the old world of habitual thinking. In these early days, you begin to lose touch with who you were, as you start to become who you really are. Fear enters as you worry about how you will be perceived by all the unconscious people you still interact with every day. You worry about losing your old relationships with these people, so you try to bring them along with you. But you soon find that most are not ready to go where you are going and you allow them to find their own way at their own pace.

You worry about being seen as different with your new ideas about life. You start to reanalyze and realize that all the things you once believed were right might not be right for you. From your new perspective, you now see that many of the old beliefs were limiting and do not serve who you are becoming. You control what you say, even though you want to talk about what you've learned, fearing that others might think you're strange. You start to look for others you can talk to about this wonderful new perspective on life.

Soon you attract others who are also beginning the process to consciousness. You form small groups and go to gatherings where you discuss the nature of physical reality and the laws of the universe. You read more books and learn from others who are living more consciously. You start to see signs that support your new beliefs. You see examples of universal laws in everyday life and on film and TV. You delve deeper and deeper into the study of these universal laws.

You begin to practice creating your reality as you prefer. You start to become aware of your thoughts for the first time. You ask for things and look for the answers. You get the first spot in the parking lot over and over. You see that your mood attracts others in the same mood. You notice the time of day when all the numbers on your digital clock are the same. You notice the times when it reads 1:11, 2:22, 3:33, and so on.

You become more aware of coincidences and now realize that they are signs of alignment rather than random events. You start to see amazing alignments happening all the time and you recognize these events as purposeful and meaningful. You might think of an old friend when suddenly the phone rings and it's your friend calling you out of the blue. You begin to realize that your thoughts and these events are related.

You start to feel inspired to do certain things. You wander down new aisles in the bookstore, and a certain book will catch your eye. You overhear conversations and new subjects catch your ear. You watch stories on TV about things you've never heard of before, but you find yourself really interested in these things for the first time.

In these early stages of consciousness, you progress quite rapidly from who you were to who you're becoming. You look back just a few months before to who you were and recognize that you've come a long way. It seems like a big shift has occurred, and it has. The difference between a life lived mostly unconsciously and one that is awakening to conscious living is quite large indeed. But at these early stages, there is so much more to come.

At some point in the early stages of consciousness, you will start to hear a subtle voice coming from within. You may have been aware that you have a certain knowledge within you that knows what's really going on. You might have called it your gut feeling or intuition. Even in your unconsciousness, you may have been utilizing your inner self to some degree. But the next step in the process to consciousness is building the relationship between you and your inner self.

II.

The second step in the process of consciousness is understanding that there is an inner world. Communication, insight, and knowledge are coming from within. There is a place that is felt where guidance is offered. There is a larger part of you that is able to see your path from a higher perspective. You know that part of you as your inner self. Others who are beginning the process to consciousness are starting to feel for their inner selves and are becoming aware of the guidance and insight that comes from this source.

Conscious living starts with the acceptance and integration of your inner self. You must come to understand that your inner world affects your outer world. You will begin to realize that certain aspects of reality are created from your feelings, thoughts, and beliefs. As you realize you have some control over what happens in the physical world, you move into a higher level of consciousness. You make a great leap over the chasm of the victim mentality. This is a step that brings you into true consciousness for the first time.

You experience the outer world through the translation of vibration by utilizing your five senses. You can see colors, touch objects, hear sounds, smell odors, and taste foods. The world comes alive through your senses. It's quite a vivid world. When living unconsciously, it's rather overwhelming and it captures much of your attention.

There is another important component of this physical reality and that is your inner world. Your inner world is translated through your feelings, thoughts, imagination, and emotions. Your inner world is more subtle and if you're not conscious to it, you might believe that it does not really exist. But your inner world is just as important, just as real, as your outer world.

Your inner world creates your experience in the outer world. This is a huge distinction that you would not be aware of if you were living unconsciously. This concept distinguishes unconscious thinkers from conscious thinkers. When you understand that your feelings, thoughts, and emotions dictate what occurs in your physical experience, you are living consciously. When you believe that your thoughts, feelings, and emotions are simply reacting to what happened in your physical world, you are living unconsciously.

A conscious creator knows that what happens in physical reality is an expression or manifestation of what has been happening in his inner world. He realizes that the way he has been feeling has caused the event to unfold. He knows that there is a reason for the event and that reason is to serve what he wants. Even if the event is unpleasant, he knows that its lesson is purposeful and the event, when seen in a positive way, has helped him change his stance so that he is in a new position to allow what he really wants to come to him.

An unconscious creator reacts to events with shock and surprise. He sees the event as happening to him rather than for him. This is the distinction. He feels like a victim rather than a creator. He believes he feels bad because something bad has happened and he feels good only because something good has happened. He has it all backward.

An unconscious thinker reacts to events in the same habitual way, while a conscious thinker reacts to events by consciously choosing his or her reactions. An unconscious creator judges the conditions as good or bad and focuses on that aspect of the event. A conscious creator sees each event as neutral, setting judgment aside and focusing on the positive aspects of any condition or event.

An unconscious thinker lives mostly in the past or the future, while a conscious thinker lives more in the present.

The unconscious thinker is fear-based, survival-oriented, and ego-driven. The conscious thinker is love-based, thrives on uncertainty, and is purpose-driven.

The unconscious creator seeks to justify his existence by proving his worthiness. The conscious creator accepts that she is worthy and only seeks to become the highest version of who she really is.

The unconscious creator operates in the world by making decisions based on her limited perspective. The conscious creator navigates physical reality by aligning with the higher perspective of her inner self.

The difference between an unconscious creator and a conscious creator is in the relationship with their inner self.

You are not living consciously until you understand and acknowledge that there is a wiser part of you that remains nonphysically focused. This is your inner self. Your inner self is you. You are one. You are always together and never apart. You cannot know the fullness and completeness of you without coming to know your inner self.

Your inner self is focused on you and your life. This aspect of you knows who you really are, knows what you really want, knows what you intended to experience in this life, and knows how to get you everything you really want. Your inner self can see your path from a much higher, broader, deeper perspective. Your inner self is your guide.

The first step in building a relationship with your inner self is acknowledging its presence and asking for guidance. When you ask for something, it will be delivered, as long as you allow it to be. Therefore, it is in your best interests to believe that your inner self exists and that you can open up a dialogue. You can communicate with your inner self if you want to and if you believe you can. It's as simple as that.

Your inner self communicates with you through your thoughts and through inspired action. When you ask a question, your inner self always answers. However, your mind must be quiet for you to hear the answer. You must be able to slow the chatter of your thoughts. You must learn to use your mind as it was intended to be used.

You have the ability to think any thought. But you have not been practicing this skill. Your mind is like a muscle. If you work it, you can make it stronger and it will work for you. If you don't use it, it will atrophy and become weak. A sign of a weak mind is the inability to control the quality and quantity of your thoughts.

Most of humanity is largely unaware of the need to exercise the mind to control the cacophony of thought. What is the purpose of controlling what you think? Is it even possible? What benefit comes from exercising the mind?

There are many benefits to be derived from exercising your ability to control the thoughts that flow into your mind. The first is that you can only hear guidance from your inner self when you clear your mind and listen to what is being communicated. You can't have a conversation if you're doing all the talking. You can't hear what another is saying if you're always shouting. The flood of thoughts that is constantly in your mind is drowning out the messages being sent to you by your inner self. You're missing out on a lot of useful insight and guidance.

The most effective way to strengthen your mind is through the consistent practice of meditation. This ancient art has been practiced by many cultures and is now gaining traction in your society. It is a simple and effective tool for controlling the frequency of your own thoughts. It is also quite enjoyable.

When you meditate every day, you gain the ability to slow down the thoughts that enter your mind. The practice of meditation is just like any other practice. Imagine that you have never run for any significant distance in your life. Now you begin the practice of running. You start with short runs or even walks. Soon, as your body gains strength and endurance, you are able to run farther and faster. Within a very short amount of time, you are running with ease. You begin to feel better during and after each day's run. The same is true of meditation.

If you have never attempted to control your mind, the practice of meditation will seem challenging at first. It will be difficult to quiet your mind in the beginning. You might be unable to meditate for more than a few moments each day. But if you stick with it, you will gain strength and endurance, just as in any other practice. In time, you will be able to slow your thoughts and maybe even to stop thought for a moment or two. Your meditations will become pleasurable.

Meditate once each day for fifteen minutes or so. This is all the time you need to exercise your mind. Unlike other forms of exercise, there is no need to meditate for longer periods of time, even though your endurance will increase. There is also no need to judge your progress. If you are able to slow thought for just a few moments, that's just fine. It is the consistency that is most important here. Meditate each day and do not keep track of your progress.

The meditation process helps connect you to your inner self and your inner world. This is the most important aspect of meditation. It allows you to feel for the existence and reality of what is inside you. It allows you to begin a dialog with your inner self. In time, you will ask your inner self questions and soon you will begin to hear the answers. Your inner self is always communicating with you, but until you've begun the practice of meditation, you might not be aware of this form of communication.

Your inner self sounds like you. The thoughts you receive from your inner self feel like your own thoughts. It feels like you answering you. This is because your inner self is you. However, the answers that come from your inner self are very different from the answers that would come from you. Your inner self provides guidance that is always positive and for your highest good. Your inner self will never, ever be negative or derogatory in any way. Your inner self speaks from a position of love for you and love for your world. Any communication coming from your inner self will be positive and loving.

If you receive anything negative or fear-based, understand that these thoughts are not coming from your inner self. Your inner self would never say "Don't go that way," but instead, "Do go this way." Your inner self will never tell you to avoid something, but will instead ask you to do something else. Your inner self will point you in the direction of what's wanted and never away from what's unwanted. Your inner self will never caution you against something, but will instead inspire you toward something else.

This communication is initiated during meditation. When you have come to the point where you have slowed down thought while meditating, you will be able to speak to your inner self through your thoughts. At first, you might doubt the information that is coming through. This is natural because this process is new to you and still requires practice. But if you can trust that your inner self is there and that you're making progress toward better connection, in time you will become better at communicating with your inner self.

III.

You have been thinking thoughts for a long time and these thoughts feel as if they are being created in the moment by your mind. This is not quite accurate. You attract thoughts that exist in the nonphysical. You bring thoughts to you through the way you are feeling. Your feelings attract thoughts. When you feel the same way often, you will attract the same old thoughts. When you begin to deliberately choose the way you feel, you will attract different thoughts that come from that feeling.

If you feel bad, if you are depressed, you attract thoughts that match your feeling. Since your inner self is always feeling good, you will have little access to communication from within when you are not feeling good. Your inner self exists as pure positive energy. When you are not aligned with that high-vibrational energy, you will not have access to the communication that comes forth. This all points to one conclusion: if you seek to have an open dialog and gain the higher perspective of your inner self, you must simply choose to feel better.

Yes, your feelings are a choice. Yes, you have the ability to feel better anytime you consciously choose. Yes, there's a reason you must strive to feel good. If you cannot alter the way you feel, you will have difficulty attracting positive, beneficial thoughts and guidance from within.

Conscious creators have the ability to feel better through the practice of seeking thoughts that feel better. Conscious thinkers do not let themselves sink into darker, fear-based thoughts. When a negative thought enters their mind, the conscious thinker realizes it's there and habitually and automatically thinks a better-feeling thought. The thinking has been practiced so that the feeling improves. As the feeling improves, the thoughts automatically get better.

When you think good-feeling thoughts, your feelings improve and you attract better-feeling thoughts. It is a flow of energy that is rising and brings you with it. When you allow a bad-feeling thought to linger, your feelings dampen and you naturally attract more bad-feeling thoughts. This causes your mood to spiral downwards and you sink deeper into a lower vibration. As you know, lower vibrational states of being align you with unwanted conditions and experiences. Higher vibrational states of being align you with better conditions and the manifestation of pleasurable experiences.

Conscious creators understand that this is the basis of the attraction process. It is not as necessary for you to constantly think thoughts of what is wanted. All you really need to do is become chronically focused on feeling good. It is your vibration that is the attraction factor more than your thoughts. It is your feelings that bring you manifestations, good or bad. When you feel good, you attract things that are a match to your feelings. When you feel bad, you also attract experiences that match your feelings. Therefore, if you want to attract good things into your experience, you must strive to feel good as much as possible.

We do not want to discount the value of negative emotion or try to tell you that you must never experience a bad-feeling moment. These moments have value as well. We are simply stating the fact that you have the ability to choose to feel good and that feeling good more of the time will allow you to receive more good-feeling moments as manifestations. What you predominantly feel is what you predominantly receive.

Most of humanity does not recognize that how they feel: 1) is a choice, and 2) affects their own future. A moment lived in joy will cause future moments to be joyous. A moment lived in despair will attract similar moments until the person chooses joy. You are given the free will to choose happiness or sorrow. Your choice is displayed by your decision to feel a certain way.

Many people enjoy feeling miserable. They get something from the attention this type of feeling brings from others. They like the pity. They like being soothed. Yet they do not realize that misery loves company and that they will attract more of the same through their choice to feel bad. If they knew what they were doing, they would seek to change their state of being. If they understood the ramifications of their feelings, they would choose to feel better. If they were conscious thinkers, they would understand that how they feel leads to what they will experience.

As you become immersed in the process to consciousness, you will learn that how you feel affects your journey toward becoming who you really are. A radical change in your approach to life will come from consciously choosing how you feel in each moment. If you feel good, you will attract more good-feeling thoughts and you will ease your way into a state of bliss. As you notice that you are not feeling good, you will learn to seek better-feeling thoughts to improve your mood and your emotional state of being.

Your mood is highly attractive and builds momentum easily. Your mood is your present state of being. Keep your mood good and you will allow what you want to come. You will attract other people who are also in a good mood. Your good mood will spread and you will receive indications that you are getting what you want as good things come that are a vibrational match to your mood.

If your mood changes, you must stop and realize what's happening. If something has occurred, if something has been said, or if you have seen or read something and your mood has changed as a result, you have encountered a trigger and you must stop and analyze the new thoughts. You have come across a limiting belief. You have stumbled into a block in your path. This is a very important moment and in order to move to the next level, you will have to analyze what is happening in this very moment.

You can only find triggers when you are in a good mood and something causes you to lose that good feeling. If you are constantly in an unhappy, depressed, or despondent state of being, you will experience negative energy and every moment will seem like a trigger. You won't notice the individual blocks in the road because the whole road will be blocked. You won't want to evaluate anything because there will be way too much bad stuff to look at. You'll just want to give up.

Conscious thinkers know that not every moment will be sunny and bright. Some dark clouds will appear to create bad-feeling moments. Yet when life is lived in a happier state, one can see the blocks for what they are. Anytime a limiting belief is brought to the surface it is a good thing because only then can the trigger be inspected. Ironically, you will only discover your limiting beliefs from a place of joy.

IV.

The next step in conscious thinking involves how you come to evaluate your own emotional road blocks. This phase is best described as becoming "neutral." An investigator can only solve the problem if he becomes detached from the situation. A surgeon does not operate on her own children because she is too emotionally involved. You cannot see your own triggers when you allow judgment to cloud your view. You must become neutral to whatever is going on that you do not like in the moment. When something bad happens, the conscious creator sees it as a learning opportunity. Neutrality is the key.

You are designed to determine what you prefer. You use judgment to evaluate everything in your physical world. Judgment is a significant tool in navigating this physical environment. You have two choices in front of you. You must decide which choice is best for you in the moment. So you use judgment to determine which choice is better. Judgment helps you make decisions.

However, many of your decisions are made unconsciously, as you are quick to judge. Unconscious thinkers are stuck in duality, which says that if one thing is good, the other must be bad. When you judge something, you judge one thing as good and the other as bad (less good). You seldom say that this is good and this is also good. You rarely believe that one choice will take you where you want to go and that the other choice will also take you where you want to go. You believe that one thing is always better than its alternative. But this is not the case.

Since you view the world from a narrow and limited perspective, you cannot see the path as it unfolds ahead. There are hills and you cannot see the other side until you climb the hill yourself. There are blocks in the road and you cannot see over the blocks until you come to them. The trait that does not serve you is the belief that you know what lies ahead and exactly how to get there. You cannot see very far up the road.

When you come to a fork in the road, you believe there is only one right choice. You believe that one path will take you where you want to go and that therefore the other path must lead in the opposite direction, where you do not want to go. One path heads toward what is wanted, so the other path must lead toward the unwanted. One is good, so the other must be bad. But what if we were to tell you that either path will lead you where you want to go and that it makes no difference which path you take? That would mean that every decision is right and that you can remain neutral.

You were raised in an environment of duality and now you must make your way to neutrality. Duality means that everything can be evaluated and in it you will find the good and the bad. Neutrality means there is nothing inherently good or bad in anything, it's only your judgment that makes it good or bad. Therefore, when you can move from duality to neutrality, you can decide what anything means based on what serves you. This is power. Duality is victimhood and neutrality is creation.

Let's look at an example. Imagine that you have just graduated high school and are preparing to go to college. You studied hard in high school because you really wanted to go to university and receive a college education. There is a lot more we can talk about here, but for now we'll keep this example simple to illustrate a point.

You are influenced by your parents, peers, teachers, and society and you have come to believe that it is important for you to go to a "good" college and earn a degree. You think that this will greatly affect your future. You do not know anything about the laws of the universe or the mechanism of physical reality; you simply accept the beliefs that have been transferred to you by others. You also think it will be fun to go off to school and you are inspired to do so.

You have applied to many schools, but you have a list of favorites and there's one in particular that you really like. You have applied to some schools even though you believe that you will not be accepted. Other schools fall below your standards and you've applied to them just in case. But you think realistically you have a good chance of being accepted into your favorite school.

The lesser schools accept you just, as you thought they would and this proves to you that they are not worthy of you. The better schools reject you and this proves to you that you are not worthy of them. You do not feel strong emotion in either case. It comes down to the last school. This is the one you want. This is what you've been waiting for. The envelope arrives and you firmly believe that your fate is sealed by the answer waiting inside this letter. How will you react to what's inside that letter?

If you open the letter and read that you've been accepted, you will be elated. You will believe that your efforts have been rewarded and that you're finally on the road to what you want. Your dreams are coming true. You are filled with positive emotion.

If you open the letter and find that you've been rejected by your favorite school, you'll feel like your life has been ruined in that moment. There is nothing now to live for, as you believe that your hopes and dreams have been shattered. You are filled with negative emotion.

In this example, if you are accepted by the one school that you really wanted, you will be happy and if you are rejected by this school, you are unhappy. But since you cannot see the future, since you cannot see the road ahead, why on Earth would you have any emotion one way or the other? You can't tell from your perspective that this event was good or bad. You're bringing judgment to the event. You are determining whether it is a good thing or a bad thing because you think you know the outcome. You cannot know what the future will bring, and therefore there is nothing inherently good or bad contained in the letter. The letter is neutral. Everything is neutral.

Now imagine that the acceptance or rejection would both lead you to the same outcome. Imagine that either outcome has the exact same potential to bring you where you want to go. What would that mean? It would mean that everything is right. It would mean that if you were accepted to that school, you would end up where you wanted to be and if you were rejected, you would also end up in the same place. This is a radically different way to look at the decision-making process.

You can realize this new paradigm only after you come to fully understand the laws of the universe and the mechanism of physical reality. You are a vibrational being and what you want in this life emanates from your being through the signal you are sending. You receive what is wanted based on that signal. You get the essence of what you really want in a never-ending series of unfolding events. It doesn't really matter what you do or which road you take because the universe sees where you are and brings everything to you. The path itself is much less important than the signal you're sending. All paths lead to the culmination of your desires. It just depends on how you're operating on whatever path you're on.

Let's return to our example and see your life as a teenager about to graduate high school. You consider yourself intelligent and you are interested in many things. When you look at your life ahead, you want to live life in a certain way. You want a good job that pays well doing something you like to do. You want to be interested and challenged by the work you do. You want a family someday, so you would like to find a mate and have children. You want to make enough money to support your family, buy a home and a nice car, travel the world, and provide for your children's education. This is what is emanating from you. This is your vibration.

There are two ways to approach life. Most humans believe that they must do something to achieve what they desire. They believe that it is their action that causes results. And they are right in that action does create outcomes, but action alone does not have the power to create preferable outcomes.

The other way to approach life is to understand that you receive what you are vibrating and therefore you must allow what you want to come to you. This way of life involves feeling for what you want, not doing. You'll be inspired to the proper action at the right time, yet you are not focused on doing, you're focused on allowing.

When you are focused on doing, you will believe that your acceptance to the school of your dreams is a very good outcome and rejection is a very bad outcome. You will believe that your action was successful if you're accepted or a failure if you're rejected. Your attention is focused on the action and its outcome. Yet you have no idea if your action or its result is going to lead you to the things you really want.

When you are focused on allowing, you are neutral to the outcome. From this stance, you understand that both acceptance and rejection are good. From your position of knowing that you cannot see the road ahead, you understand that both outcomes have the same potential to lead you where you want to go. If you are accepted, you are eager to experience this new phase of your life. If you are rejected, you are eager to see where the next fork will take you.

In reality, it does not matter whether you are accepted or rejected. It doesn't matter whether you go to an Ivy League school, a community college, or straight into a career. You might read statistics that say otherwise, but it is always your vibration that will lead you toward what is wanted. It is your approach to life that determines the quality of your experience. What matters is whether you are living consciously and making choices that allow you to discover who you really are or whether you are making choices based on who you have been told you should be. There is an easy way to approach life and a more difficult way. It is always up to you.

When you have come to view an event as neutral, you will have made one giant leap to becoming who you really are. When you can trade judgment for neutrality, you've radically changed your approach to life.

From our simplified example, it is easy to see that the unconscious thinker who becomes emotionally tied to outcomes chains their happiness and well-being to these very outcomes. If an outcome is judged as good, they are happy. If it is judged as bad, they are unhappy. They relinquish control over how they feel to the outcome. They are at the mercy of fate.

The conscious thinker is tied to the process of consciousness and realizes that the outcome is neutral and therefore has no effect one way or the other on happiness. The conscious thinker lives a happy life just by feeling good. The universe must match that feeling, since that is what is emanating from the thinker. When the conscious thinker experiences an event, the event is completely understood to be part of the process that will bring them to what they want.

V.

Consciousness is always evolving to higher and higher levels. It does not matter where you are because you can always grow in consciousness. The development of the conscious creator is through a linear process. You move from one level to the next and the next and the next, always reaching for higher and higher levels. However, the joy of physical existence is never lost or subjugated to the process.

The ultimate purpose of the process to consciousness is a blending of you and your inner self here in this physical reality. This is the basis of the design of your environment. It was always thought that you would grow and evolve to become one with your inner self living here on this planet.

The benefits of living as a blended being, incorporating the best parts of your physical experience with the deep understanding of your inner, nonphysical self, are many. Your experience of life in this world would be so much deeper. Your expansion would be greater. You would be able to exercise your powers of creation in a more leveraged manner. You would live in joy more of the time. You would live as a nonphysical being in a physical body, because that is what you really are.

You cannot reach the goal if you do not know the goal even exists. So we are here to let you in on a little secret. The highest version of you is one that lives as your inner self would live. Who you really are is who your inner self is. What you really want to do is see your world from this higher perspective and live your life as your inner self would live it. You can do all this now. Just ask yourself, "What would my inner self do?"

Let's talk about what your inner self sees when it experiences your world through your eyes. Your inner self has no fear. There is no survival instinct. This makes life much easier and less stressful. If you don't have to worry about dying, then there's really nothing to fear. Since your inner self is already nonphysical, there's nothing to lose. Can you imagine what life would be like knowing you're immortal? It would be carefree.

When you reach the stage of living life blended with your inner self, you become immortal in physical experience. You are an eternal being living a brief, physical life. It is one of many. You have lived many lives before and you'll live many again. To your immortal soul, a lifetime is like a day in your own physical life. Each day brings a new opportunity for growth, experience, and expansion. If it doesn't work out today, you always have tomorrow. This day can be extremely fun and exhilarating and so can the next. When you understand that you are an eternal being, simply experiencing a life in which there is nothing to accomplish or get done, then you can relax and seek experiences.

Your inner self experiences oneness with all that is. Your inner self does not feel separate from anything. In your physical body, you experience the illusion of individuality. This is false. You remain one with all that is. It just seems like you do not. In reality, this environment revolves around you. You are the center of attention and everyone and everything is connected to you. This environment was created for you to have experiences and to provide for your expansion. Live like that statement is a fact and you will radically change your approach to life. We will talk more about the oneness that is absolute, but for now know that your inner self exists within All That Is and as a blended being, you will live this way as well.

Your inner self is completely focused on your preferences and never wavers from that. It exists in a stance of neutrality, withholding judgment of good and bad. Your inner self only sees the good and is focused on the positive aspects in every situation. It does not gripe, complain, or wish anything to be different than it is. Your inner self fully understands the laws of the universe and leverages those laws to create what is wanted at all times. When you become clearly focused on what you want without judging the events that come your way, you will live as your inner self would live. You would operate within this physical reality from the perspective of a higher, more evolved being.

As you come to be more neutral in situations, you will begin to see these events from the higher perspective and your fears will be alleviated and gradually dissipate. When you really know that there is no death and no separation, your fears about death will start to fade. You will not become emotionally distraught over the loss of life because you will know nothing was lost.

This understanding that there really is no death, just the transition into another form of life, will allow you to see death from a higher, fearless perspective. You will see funerals as parties. You will understand that suicide is no different from any other form of death. You will not try to dissuade those you love from making their own transition. The highest form of love is allowing people to transition when they are ready and not keeping them here, which will create suffering and pain. Can you imagine the freedom you would gain by understanding that death is not the end, but rather a new beginning? It would allow you to return your focus to living while you are here.

Your inner self has no need to prove its worthiness. Your inner self does not need to fit in. Your inner self is not self-conscious. It cannot feel embarrassed. It does not have an ego. It is afraid of nothing. It knows it can do no wrong. It knows it cannot make a mistake, for it understands that everything is right. Wouldn't it be nice if you could live this way?

Your inner self does not feel superior to anyone, for it knows that everyone is equally worthy. It does not worry that someone else is different, because your inner self knows that everyone is unique. Your inner self does not seek control over another or the conditions, for it knows that control is an illusion. Your inner self knows that it cannot create in the reality of another, nor can anyone create in its reality. But furthermore, your inner self knows that to help another is to stand as an example of the benefits of living as who one really is rather than who one is not.

Your inner self can only live as who it really is in this environment. It is not possible for it to live any other way. You believe that you can modify your behavior to coerce others into loving you or liking you. This is never true, because when you act in a way that is not true to yourself, it's an act and you're not a very good actor. Eventually, people will see right through who you are pretending to be. You cannot keep up the facade indefinitely. Cracks will form. Your inner self would only be who it really is.

Your inner self is a being of pure love without a trace of fear. Imagine living life this way. All decisions are based in love and not in fear. If someone asks you for something, you give it. You do not try to protect yourself, because this would be acting out of fear. You are not worried that if you give something away you will not get it back because this worry is based in fear. Every time you have a decision to make, it is made with a profound absence of fear. All decisions would be made from a position of love.

In every decision you would think, "What is the best thing I could do here?" You would not consider what was best for you. You would not separate yourself from another. You would not seek to gain the upper hand. You would have no desire to win when another could lose. What is good for another is good for you.

You would not worry about being taken advantage of because you would know that this is not possible if you are able to live without fear. It is only the aspect of fear that draws your focus away from what is wanted and toward what could go wrong. If you lived without fear, you would live in love and the universe would completely submit to you as a powerful creator. Everything you wanted would be delivered at exactly the right time. This is how you will live as a blended being.

The universe is a desire factory. It creates for you whatever you desire. All you have to do is allow it to flow to you. As a blended being, you will live as your inner self would live. Your inner self would live in complete allowance, and thus everything would be delivered. You live in fear and the fear blocks much of what you want from coming to you. That's just the way it is.

Those aspects of your life where fear is less prevalent are the parts where you experience the most abundance. Those areas of your life where you are fearful are the parts where you experience the most lack. Reduce the fear and you will increase the abundance.

If you do not have enough money, you experience fear about the subject of money. You think about not being able to pay your bills. You worry about losing your house, your car, or your credit rating. You worry about your retirement. You fear the loss of your job or your spouse's job. You feel lack and this is a fear-based feeling. Reduce the fear in this area and you'll create more abundance.

If you do not have a mate, it's because you experience a lot of fear about the subject. You worry that you won't be loved. You worry that the relationship might end in heartbreak. You are afraid that if you don't find a mate soon, you might not have time to bear children. There is so much fear around this subject that you do not allow the mate in. Reduce the fear and you will allow love.

Living from the higher perspective of your inner self allows you to navigate your reality with less fear and more abundance. This is how you intended to live prior to your birth, but you were influenced away from your inner self by those others who dominated your world when you were a child. Fear was allowed to intrude into your consciousness. It is now your job to rid yourself of irrational fear. The process to consciousness is the conscious dismantling of fear.

Chapter Nine

How to Deal with Fear

As we have discussed, there are only two emotions: love and fear. We've talked about love and now we will try to unravel the secret behind fear. Let's look at what fear really is.

You are born into a physical world and it is a much different environment than that of the nonphysical realm. You are given an earth suit called your body that is also physical. Your body is alive with countless points of consciousness known as cells. The cells are not you and your body is not you, yet you are bound to your body through your consciousness. Each cell is a living being also existing with you in this physical body. You all have the desire to experience physical reality and to experience expansion in joy.

You desire to exist as you did in the nonphysical realm, which is the state of bliss. However, you have certain unique needs that come with being physical. The first need is to survive. This is something you were born with because without the survival instinct you could not navigate this reality. This survival instinct uses a tool called fear to keep you alive. Without fear, you would simply follow your interests without regard to the fact that you must stay alive in order to experience this life.

Fascination is what drives your inner self in the nonphysical realm. Your inner self is fascinated with many aspects of existence and with the world in which you live. Like your inner self, you have interests and follow those interests where they may take you. If it were not for your survival instinct, your interests would send you off cliffs and into the mouths of lions. So as part of the survival instinct, fear is a pretty useful tool.

Earth is a playground designed to serve the expansion of countless life experiences. If not for the survival instinct and fear, there would be far fewer lives to be lived and they would indeed be shorter. So we know that fear, in and of itself, is not bad or wrong. There is no wrong anywhere in the universe and therefore fear is not wrong. It's just that irrational fear stalls the process to consciousness.

Another important aspect of physical reality as a human being is the need to breathe air, drink water, and eat food. These activities are not necessary in the nonphysical realm. On Earth, however, if you are unable to complete either of these activities, you'll end your physical experience. So you must constantly maintain your body by eating, drinking, and breathing. You must constantly be on alert.

You must also care for the ongoing health and well-being of the body. You must pay attention to the weather and the environment. You can't let the body get too hot or too cold. You must keep it out of danger. You have to be careful. Fear allows you to keep the body out of harm's way.

These are all examples of how the proper use of rational fear is completely appropriate and necessary for navigating this physical environment. We have established that fear is an important and primary aspect of physical reality. It is part of the physical experience.

In order to allow more life experiences to come to this planet, its inhabitants must bear offspring. This is simply the design of physical reality. It is natural. Just like the survival instinct, you are given the instinct of love. As soon as a baby is born, the parent naturally feels love. Love is the method physical reality uses to keep newborns alive long enough to survive on their own. The feeling of love is so powerful that it causes fear of loss. Here, again, fear comes in handy.

Parents protect their offspring from the dangers of the environment because their love causes them to fear anything that might harm their children. The survival instinct causes people to protect themselves using fear. The love instinct causes people to protect that which they love. This is all done by design and it is all good.

It is interesting to note that in the nonphysical realm, love does not bring in fear. There is no need to fear anything in the nonphysical and therefore fear does not exist there. Love exists, but fear does not. Therefore, your inner self loves you but has no fear because it knows it cannot lose you. You believe that you can lose your child, but from the higher perspective, you cannot really lose anyone you love. They will always be with you.

So fear is built into the fabric of physical reality. Rational fear is part of the game of life. It is good and necessary. But fear has made its way into other parts of your experience. When fear is not natural or necessary, we call it irrational.

Fear exists in the inner world of your mind. Fear does not exist in your outer world. You cannot see, taste, touch, smell, or hear fear. You might sense fear, but that remains part of your inner world. You can feel fear yourself and it is always an unpleasant feeling. All unpleasant emotions are based in fear. All pleasant emotions are based in love. This is your guidance system. You are designed to move away from fear and toward love naturally. Yet you do not do this. You allow fear to reside in your experience. We don't really understand it, but through this analysis we can see how it might occur when one is not conscious of universal laws or the mechanism of physical reality.

You exist in the physical environment in a body that is your link to this world. You must protect the body and survive so that you can continue to experience this life. You are born with a very powerful instinct to survive and fear is the main tool of survival. You must protect yourself and those you love. If you do not get enough water, air, or food, you'll die. If you are not safe, you'll die. If you are not alert to the dangers of the world, you'll die. And you think death is the end of life, so you definitely do not want to die.

II.

You must protect what you love. You love your children and you must protect them. This is part of the survival instinct. You fear that something might happen to your children or to those you love. Fear causes you to seek safety for yourself and for those you love. You want to protect them from harm.

To keep safe, you must have food, water, shelter, and a means of survival. You begin to fear that you might lack the things you need to survive. This fear of lack causes you to doubt the abundance that exists. Your focus is on having enough to survive and to keep those you love alive as well.

This fear of loss carries over to things as well. You learn to love your things and you want to protect them from harm. You fear the loss of your possessions. You have an ego and you begin to build up a view of yourself in the world. You might be defined by your possessions and come to fear the loss of status. Soon you fear the loss of anything and you try to protect everything. Fear becomes pervasive if left unchecked. It is now time to analyze your fears. Are they rational or irrational?

We are not saying that rational fear is good and irrational fear is bad. We are simply asking you to analyze the fear and understand whether it supports who you really are and what you really want or not. Rational fear is a component of the survival instinct and has helped man survive for eons. Yet your world is quite different from almost all of man's history on your planet. Now you must look at what serves you and what does not.

Fear is here and without it you would not have made it to this point in your life. In this respect, fear is a wonderful aspect of life. However, most of your fears have been learned through the warnings of others or completely fabricated in your own mind. Fear is what keeps you from anything and everything you want. If you don't have something you want, you can bet it's due to some irrational fear. Once you are able to release that fear, you will allow whatever it is you want to flow effortlessly into your physical experience.

There are many types of irrational fears and as they arise, you can inspect them and then come to understand if the fear serves you or not. It is unlikely that any fear you see in front of you serves what you really want. Now your job will be to deal with the fear and reduce its intensity.

Let's take a look at the fear of loss. You believe that once you have acquired something or someone that it now belongs to you forever. From this stance, you automatically fear its loss. When you enter a relationship and develop feelings for the new person, you suddenly fear the loss of the relationship. It happens quite naturally, but it is completely irrational.

First of all, this person and your relationship have nothing to do with your survival. If the relationship ends, you will still be alive. From this perspective, we can label the fear irrational because it does not affect your survival. Irrational fear is limiting. It always keeps you apart from what you want. In a relationship, you want the freedom to explore the other person as well as what you experience in union with the other person. You want to be free, fall in love, and then see where the relationship takes you.

Imagine a relationship free from fear. This would be the natural state of any relationship, since it falls outside the realm of survival. In other words, your survival in these modern times does not require another person or a romantic relationship. Today, a mate is simply something you desire and therefore fear is not a necessary aspect of the dynamic.

If your desire were to go into the wild and photograph lions, then fear would be a natural aspect of your desire. Your survival would depend on the proper dose of fear. Too much fear would keep you away from the adventure and too little fear might get you eaten by your subject.

So what are the irrational fears involved in relationships? These are is the fear of rejection, the fear of failure, the fear of change, and the fear of loss. These all seem like valid fears, yet they are all irrational (since your survival does not hinge on the success of the relationship) and they are all limiting.

When you enter a relationship and allow fear to come into play, you behave differently. You will be more cautious. Your guard will be up. You will look for reasons to end the relationship before you get too involved. The relationship will never get off the ground, and it's the fear that will prevent you from getting what you really want. Reduce the fear and you clear the blocks so that you can allow what you want to blossom naturally.

This is true of any aspect of life in which survival is not a factor. Imagine going to a job interview without fear. Imagine working in a job without fear. Imagine quitting a job without fear because you know you'll find a new one.

What keeps you from applying for your dream job? Fear. What keeps you from performing at your best in your current job? Fear. What prevents you from quitting your job? Fear. Irrational fear does not solve your problems. It does not keep you safe. It simply blocks your path to where you really want to go. That's all it does. There is no benefit to entertaining irrational fear.

Imagine applying for that job you really want or talking to that person you find attractive. What's the worst that could happen? Rejection. That's all. So why is the concept of rejection so frightening? What does it really matter? Does it make an actual difference? No, it doesn't matter at all. It has no effect on your life unless you think it does.

Rejection has very little to do with who you really are, but it has a lot to do with who you are being in the moment. Who you really are is one who lives free from irrational fear. We will term this "fearlessness" (it is really "irrational fearlessness"). Who you really are is fearless. Can you imagine what that would be like? That concept is so alien to you that you cannot even picture it. Yet who you will become, who you really are, is fearless. When you become the highest version of you, it will be the you with the least amount of irrational fear swimming around in your personality.

All that really separates the current version of you from the highest version of you is the amount of irrational fear you carry with you. The process to reaching the higher version of you comes with the intentional reduction of irrational fear. All you have to do to become who you really are is remove fear one layer at a time as it comes up. The way you progress to higher and higher expressions of your finest self is by stripping away these irrational fears one day at a time. That's all there is to do.

III.

Releasing irrational fear is easier said than done. If it were easy, you would have done it already. You know that most of your fears are irrational. You know that there are no negative ramifications to talking to that person you find attractive or interviewing for that job you really want. There are no real downsides to asking for a raise or a date. It's all made up in the confines of your own mind. You create the ramifications yourself.

Obviously, confidence is helpful when overcoming fear. As you increase the intensity of your confidence, you reduce fear. Confidence is gained with practice and belief. When you believe in your abilities, you create confidence and this reduces fear. Most people gain confidence through practice, but some things can't really be practiced and confidence doesn't always work when you are overcome with fear.

How do you practice talking to your ideal mate when you're too scared to approach anyone you find attractive? How can you practice interviewing for your dream job when there is only one dream job? How do you practice asking for a raise when you can only ask one time? Can you see where we're going with this? The answer is simple: just ask for easier things. This is the practice you need and this is one way to gain confidence.

If you're afraid to talk to someone you're really attracted to, then talk to someone you're not attracted to. This reduces the risk and when you reduce the risk, you reduce fear. Apply to jobs you know you are over-qualified for. When you're being interviewed, recognize how interested the interviewer is in hiring you. Feel that feeling of being desired and allow yourself to gain confidence. If you fear asking for a raise, then ask for something smaller. Notice that they are quite willing to give you what you deserve. Ask for a new chair or a new computer. Ask for a new office and see what happens. If they say no, who cares? It's not that important.

Practice creates confidence and confidence reduces fear. You can offset fear by believing in yourself. You can also lower the intensity of fear by understanding and believing in the laws of the universe and the mechanism of physical reality.

When you come to know that fear is simply a necessary component of physical existence, you can see it for what it really is. When you can define a fear as rational or irrational, you can change your perspective. How you face fear really determines the quality of your life experience. If your stance is confident, then fear is relegated to the second position. It has less effect on your behavior. It is less of a barrier to what you really want. The way to radically change your life is to change the way you respond to fear.

It is your response in the moment that creates your future reality. When you respond with confidence, you create the reality you truly desire. When you react in fear, you create a reality that does not allow what you have asked for to flow to you.

Courage is the ability to face rational fear and overcome the feeling. Bullfighters and mountain climbers have courage. But no bullfighter started out fighting bulls; they started with something smaller, like a wooden post or a small calf. No mountain climber started with Mt. Everest; they started with a ladder or a small hill. They started small and built confidence over time. By practicing on smaller things, they learned there was a way to overcome the fear. Somehow they realized they could do it. They felt the challenge yield to them.

IV.

All fear is limiting. Both rational and irrational fears keep you from doing what you really want to. Rational fear keeps you from feeling what it's like to dive off a cliff or pet a lion. This fear limits what you can experience so you will stay alive. Irrational fear limits your experience also. But since there is little risk of death when asking for a date, the limitation of irrational fear places restraints on experiences that are both desired and safe.

The problem with fear is that it makes you feel unsafe. If you can figure out a way to feel safe in the pursuit of the experience, you can reduce the intensity of the fear and then overcome it. One of the most satisfying feelings is overcoming fear. It is exhilarating. When you consciously figure out how to feel safe in the face of fear, you'll gain the satisfaction of overcoming that fear.

You might be afraid of roller coasters. They're designed to scare you. You are supposed to feel fear. Yet the exhilaration comes from riding a roller coaster despite your fears. So how does one overcome this fear? You simply soothe the fear by rationally analyzing the basis of that fear. In the case of roller coasters, you might realize that it is designed to be scary, yet the fear is irrational because the vast majority of rides end in the survival of all passengers. The same could be said of airplanes. The easiest way to soothe the frightened passenger is to remind them that air travel is the safest form of transportation.

We will call the method of overcoming fear, "a device." Think of a person who would like to jump off a cliff. The fear causes him to resist his temptation. He needs some kind of device to make it safe. If he can figure out how to jump off a cliff safely, he can overcome his fear. So he straps on a parachute. This device eases his fear enough to allow him to jump off the cliff.

Let's look at a person who would like to pet a lion. Her fear prevents her from doing what she wants to. So she looks for a device that will allow her to experience what it would be like to pet a lion. She gets a tranquilizer dart and shoots the lion. The lion falls unconscious and she is able to pet it. Her device allowed her to feel safe enough to overcome her fear.

Whenever you feel fear, simply find a device that will make you feel safer. Generally that device will be a thought process that will lessen the intensity of the fear. The fact is that irrational fear limits your experience and blocks what you want from coming to you. It is so pervasive that you don't even acknowledge it. You don't even analyze the fear. It just consumes you and you wave off your desire as if it were some unrealistic dream. But there is nothing you cannot do, have, or be. It is only fear that keeps you from all that you want.

V.

There are four primary fears: the fear of failure, the fear of rejection, the fear of loss, and the fear of change. The first three fears are implanted in you during childhood, usually by your well-intentioned parents. Your parents wanted you to do well in school. When you brought home a report card with good marks, they were proud of you. If you received a low grade in a certain subject, they voiced their disappointment. How you felt became dependent on their approval. Since you are designed to feel good, you endeavored to succeed. When you succeeded, they were pleased and you felt good. When you failed, they were displeased and you felt bad.

Depending on the way you were raised, you either have little fear of failure or are absolutely paralyzed by fear of failure and simply will not attempt anything. Those without much fear of failure were brought up in a home where their parents were either supportive or absent. In the supportive home, the parents did not view failure as a problem or a setback. They encouraged the child to keep trying or to approach it in a different way. This style did not bring on the fear of failure and the child grew up to have the confidence to try new things.

In the home where the parents were absent or not particularly involved in the activities of the child, the child had little incentive to impress its parents. It did not matter to the parents if the child succeeded or failed and the child grew up without the fear of failure. The child may have developed other issues, but this is usually not one of them.

Fear of rejection is also often instilled in childhood by parents. All children seek to be loved unconditionally by their parents. When parents attempt to control the behavior of their child through the manipulation of love, they instill the fear of rejection. When you love a child when he is good, you accept the child as he is. When you withhold your love when the child does something you do not like, you reject the child for who he is. This rejection is extremely painful and leads to a consuming fear that is difficult to overcome later in life.

Fear of loss is the third primary fear and has to do with the survival instinct. Parents have a natural instinct for protecting their offspring from the dangers of the world. What you are fearful of now has to do with your parents' fear of losing you. You look both ways when you cross the street. You wear your seatbelt while driving. You stay out of dangerous neighborhoods. You cross the street when some unseemly character lies in your path. You lock your doors and clutch your purse. You purchase insurance policies of every description. Fear of loss is mostly instilled in you by your parents at a young age, but this fear is propagated by your society and as you grow into adulthood, it matures with you.

Fear of change is the fear of the unknown. Why is the known safe and the unknown dangerous? What is there to fear under the bed or in the darkened closet? This fear is part of the survival instinct and says that if you're alive now, it's because you're doing something right. We want to stay alive, even if we're miserable, so let's not change. But if you don't change, you can't thrive. So man has always needed to challenge the unknown. Your society is where it is now because of those courageous and miserable people who wanted something more. Wanting more is the device that allows you to conquer your fear of change.

There are devices to deal with all of these fears. These fears are limiting, so overcoming each one will enhance your experience of life and allow your desires to flow to you. Let's take a closer look at each one and find devices to reduce their intensity.

The greatest device for dismantling any fear is the improved understanding of universal laws and the mechanism of physical reality. When you know how the system was designed and how it operates, you can see that fear is simply a necessary component of the design.

Let's start at the beginning. The physical world you live in was created to allow nonphysical beings like us to explore a new experience of beingness. In the nonphysical realm, we can do anything, so desire is not so strong. There is nothing that pushes the envelope. Physical reality was created primarily for our growth and expansion. We live in joy in the nonphysical realm, so it was important that joy was made an integral part of the physical experience.

The nonphysical realm is light and limitless. The physical realm is dense and limitations are part of the plan. In physical reality, there are the limits of space and time. In the nonphysical realm, there is no time and you are an eternal being. In the physical realm, you are given an entry point (birth) and an exit point (transition/death). You are given a physical body and that body ages over time so that you can experience life from a new perspective every day. It was all designed for your individual growth and expansion.

Most nonphysical beings desire the experience of being physical. But it is such a different experience from nonphysical life that many would just want to try it out to see what it's like. If it were not for the survival instinct and fear, most would leave as soon as anything unpleasant occurred (like birth, for instance). It is the survival instinct and fear that keeps you here, even though it can be unpleasant at times.

If you understand that you are an immortal, eternal being who can never die and who can experience as many physical lives as you want, you have nothing to fear. If you know that nothing can really be lost, you can't fear the pain of loss. If you understand that the universe has the ability to provide you with all you want when you want it, you can't lose anything. If you believe and trust in the laws of the universe, you will see the loss of something as the opening for something new to enter.

It is your perspective on life that allows for the presence of fear in almost everything you experience. When you change your approach to life from a narrow perspective to the higher perspective, your experience of fear will radically change as well. Since irrational fear keeps you from getting what you really want, it is critical that you work to reduce fear whenever possible. Irrational fear is best dealt with through close scrutiny. This analysis will be your device for overcoming fear.

Let's look at fear of rejection. You could say fear of rejection might be a rational fear based on survival if you were an infant and were rejected by your mother. Without your mother, you would not survive. But since you've made it this far in life and are able to care for yourself, the fear of rejection is now irrational. All fear is limiting, so how does fear of rejection limit your experience of life?

If you fear rejection, which nearly everyone does, you stop yourself from having all sorts of opportunities. You avoid talking to new people. You might even avoid smiling at people. You might walk with your head lowered to avoid eye contact. You might not ask out or be asked out by the person you find attractive. You might not make new friends. You might not apply for new jobs or business opportunities. You will miss out on all sorts of experiences. But most importantly, you will not discover who you really are.

Who you really are has no fear of rejection. When living the highest expression of you, you are not afraid of rejection. You are eager to meet new people because you know this will allow you to experience new things. You are eager to talk to anyone and everyone regardless of their beauty or status because you are not fearful of being rejected. You know that if you are a vibrational match to them, they will enter your experience. If they reject you, it is simply a matter of mismatched frequencies. It has nothing to do with you.

You will be aligned with those to which you are vibrationally compatible. As you raise your vibration by living consciously, you will meet many new people who also vibrate at this level. There is never anything to be worried about. If you were not a vibrational match, you would not meet. If they seem smarter or prettier or more accomplished than you, that's a very good thing because you are rising to their level. You are moving up and they are there to greet you.

If you resist your new level of vibration and hide out in fear, you will cause inner conflict and pain. You will be thrust into situations that force you to confront your fears. The universe will throw you into the swimming pool whether you believe you are ready or not. That cold water will be a shock to your system, but you'll get over it. Or you could simply face your fear and wade into the water at your own pace. Once you're fully immersed in the water, you will acclimate to the water's temperature.

You cannot resist your vibration for very long. Once it has been raised, it is not possible to lower your vibration for any significant length of time. Once you have expanded, you cannot contract. Your fears will cause resistance and make the journey more uncomfortable than it needs to be. You will have to practice reducing the intensity of these fears so that you can smooth out your path to becoming who you really are.

Another device for dealing with fear of rejection is to love and appreciate yourself as you had intended prior to your birth. If you were to fully love yourself, unconditionally, you would never fear rejection. If you saw yourself as the perfect being we see, you would understand that if someone does not see your worthiness, it is because of their own limited perspective. It has nothing to do with you.

We will tell you a secret. If you were left alone with just about anyone you have ever met and had a conversation with, you could grow to love that person within five days. Think of anyone you have ever known. Think of someone you met on an airplane or at a party. Think of someone you know as an acquaintance. If you were left together without the influence of the outside world or your normal lives, you would start to see their perfection within a matter of days. If you removed fear from the equation, you would love them within five days. It is only fear that keeps you from loving that person.

We are not talking about romantic love, though this would be very likely if you had a physical attraction to this person; we are talking about natural love. Without the presence of fear, you would not just like someone, you would come to love them very quickly.

If you were left alone with just about anyone and there was nothing to fear because you were removed from society and your present conditions, it would be natural to love that person. You would have no reason to dwell on their faults because it is only fear that allows you to become consumed with another's idiosyncrasies. We'll talk a little more about this later. But for now, just realize that you are naturally able to love another person when there is nothing to fear and they will all naturally love you as well. You will also naturally love yourself when you remove fear from your life.

When you reduce the intensity of fear, you automatically gain confidence. Have you ever seen an unattractive man approach a beautiful woman? The confidence he exudes makes him more attractive. Have you ever met a woman who seemed beautiful, but once you got to know her, her insecurities made her less attractive? It is the fear or the confidence that everyone senses. It is the vibration that causes you to be attractive or not. A confident vibration is attractive, while a fearful vibration is not.

The belief that fear keeps you safe does not serve you. We will not say it is wrong, for there is no wrong anywhere in the universe. We only stress that irrational fear places extreme limits on your experience of life. You are here to experience physical reality. It is a safe environment. You need not fear anything that does not affect your survival.

VI.

Another device for reducing the intensity of fear is the question "What is the worst thing that could happen?" If the answer is death, then this is a rational fear. If the answer is the pain of loss, rejection, change, or failure, then it is an irrational fear and you can deal with it. Whenever you face a fear, just ask yourself, "What is the worst thing that could happen?" and it will put the fear in perspective.

Understanding the fear from a higher perspective will give you confidence. When you can look at a fear and see what is really at stake, you can move through it. Sometimes, you stop yourself from doing something because you fear looking foolish. Where does this fear come from? What makes you care what others think? Is it really a fear of rejection? Usually not. It's most likely a fear of the pain associated with loss.

Fear of loss involves physical objects that you mistakenly believe you own. But that fear is not so profound. You can insure your valuables and replace almost any object. Fear of loss really surrounds your life and the lives of your loved ones. You fear skydiving and rock climbing and white-water rafting because you could die. But you also fear public speaking, being wrong, or saying something inappropriate just as much or even more so. Most people would rather skydive than speak in public, even though there is little chance of physically dying on stage. So what does this mean?

It means that your persona is as real and as alive as your physical body. You have created a version of you, your persona or your personality, which you are as tied to as you are your body. Yet, neither of them really exist. Your body is a community of cells, some of which you control but most of which you do not. Your body is not you; it's simply your space suit. You can clean it and mend it, but it is not you. Your persona was created by you and you are just as tied to it. But, unlike your body, you completely control its existence if you think about it.

Your ego fights to keep your persona alive and valid. It is neither alive nor necessarily valid. You can alter it at any time. You can change your personality and in fact, as you become who you really are, you must change it. It will be different as you emerge into higher levels of consciousness. Your ego fears for the loss of the persona and fights to keep it just as it is. It uses fear to restrict you from altering it. Your ego is in a fight for the survival of the persona. It is a battle against change.

You have created your persona to be what it is right now. If you believe that you (your persona) is smart, then you must constantly prove it. When challenged by someone on a certain topic, you might resort to making them wrong so that you feel right. But, since you are inherently intelligent when you live as the highest version of who you are, you would never need to prove yourself to anyone or to make another wrong. This is simply a tactic of the ego.

You have nothing to lose by altering your persona. Therefore, you have no need to fear its loss. In fact, you must lose your current persona as you ascend to who you really are. Think about it this way: when you make your transition to the nonphysical realm, what of your current persona will you take with you?

There are no fears in the nonphysical realm, so would it be possible to take your fears with you? No, of course not. If you could not take your fears, would you need to prove your intelligence? No, never. Would you take your sense of humor? Absolutely. Would you take your love of animals and nature? Yes, definitely. Would you take your pride and accomplishments? They would do you no good. Would you take your interests and passions? You sure would. So look at yourself honestly and decide what you would take. This is the highest version of you that you are moving toward. Everything else is holding you back.

So now do you fear embarrassment? Why would you? It is irrational and it keeps you from trying new things. You are an inherently worthy being. You're as worthy as anyone who has ever lived and as anyone who will ever live. You need not prove anything. You cannot be embarrassed, you cannot fail and nothing of value can ever be lost. There is nothing to fear in change because you must always be changing.

VII.

There is more to life in the current times in which you live. The earth is vibrating at a higher level than ever before. It is the most interesting time to be alive and the fact that you were born in this time means that you are truly successful.

You came here to explore this world at this time. You intended to expand through the experience of physical reality. You are supposed to push the envelope and try new things. In this sense, from the higher perspective, it is not possible to fail.

Failure is another powerful irrational fear. It is not possible to fail, since all experience is expansive. In fact, you usually learn far more from failure than from success. But it is this fear of failure that keeps you from attempting that which you know you would enjoy.

If you lived naturally in the world without the influence of others, you would not fear failure. However, you have a persona and you want to be seen by others as successful in everything you do. Your ego keeps you from taking risks that might harm the persona. If you want others to believe that you are good, worthy, and successful, then you cannot risk failure. However, it is a false persona.

Any persona other than who you really are is a false persona. If you are afraid of failure, you are not living up to the highest version of who you really are; you are simply acting in a way that is not true to you.

It is one thing to carefully assess the idea to see if it is valid, but certainly you must look at the decision to try something new without worrying what others will think of you. Only you know what's right for you. You must not let others guide you away from what it is necessary for you to explore. You must not concern yourself with everyone else's fears.

If you have a desire or a dream, it is up to you to pursue that dream. If you do not succeed to the expectations of others, you must not consider it to be a failure, for it is the pursuit of this dream that raises your vibration so that you will be ready for the next real dream to come to you.

Everything in life is a series of steps. As you follow an interest that is true to who you are, you climb steps. You are always moving forward and climbing up steps. You are never stuck in one position, nor can you ever move backward, even if sometimes it feels like you are. Your vibration can only be raised through experience, never lowered. Once you've moved one step, you're ready for the next. You can move as slowly or as quickly as you like.

When it seems like failure, you believe you've moved backward. You feel as if you were in a better place prior to the event that felt like failure. But this is an illusion. You are actually quite a few steps ahead in your failure than you were before you started. In fact, your vibration almost always moves higher after what you perceive to have been a failure rather than what you would have perceived to have been a great success.

Those who seem to be the most successful among you have faced what you would call significant failure. Yet, it is precisely theses failures that have allowed the most growth and the most raising of vibration. If it were not for these apparent setbacks, the real, true successes could not have occurred. Without failure, significant growth cannot occur.

If you are afraid to attempt that which you are here to explore, you create resistance to who you really are. This causes inner conflict and pain. It is not advisable to play it safe when it comes to exploring your passions. You will come up with many reasons not to try something. This is your ego speaking. If you are afraid of failure and do not do something you want to, only then have you really failed.

If the thing you want to attempt is life-threatening, then your fear is rational and you must carefully weigh the risks. This is not what we are talking about here. We are speaking of an irrational fear of failure where there is no danger to your body, only to the perceived, ego-created persona. If you are worrying about what others may think of you, then you are primarily concerned with the risk to your persona and this is limiting.

Your ego will make you want to protect your persona. But you must not protect it. You must challenge it at every turn. If you have a choice between trying something new and doing what appears to be safe, then you must try that new thing. Don't worry about your finances, your possessions, or your relationships. If you are called to do this new thing and it interests you, you must explore it. The only thing you can lose is this opportunity.

You intended to explore certain specific subjects as you made your decision to enter physical reality prior to your birth. This physical world is vibrant and the environment is harsh compared to the nonphysical world. It is a very dense environment and your instinct is to play it safe and seek comfort whenever possible. But this is not why you came. You wanted to grow and understand more about who you really are. You wanted experiences and expansion. Your interests and passions lead you there step by step. There is really nothing to fear, so don't fool yourself that not doing something is safe. It is quite the opposite.

In the nonphysical realm, you will never regret the things you did or did not do, so there is nothing you can get wrong. This life experience will be more satisfying and intense when you fearlessly follow your interests and passions. We want you to come to know who you really are because life is much more interesting when you are on this path. Life is meant to be fun, exhilarating, and filled with passion. It is just a little fear that keeps you from that which you very much want out of life.

VIII.

The most irrational of the irrational fears is the fear of change. Since you are always changing, how can you possibly fear change? Change is your natural state. You are not static beings. It is not possible to stay in the same place. Time changes everything. You could sit still in your chair and stare at a spot on the wall for an hour, but you would still change. You would be a different person as a result of the experience of sitting in a chair and staring at the wall for an hour. Everything you do, everything you think, everything you experience, changes who you are.

You are quite different now than you were a decade ago. Think about who you were, what you were doing, and what you wanted just a decade ago. You are not the same persona at all. You are not the person you were a year ago, a month ago, a week ago, or even yesterday. You are constantly in a state of growth and change.

Is it not irrational to fear change when the basis of what you are is a changing being? You think you can stay the same, but you cannot. The world changes right along with you. Everything changes. Everyone changes. To resist the change that is happening to you and the world around you is to stop becoming who you really are. This causes inner conflict and stress.

Embrace change. Do not fear change. Seek change.

This entire book is about change. As you radically change your approach to life, you move rapidly to who you really are. This book is not just about changing, for you can't help but change. This book is about changing on purpose. It's about changing with purpose. It's about moving the concept of change forward so that you begin to enjoy change and relish the newness of everything.

When there is change, you judge whether the change was good or bad. You often believe that the change might have negatively affected you in some way. This is not possible, since all change leads to growth and expansion. It might not have appeared to be a good thing at the time, yet ultimately your growth depended on it.

Let's say you have a family member who has made their transition to the nonphysical. You feel pain in the apparent loss of this person in your world. You believe this change was a bad thing. You judge it as being wrong. Your limited perspective tells you that your life has worsened as a result of this change.

When you are living less consciously, you are operating under a system called "duality." If something is good, its opposite is bad. Up and down are two opposing things because you believe that something cannot be up *and* down at the same time. Something cannot be good *and* bad at the same time. Something cannot be physical *and* nonphysical at the same time.

When you start living consciously, you give up your attachment to duality. You can experience the loss of a loved one as good and bad at the same time. You can realize that we are all physical and nonphysical at the same time. If you remove the word "time," duality ceases to exist.

So when you experience change and remove your judgment from it, you lessen your resistance to the change. You allow yourself to expand from the change as it was meant to happen. Even though your loved one's transition primarily affected their experience because it was their decision, your life still changed as a result. But it's your reaction to that change that affects your experience from here. You can either accept the change or resist it. Guess which reaction is more beneficial?

This is true of any change you judge to be negative. You can either see the benefits and the positive aspects of the change or you can feel sorry for yourself as you judge the change to be wrong.

When you are fired from that job you hate, you judge it as wrong. Yet this will only lead to another job or another experience. When you react negatively, you set up the conditions of your future. When you believe that you are the victim of someone else's decisions, you will continue to reside in the less conscious state of duality.

It is when you are consciously able to choose your reaction to change that you drop resistance to what is. When you accept the change as a step in your progression to who you really are, you build forward momentum. When you allow for the brilliance of universal laws to work this all out for you, you begin to live from the higher perspective.

Things are always working out for you. Your critical judgment of the design holds you in a resistant stance against what is. When you believe you know what's best from your limited perspective, you fight the natural flow of the universe that is bringing you to where you say you want to go. Give up your resistance, because you cannot resist the power of the universe. Resistance is futile!

Chapter Ten

A Conscious Approach to Life

All fear is limiting and all love is beneficial and expansive. Reduce the fear and you'll allow more love. There are no negative consequences to overcoming an irrational fear. If the consequences seem as though they would be negative, it is simply your inability to see the whole picture because your perspective is limited. When you face an irrational fear and overcome it, you expand and grow from the experience, regardless of the outcome.

Let's imagine you want to quit your job and start your own business. We'll also imagine that you have done the necessary vibrational preparation needed to ensure you are ready to start your own business and you are doing this because it is fun and exciting, not because you are trying to escape your nine-to-five job.

You have a passion, so you build a business around your passion. You have some great new ideas for the business and you add something unique to it. You have felt the inspiration to start this business and because you have reached a new, higher vibrational state as you mentally prepared for it, you received insight in the form of an innovative idea.

However, you face obstacles in the form of fear. You must quit your job that you like and that has provided the lifestyle you enjoy. You must risk your savings and the investments of your friends and family. You must commit to a lease and other loans. And you must face the unknown changes that will come.

You overcome your fear by soothing yourself. You notice that many other successful people have started their own businesses. You believe that your idea is a good one and you know that people will see the value in your innovation. You believe that you will be happy running your own business and that it's worth the risk.

You come to a decision to quit your job, sign a lease on a building, and invest your money and the money of many others who also believe in your idea, and you open your business. You hire employees, you develop strategies, and you create a marketing program. Slowly, you start to sell your product and money begins to flow.

As you run the day-to-day operations of the business, you encounter more fear and you overcome your fears. You have success and you enjoy those successes. Things are going well, and you begin to pay back your investors and yourself. But then something happens and you are forced to close the business. You have lost your money, your employees have lost their jobs, and you cannot repay your investors the balance of their investment. You have personally obligated yourself to a lease you can no longer pay, as well as many other debts. You have lost everything and are forced to declare bankruptcy.

You could view this entire event as a total catastrophe. You could feel as though you were much better off when you were working at your old job. You had some money in the bank and your friends and family all had their money safe and sound. Your credit was still in good standing and all those people wouldn't have lost their jobs. You might believe you would have been much better off just ignoring your dream and playing it safe. You might even believe your fears were justified all along. You should have listened to your fears, for they would have kept you safe.

When you believe that your irrational fears keep you safe, you're living in duality. Submitting to your fears only gives you the illusion of safety. You are always safe unless you are risking your life. If you're only risking money, or time, or your credit rating, then you are not risking anything real. Money, time, credit ratings, and all these things are fabricated aspects of your society. They're not real. What's real is the experience.

As you move through your fears into a new experience, you expand as a result of the process. Your vibration rises. You become more. Your fears kept you small, but you moved through them and became more in the process. You made a dramatic shift in your reality and moved one step closer to becoming who you really are.

You lost nothing of value in what you perceived as a failure. You expanded and that is what is truly valuable. You now stand in an entirely new position. You are now so much more than you once were. It is from this point that you shape the rest of your life.

There are two ways to react to the culmination of your venture. You can see it as a failure or as a success. You must decide right now what it is and what the experience meant to you. You must make that decision on your own from your individual level of consciousness.

There is so much we can say about the vibrational preparation that must be done before attempting a new endeavor like this one, but for the purposes of illustration, we will assume that you completed the vibrational preparation needed to ready yourself for your new business. In this case, we will simply say that the business ended and you must realize that ultimately you created the end to your own business whether you consciously wanted to or not. Had you been vibrationally aligned with the business, it would have continued to prosper and thrive. Since you create your own reality, we must submit to you that it is always you who controls the fate of your business and every other area of your life as well.

The economy could have collapsed, a competitor might have entered the market, or a lawsuit might have ended the business. But no matter what happened, it was your creation. We understand the laws of the universe and the mechanism of physical reality well enough to know that you are the creator of your own reality. If it happened to you, it was your creation.

If you are a conscious creator, you can only view the collapse of your business from one perspective. You must know that it was an expansive experience and that you are more now than you were before. You must conclude that there was knowledge to be gained from the experience. You must come to the conclusion that the experience was ultimately for your growth. This is the only possible logical conclusion that any conscious thinker can come to.

The unconscious person who is unaware of the laws of the universe might believe that the failure of the business and the resulting bankruptcy left him less than he was before. His reaction to the experience is one of denial. He believes that outside conditions led to the failure of the business. He is certain that something happened to him, not for him. He now lives in a resistant stance to the version of himself that has expanded as a result of this experience.

So here you have the two sides of awareness. The conscious thinker knows that the result of his dream, which culminated in the opening and closing of a business, has left him in a certain place that was different from where he started. He knows that he moved through his fears to create something that had not existed before. He tested his idea. He did things he had never done before. He can feel that he is a different person now than he was before he started the business.

While he may observe that he no longer has a job or a business, he no longer has money in the bank or a good credit rating, and he no longer has many of his possessions and some of his friends refuse to talk to him, he realizes that the experience was necessary for his growth. It was all part of becoming who he really is. He understands that something inside him caused the business to end and he does not blame outside conditions. He realizes that the universe has led him step by step to this place and he is eager to move forward from here.

The unconscious thinker believes he is a victim of circumstances beyond his control. He will complain about the unfair business practices of his competitors, or government regulations, or lazy workers, or any outside condition he feels caused the collapse of his business. He blames everyone but himself. He too has expanded, yet he denies this expansion. He feels ruined and acts as if he's been ruined. But his expanded self is ready for something more. He has grown, but he denies his growth. This resistance to what he has become results in inner conflict and stress on the body.

When an unconscious thinker expands through an experience like this but denies their expansion, they harm themselves with thoughts that revolve around failure and other negative aspects of the experience. They wish they could go back to the way things were before. Their negative reaction to what occurred greatly affects their future experience. As they feel broken, they attract more conditions that represent their feelings. Soon, everything is lost. If they live long enough to reach rock bottom, they will begin to emerge and their expansion will help them regain their stance quickly. Once they give up their resistance to the new conditions, they will rebound quite naturally. When they release their negative thoughts and begin to focus on the positive aspects of some new endeavor, their expanded self allows them to rise once again, often much higher than ever.

However, failure need not bring anyone down. A conscious thinker can move from this place to the next without dwelling on anything in a negative way. The conscious thinker can speak words to himself from a place of understanding.

"This was an expansive learning process and I expanded as a result."

"I am now more than I was before."

"I know more than I did before."

"I am able to do things I did not know I could do.

"I am worthy."

"I have value."

"What do I really want now?"

Imagine if you could say these things in the face of what many would call "failure." Imagine how powerful you could be. If you could see that the result of this experience has caused you to become more, then you could leverage the growth you gained into something so powerful you could not be stopped. Imagine if you viewed failure with the same enthusiasm with which you view success. This is how you use what you have learned about universal laws for your direct benefit here in this life experience.

ll.

All events in your life work to shape you into vibrational readiness for what you want. If you judge an event to be bad, you are not seeing the purpose of the event. Your judgment and your resulting reaction to anything seen as negative stalls your growth. One who approaches life from a high level of consciousness knows that all events are neutral and that it's your your judgments that make them either good or bad. However, you now see that this judgment is a part of a dualistic approach to life.

Duality is the mode of the unconscious thinker. Neutrality is the basis of the conscious thinker. When you start living your life from the higher perspective, in a more conscious manner, you will begin to reduce your rush to judgment. You will stop seeing people as beautiful or ugly. You will stop noticing drivers as good or bad. You will not judge strangers as friendly or scary. You will begin to understand that it is your perception that makes things seem one way or the other.

Imagine a day in your life free from judgment of good or bad, right or wrong, preferred or disliked. You are able to be with everything as it is. You allow it all just to be without trying to figure out if it's right or wrong.

You wake up in the morning and as you lay in your bed, your senses come to life. What time is it? Does it really matter? Did you sleep in late or did you wake too early? It's fascinating to break this down and realize that you make judgments about every little thing and you often make them unconsciously.

Let's say you wake up twenty minutes later than normal. What would the unconscious person say to himself? "Oh, no. I'm late. I must hurry. This is going to ruin my whole day. I hate being late. Why didn't the alarm clock go off? Why is this happening to me?"

You can see the victim mentality at work within the unconscious mind. The question "Why is this happening to me?" ignores the fact of your own creation. The unconscious creator believes that things happen to him, not for him.

The conscious thinker would look at this event from a higher perspective. He might say, "Wow, I slept in late and the alarm clock did not chime as I expected it to. I wonder what's going on here. There must be a reason this is happening. I created this for a purpose. I wonder what there is to discover. Let's see how this all plays out."

The conscious creator does not judge the event as good or bad. He sees it as a neutral event that might have meaning. He sees the fun and challenge in learning what there is to be learned. His day is not ruined and he is not bothered. His reaction is one of interest and speculation. This is quite a different reaction to that of the unconscious thinker.

If we can convince you that it is your reaction to events that set forth the construction and design of your future, you will understand that how you react to events will have a great impact on the quality of your life. If you can learn to modulate your reactions so that they are more balanced and are based on observation rather than judgment, you will make great strides towards the improved life experience that you desire.

We think it is quite easy to see the difference between the reactions of the unconscious thinker and the conscious thinker. The first reacts negatively based on the judgment that something wrong has happened. You can see that this negative reaction is likely to affect his entire day. You can sense that he will be scrambling to catch up and will likely make things worse. He will rush to get ready and might forget something. He will drive too fast to work and will undoubtedly become annoyed with other drivers. He will not give proper time to something important because he feels he has run out of time.

The conscious thinker remains calm. He realizes this has happened for him, not to him. He knows all about the laws of the universe and the design of physical reality. It would not be happening if there wasn't something in it to be learned. He knows it could not be happening unless he needed some vibrational adjustment. Maybe he was getting into too much of a routine and this event happened to shake things up. Maybe he was becoming too focused on time and this event caused him to rethink his relationship to the clock. Maybe this event caused him to take a new route to work, or to skip work that day, or to cancel some appointment, or many, many other possibilities. The conscious thinker realizes that things are always working out for him and is confident that this event occurred for his personal benefit.

So, based on his reaction to the event, how do you believe the rest of his day will go? We believe that from his stance of awareness and readiness, he will allow the event to play out and will become an observer. He will be fascinated by what will come and will be open to the change that will occur in his vibration. He understands that the universe is molding his vibration and he allows the change to occur.

This example occurred within minutes of waking. The person in our example was given the choice to react in any way he pleased. But the reactions as seen from the perspective of the conscious and unconscious thinkers were quite opposed and this was only the first of many events that would occur that day. Depending on the reaction to this first event, the day could unfold in so many different ways. It was the reaction to the event, not the event itself, that created the rest of the day and the future of this person.

III.

Consciousness involves being aware of what's going on. The conscious thinker is able to step back and take an honest look at each segment of his or her life. If something is not working, the conscious creator realizes that a radical change is needed. The analysis of this segment of one's life will reveal something about the person, not about the situation or condition.

For instance, imagine that you are a conscious person who understands that each area of your life should be working. While you realize that you are an expanding and growing being and that things are always moving, you also know that everything should be moving in the direction of what you want. In other words, each part of your life should be enjoyable as it is, even though it's in a constant state of evolution.

Imagine you are happy with your work life, your health, and your relationships. Everything is going very nicely. You are an expanding being and you're primarily focused on conscious living while pursuing those aspects of physical reality you find interesting, stimulating, and enjoyable. You have a great job that allows you the freedom to express who you really are. It is satisfying, challenging, and very interesting. You have found your passion in life and are immersed in your work. However, there are aspects of the job you perceive not to be working. Why is this? Why can't it all be the way you want it to be? If you create your own reality and you've made it to this high level of consciousness, why are there still so many things that are not the way you would choose them to be?

As an evolving being, you are on a never-ending path of expansion. As soon as you reach one level of consciousness, something will present itself in the form of a block or a challenge. If you experience negative emotion, you can be sure that this challenge has been specifically orchestrated for your personal growth. In order for you to move to the next level of awareness, you must move through this block.

Let's present you with an easy example. You've attracted this wonderful job, you are well compensated, you enjoy your work, you feel fulfilled, and you love your co-workers - all except one. There is one person you find annoying and you don't really see how they fit into your reality. This person grates on your nerves. You are able to be nice and to tolerate him, but you would prefer that he did not exist in your reality.

If you could, you would make this person vanish. You can't understand why he is even here. It's odd how your co-workers are not nearly as annoyed by him as you are. Some of them even like him. It just seems so strange. Every time you're near him, you tense up. You avoid conversations and are very short with him. You feel negative emotion and this allows you to realize it's not him, it's you.

This person represents something you do not like about yourself. As you evolve to who you really are, you are coming to love yourself unconditionally. When you reach the highest version of you, you will love every aspect of yourself. Until then, you will be uncovering those areas where you don't love yourself. This co-worker you find annoying is here to help you discover the truth about who you are being right now.

This system of reality is designed to allow you to be, do, and have anything you want. You desire to become who you really are. You want to love yourself unconditionally so that you may love everything else unconditionally as well. You want to expand and evolve. In doing so, the universe is helping you achieve your desire by modifying you. You are the one who must change.

When you look at this annoying person you work with, you want him to change. Isn't that funny? You think that if he would just change, or if the conditions would change so that he was not there, you would be happy. You see how the first thing you want to change is the other person or the conditions. You can't change the environment, because you take the issue with you as the environment changes.

Let's say you quit your job because you can no longer tolerate this person. It was becoming unbearable, so you decided to leave everything behind and find another job. By quitting, you would be rid of that person. Do you see that this is an unconscious reaction to these blocks? Once you found a new job, a new annoying person would pop up in your experience. This is the mechanism of physical reality. It cannot work any other way unless you change your desire, which you cannot do. You cannot decide that this becoming-who-you-are business is too hard and then desire to become unconscious once again. It doesn't work like that. You can't go backward. You already know too much.

So, leaving the situation just brings up newer and tougher blocks. A conscious creator realizes that this person was delivered for the specific purpose of growth and expansion. This is a gift from the universe to help you move to where you say you want to go. In this case, this person is here to illustrate an aspect of you that you do not like. Once you make the necessary change, the situation will resolve itself.

Have you ever watched a movie or television show about time travel? In these stories, the hero always does something in the past that solves a problem in the present. As soon as the challenge in the past has been overcome, we see the resulting present time as if the problem never occurred. The hero knows all that went on to make the future better, but those in the future are oblivious because they knew nothing of all the challenges that took place to create the outcome they now enjoy.

The same is true with the block that has been presented to you. As soon as you make the necessary change to overcome the block, it will vanish and there will be no signs that a problem ever existed. This is because your change has created a new reality, one in which the perceived problem was never an issue.

Let's continue with our example of the annoying co-worker. Let's say you realize that he has been specifically placed here for your growth. Now, this is a leap of faith because he was working here before you even applied for the job. He was part of the landscape before you even stepped into this environment. How could he be here for you? If the universe was going to bring in someone for you, wouldn't it bring in someone new?

If this person causes triggers to fire within you, then he is here for your specific growth. Don't worry how the block arrives or what shape it takes. If you feel negative emotion, it's here for your growth. When you no longer feel negative emotion, you have resolved the issue by making the necessary changes in your approach to life. Once you have changed, the block will be removed.

You know that this person is your block because you feel negative emotion. That's all you need to be aware of. So, now that you know the reality of the situation, what are you to do? How are you going to remove this block? How will you move forward?

You must radically change your approach to this person. You must uncover what it is you find so annoying and how it relates to you.

This is not a pleasurable experience because you will be battling your ego. Your ego is trying to keep you safe. Uncovering the truth about who you really are makes you vulnerable. You must expose yourself and your deepest fears as you confront this aspect of you, which is not happy with this other person. But this is the only way to remove the block and to grow from the experience.

As you analyze what it is you do not like, you must pinpoint it and see that it is related to something in you that you do not like. This is an awkward concept because it's hard to admit that this person is like you. You believe that this person is the opposite of you. Now you have to convince yourself and your ego that it is okay to look deep inside yourself to find out what your fear is all about.

Every block is different and each block affects you in some way. But let's say that in this case you find this person to be less intelligent than you think he should be for his position. Everyone else is smart as a whip and you all work together to make the company run smoothly. This guy just doesn't seem to be able to understand anything. He was here before you and may even have seniority over you, yet you are ten times smarter than he is. He may even make more money than you and this drives you crazy. He may even have more experience and more education than you, which doesn't seem to make any sense at all. In fact, when someone else looks to him for advice, you go stark raving mad.

Okay, we think we've found the answer here. You are feeling insecure about your own intelligence. You are feeling insecure about your own lack of experience or education. You are probably thinking about going to school at night to earn another degree. You might be reading books to learn a little more about what it is you're doing. You might have the stance that you know more about this business than anyone else because you are just smarter. You might try to convince yourself that your lack of experience or education doesn't have anything to do with your ability to perform. You might believe you have a natural talent or knack for this type of work.

Aha! It was you all along. Your insecurities made this person become annoying to you when he wasn't that annoying to anyone else. Even some of the customers love him. Isn't that odd?

Now you have the information you need to move through this block. You have learned that your insecurity around experience, intelligence, and education has brought this person into your direct reality. You have overcome your ego and realized that it is you, not the other guy. You are conscious enough to allow your ego to fight you on this, but you still realize that it is your fear that makes you annoyed. You are now going to overcome your fear and move to another level in your evolution.

What you must do now is become vulnerable. You must expose your truth. You have learned that you are insecure about your depth of knowledge in this business and you must express your truth to everyone, including and especially the person who started it all. You must go to your annoying co-worker and tell him you don't think you know as much about this business as you should.

This will feel like the exact opposite of what you want to do. It will seem painful. It will seem like walking on hot coals. You will try to avoid it. You will try to deny it. Your ego will fight you. But if you have made your analysis of the situation, if you have learned what you needed to know, then you must carry it all the way through. If not, your blockage might never be removed. You will suffer through this experience for longer than is necessary. It will hold you apart from what you desire. It will begin to cause inner conflict and stress on the body.

You must go to the annoying co-worker and share the truth of who you are now and who you have been being. You must state that you have these insecurities around education, intelligence, and experience. You must seek his advice for he is the one who has already overcome the fears you now hold. He is the one who holds the key that will remove the block.

You might find it easier to speak about these truthful issues with a friend or your spouse. They will comfort you, yet they cannot resolve your issue because they do not hold the key. It is only this person you find annoying who can help you. You must go to him.

Here's what will happen in almost every case as long as you have correctly identified the right issue. You will go to this person and have an intimate conversation. This is not a meeting in the hall or casual words by the water cooler. This is a planned and carefully thought out, private conversation. You might invite him to lunch or for drinks after work. You must get him in a setting where you are alone and where you can properly express the truth of who you have been being.

You will open up to this person in as much detail as possible. You will give him everything you have about you, not him. He has nothing to do with your reality or your insecurities. You are simply expressing how you have been feeling about yourself. He has done nothing to make you feel this way. He has not been behaving inappropriately, you have. It's all about you. You are trying to change yourself, not the other person.

As you tell the story of who you were being, he will listen and hear what you are saying. Then he will offer words that will soothe you. His words are the key that removes the block. Listen to the words and feel the change take place inside you. You will start to feel positive emotion. You will start to smile at what he is saying. You might even laugh. And as you feel positive emotion, you will be changed forever. This block will be removed and your next block will soon arrive.

IV.

The conscious approach to life is simply moving away from unconscious reactions based in duality and into conscious reactions based in neutrality. It is a way of life that focuses on becoming who you really are. It is following the path to becoming the highest version of you. As you move into a conscious approach to life, you become a deliberate creator and you consciously choose how you will create whatever it is you want to create.

The unconscious creator concludes that the present conditions are wrong and wishes for them to be better. She is happy when things are good and unhappy when things are bad. Her reactions to events are based on the judgment of those conditions, either good or bad. She feels good as a result of some positive event and she feels bad in reaction to what she judges as negative. The unconscious creator seeks conditions where it will be more likely for her to feel good.

If the unconscious creator is aware of how she feels, she will desire circumstances that allow her to feel good as often as possible. This is actually a great step forward compared to many people who do not particularly seek to feel good. They feel whatever they feel and while they judge those feelings, they have become so accustomed to feeling bad that it feels natural. In fact, many will tell you that feeling too good for too long just feels uncomfortable.

The first step toward living consciously is to become aware of your feelings and desire to feel good as much as possible. This is also the most important step in the process. Since you are so used to feeling good sometimes and bad other times, you have not considered that feeling bad feels bad. It feels bad and you should not have to feel bad. You should be feeling so good so often that when you feel just a little bad you can't stand it.

Babies are tuned to feeling good. When they feel just a little bad, they scream and cry. They are not dying, yet their screams would suggest that something terrible is happening to them. They're just hungry, or maybe they have a little gas. These are feelings that would not cause even a little consternation in you, but to the baby, who expects to feel very good, this slightly-bad feeling is cause for alarm.

This is how we want you to live as well. You must expect to feel great most of the time. You must desire to feel great. You must consider feeling great to be your natural state so that when you feel bad, you really feel it, so that when you experience even mild negative emotion, you really notice it.

You cannot be a conscious creator unless you are able to be acutely aware of your feelings in each moment. You must be able to acknowledge that you feel off. The slightest shift in your mood must be seen as an indicator that something needs to be addressed. Unless you can do that, you can't really live consciously.

Your basis of feeling must be to feel good. This physical environment is a feeling reality, just as it is in the nonphysical. The basis of your experience is how you feel, not what you think. What you think always follows how you feel. If you're feeling good, you'll attract good-feeling thoughts. If you're feeling good, those good-feeling thoughts you have been thinking will manifest into a reality that matches how you feel.

Your feeling first manifests into thoughts that match it and then into a reality that matches it. Feel good and your world will be created to match your feeling. Feel bad and you will experience a reality that matches that feeling. This is why you must strive to feel good.

Feeling good is so important that it is truly the basis of your reality and should be your only goal. There is nothing else you ever have to do other than feel good. Does this sound too simple? It would be if not for the way you were raised and how you place your attention on the outside world. In a natural state, you would feel good most of the time and you would really notice whenever you were not feeling good. But because you are so focused on the conditions of your outside world, you have become numb to your own feelings.

We can see that when you are in love, you feel really good. When you have a newborn child, you feel really good. When you fall out of love, you feel really bad. When your child grows up and moves away, you feel really bad. These are the extremes and you notice how they feel, but for much of your normal day-to-day life, you vacillate between feeling good one moment and feeling bad the next.

If someone smiles at you, you feel good. If someone cuts you off in traffic, you feel bad. When you come home from work, you feel good, but when your spouse says something you don't like, you feel bad. You might bite your lip and control your emotions, but you really have no idea what purpose they serve.

As a conscious creator, you know why you have emotions and what they mean. You are aware that when you have a negative emotion you are seeing the condition in a way that is not how you would want it to be. You are judging the situation to be wrong. Since you created the condition, you judge your condition as bad and you might be tempted to seek to improve it in the moment.

Since the moment cannot be changed, your wanting it to change causes conflict. Your limited perspective and your belief in duality makes you wish it were different. But it can only be as it is because this is the way it has manifested. You are reacting negatively to your own creation and this causes you to feel negative emotion. The negative emotion is your indicator that you must analyze your thoughts regarding this matter and see the present moment from the higher perspective.

Your negative emotion is your warning sign that if your feelings continue down this negative path, your future will unfold in a way that you do not want it to. Your bad feelings are creating a future reality that is opposed to what you really want. Your feelings create your reality and your bad feelings have the potential to create that which you definitely do not want. So take a look at the situation from the higher perspective.

The negative emotion tells you that your perspective is off. You must, must, must look at the condition from a new perspective. This perspective must be so different from your first reaction that by thinking from the higher perspective, you find relief. Unless you feel relief in the moment, you have not found the proper perspective. The feeling of relief is your indicator that your new perspective aligns with what you want.

Imagine you enjoy golfing. You feel positive emotion when you hit a good shot and negative emotion when you shank one into the lake. As long as you're feeling good and enjoying your well-hit shots, you're on the right track. These positive emotions will cause momentum and the universe will bring you more good shots and a better score.

When you hit a shot you judge to be bad, and you feel negative emotion, your continued bad feeling, when left unchecked, has the potential to cause more bad shots. When you dwell on the bad shots, you set up a future in which there are more bad shots. The more you allow these bad feelings to fester, the worse your shots will become. This is why the vast majority of golfers are so inconsistent.

All golfers have hit shots that were as beautiful as any professional golfer. The only difference is that the pro golfer is much more consistent. The pro golfer has learned to expect the shot to be good, and since most shots are good, he feels good most of the time. The way he consistently feels and thinks is the only difference between an amateur golfer and a champion golfer.

Have you ever noticed that there is no single body type that makes for a good golfer? There are great variations in size and strength. A champion golfer might be tall or short, fat or lean. They could be right-handed or left-handed. In the game of golf, since it is primarily a game of the mind, the whoever is able to use his mind best to create his reality is the champion.

Everything is a game of the mind. The more you dwell on the things you appreciate, the more they become your reality. Your feelings control what your mind can think. Good feelings allow your mind to attract higher-vibrational thoughts. Bad feelings limit what can enter your mind. Low-vibrational thoughts and ideas can enter your mind when you're allowing yourself to feel bad.

V.

When you are happy, praise comes easily. You can appreciate the people in your life and good-feeling thoughts flow to you freely. In this state, you can express your love through your words and actions. When you feel good, high-vibrational thoughts and ideas come to you. You are inspired to do good things. You feel a sense of clarity and everything makes sense. You are aware of the good that surrounds you. This is all because you have reached a higher-vibrational state of being. This is the state of love.

When you're feeling bad, you have access to lower-vibrational thoughts. When you are angry, you express your anger. You say things that are out of character that do not represent who you really are. When you feel bad, you cannot appreciate the good in your life; you only see what you consider negative. Your view of the world is warped. You feel confused and find yourself in a low-vibrational state of being. This is the state of fear.

We want to express to you that it is important to be aware of your state of being and to consistently strive to be in the state of love. You are a creator and you create yourself, your life, and your world. You bring forth experiences that match your state of being. In the state of love (which is all you really want), you create from a high-vibrational platform. You create what is wanted. You experience the essence of what you really want. Your desires unfold to your delight in an elegant and satisfying manner.

You must become acutely aware of those times when you dip into a lower-vibrational state of being. This is the state of fear (which is all that you do not want), and you certainly do not want to create from this platform. The state of being known as fear includes anger, revenge, desperation, despair, depression, sorrow, sadness, fear, apathy, greed, lack, pity, etc. When you find yourself in any one of these emotions, you access thoughts that resonate at these lower vibrational frequencies.

It is like a radio station. When you are tuned to the higher frequency of love, you receive thoughts and ideas based in love and you are able to express yourself from that stance. What you say and do comes from love and powerfully creates whatever it is that you want.

When you are tuned to the lower-vibrational frequency of fear, you attract thoughts that operate within these lower frequencies. These thoughts and ideas are fearful in nature. They limit your ability to create what you want and indeed, when prolonged, have the power to create circumstances and situations you would not want to experience.

When you are in the state of love, you attract conditions that respond to that state. It is the law of the universe and cannot be any other way. You say things that are loving when in the state of love. You do things that express your love. You become the highest version of who you really are. The basis of you is love.

When the illusion of the present conditions has captured your attention, you sometimes allow yourself to feel bad. If you think that something has happened to you, you feel bad and dip into the state of fear. Your reaction to the events has caused you to slip into a low-vibrational state of being. From this platform, you attract thoughts that resonate with fear. You must become conscious and return to the higher-vibrational platform of love.

It might be helpful to think of the illustration of heaven and hell. Heaven is a place of high-vibrational thoughts, words, actions, state of being. Everything good resides in this place. Hell would be the realm of lower-vibrational thoughts, words, actions and state of being. Hell is the low-vibrational place where everything that is not wanted resides.

However, you are not damned to hell, nor are you granted permission to enter heaven. You are given free will and ultimately the choice to reside either in heaven or hell is yours to make. You get to choose where you want to be. It is your conscious awareness of your current vibrational state of being that allows you to make that choice.

Choose to feel good and you will operate from the heavens. Choose to feel bad and you will experience what it's like to linger in the nether world. It's always up to you.

Have we made our point? Can you easily see that your world is created by your vibrational tone? Let's look at an example.

Let's say you are feeling really good. You are in a high-vibrational state as you drive to work. You're driving down the road and all you see are shiny new cars and other happy people in them. Up ahead you see a car getting ready to pull into the road in front of you. You slow down and let him in and you wave to the driver and he waves back. You get positive feedback from people when you feel good.

Now let's imagine that you are not feeling good. You are late for work and you're in a hurry. All you see as you drive down the road are cars filled with slow drivers talking on their cell phones. You see a car in front of you getting ready to pull out of a driveway and you step on the gas in order to make them wait for you to pass. But the driver does not see you and pulls out into the road anyway. You are forced to slam on your brakes and swerve into the next lane, narrowly missing another car. Your low-vibrational state of being dips even lower in reaction to this event and now you find yourself in a state of rage. You speed up and come alongside this guy and give him the finger. We won't go into any more detail, but suffice it to say that things only get worse from here.

Your world is created from your stance of fear or love. Most of the time you are in a good mood and mostly good things come to you. Once in a while you allow yourself to be distracted and something happens that you don't like. This event becomes your excuse to feel bad. You still have a choice, yet you choose the lower frequency. You give yourself permission to fall out of love and into fear. You've returned to victimhood once again.

You can only feel bad when you feel like a victim. As a conscious creator, one who knows that you create every event or that every event is created to bring something for you, you can't really feel bad. How could you? If you are truly conscious and you engage the higher perspective so that you can see the right in anything you would have unconsciously perceived as wrong, how could you ever dip into a lower frequency? You could not and you would not.

If you are conscious and aware of your state of being at all times, and have long ago left the victim mentality behind, then you shall have no need to dip into the state of fear. So, following this logic, the gauge of your level of consciousness will be the frequency of your forays into fear. If you are mostly operating from this higher vibrational state of love, you are mostly living consciously. If you occasionally become angry or saddened by the circumstances around you, then you are not quite living as a fully conscious being.

You have yet to personally witness a human that is living as a fully conscious being, for you all have those occasions when you are temporarily fooled by the illusion of your outside world and you react with fear. You might never reach full consciousness in this lifetime, but you are moving in that direction. The desire we would consider appropriate would be to be more conscious more of the time by utilizing the higher perspective whenever you feel a negative reaction coming on.

We know that if you simply seek to feel good more of the time, you will engage momentum that will keep the ball rolling. The better you feel, more often, the less you will be able to tolerate those infrequent bad feelings. This will be your practice. This will be your challenge. Start operating out of the state of love as much as possible. Do not give in to the state of fear, even when you believe you have an excuse. There is no real excuse for feeling bad, only illusory excuses. The higher perspective will reveal the illusion every time.

VI.

It is one thing to live consciously while you are alone in your home reading a nice book and petting your dog. It's easy to feel good, think positive thoughts, and appreciate the joy of life while you're on your own. It is quite another matter when you find yourself surrounded by others.

One of the most important aspects of physical reality is your ability to interact with others. As you begin to live more consciously, you must realize that everyone else is living their own life as best they can. Most of those you know are on some kind of spiritual journey to an awakening. While some of them might be up there where you are, most are in the very early stages of consciousness and some remain fully engaged in the illusion of physical reality.

As a consciously evolving being, it requires patience and understanding to interact with those who are still looking at reality from the limited perspective. It is difficult to stay connected to your inner self and not allow yourself to be brought down to the lower vibrational frequencies. You must have compassion for those who want to tell you why everything is so bad. It is their mode of operation.

Most humans look at the conditions that surround them and are very good at seeing how improvements can be made. To do that they, must analyze what they do not like and make pronouncements about how bad something is. They must detail the negative in order to make it better. Yet their attention to what is not wanted never brings them what they want.

When they complain to you about the government, the state of the world, the deterioration of society, the dangers that surround them, their health, their finances, and all sorts of other unwanted conditions, how are you supposed to react? What are you to say when they are spewing negative observations and stating everything they judge to be wrong with life? How do you maintain your higher-vibrational stance?

This is the great challenge of awakening in these times. You are one of the few conscious members of your society. Most are on their way, but they're still basically unconscious. They do not yet understand what they are doing. They do not realize that they are creating their reality with their feelings, thoughts, words, and actions. They do not believe what you already know. And you can't teach them what you know.

This is the most important aspect of interacting with others in this time of awakening. They cannot reach your level by your preaching what you already know. You cannot raise their vibration enough for them to understand it. Do not try. There is a path to the awakening of everyone on your planet. They must ask for the knowledge themselves. They must desire it on their own. They must allow it. If you try to move them too quickly, they will resist.

It is fine to give a friend a book when you are inspired to do so. It's very good to speak positively about something you appreciate. It's nice to change the subject when possible. But you cannot teach someone something they are not yet interested in.

Interest is the only way anyone can learn anything. They must have a desire to want to understand the subject. You cannot make them wrong and expect them to grow as a result. If they believe something you know to be inaccurate, you will not be able to persuade them otherwise. They will simply dig in their heels and stand firm in their beliefs. Your judgment that they are wrong comes from a low-vibrational perspective.

Imagine that they are right. Imagine that whatever they are saying, doing, and believing is right. If there is no wrong anywhere in the universe, then they must be right. But how could they be right when everything they believe is the opposite of what you know to be true? They are simply saying, doing, and believing what is right for them at this specific moment in time. They are on their journey to self-discovery, just as you are. They might be a few steps behind you, but their route is the only route that will take them where they need to go. They cannot jump onto your path. It might seem like a short cut, but it does not lead them to the place they need to go. They must take a certain, specific path of their own.

So, we know that each person is on their own journey to awakening and they must travel at their own speed. You wish for them to hurry up so they can be with you, but it doesn't work this way. Even if they were to jump to your level, you would never be at the same place anyway. No one is at the same place on this spiritual journey. You're all unique and you'll always be at different levels. It is the ability to co-exist while on different paths that demonstrates your level of consciousness.

The reason you want them to be with you on the same path to consciousness is because you want them to be different than they are. This is a lower-vibrational opinion of where they now stand. You can love them as they are and still be a conscious thinker. You do not have to let them bring you down. You do not have to bring them up. You can appreciate them where they are.

If you are not yet able to maintain your stance of consciousness while in the presence of your unconscious friends, then you must limit your interactions with them until you can maintain your balance. If their words upset you and cause you to stop feeling good, then you're not ready. However, you can't avoid them forever, because guess what? They are here specifically to help you reach another level of consciousness.

You are an expanding being and in this area, you are on a never-ending journey of self-discovery and awakening. Once you make it to one level, something will come along to move you to the next level. It goes on like this forever. You have made a great leap in this lifetime. Some steps are not as big as this one has been. Most are smaller. But even the tiny steps can be challenging. Those who will challenge you most are your closest friends and your family.

Those you love, those whose opinions you deem important, are here to help you move to new levels of consciousness. When your mother asks you why you are reading all this nonsense, how do you react? Your reaction says a lot about your level of consciousness. Your reaction is your indicator of your progress. You can try to convince your mother that you have found something that works, but try as you may, she is not ready yet. Your desire for her to understand has nothing to do with it. You understand and she does not. That's just the way it is. You believe she should love you unconditionally, yet she is not conscious and therefore will have quite a hard time even understanding the concept of unconditional love. Your expectations are not in line with the reality of the situation.

It is easy to forgive the cashier at the grocery store for not being on your level of consciousness. You can see that she is living life as best she can and you are happy with the path she is on. You accept her as she is. That's because you are not invested in her. You don't even know her. But what about your spouse, your family, and all your friends? Can you allow them to be on their path, to be as conscious or unconscious as they are, and to be happy with their ignorance of universal laws and truths? If so, then you've reached a new level.

To allow others to be as they are, to say what they say, and to act in whatever manner they choose is to be a master. Are you not yet a master? That's okay, for few are. But you can imagine how a master would behave when interacting with your friends and family. You could act like a master even if you did not believe you were one. You could react in a way that a master would react. For it is simply being as a master would be and doing what a master would do that makes you a master.

Practice being conscious in an unconscious world. Do not be afraid of being around others, because you have nothing to fear and nothing to lose. Just because you allow your vibration to sink when you're in the company of lower-vibrational people doesn't mean your vibration actually becomes lower. It's just that your attention is temporarily removed from what is wanted. It's not a big deal. It's just a matter of practice.

Practice being in the company of those who are not at your level and you'll begin to get better at maintaining your stance of consciousness. As you get better and better at keeping your vibration up, you'll cause those around you to notice something different about you. They will begin to see something they admire. They will begin to aspire to be more like you. This is how you lead them along their path to consciousness. This is the only way you can help them. This is how you teach.

Chapter Eleven

Altering the Conditions

The basis of physical reality is feeling. This is a feeling environment. You are programed to seek to feel good and to avoid feeling bad. This is a component of the survival instinct. When you are hungry, you seek to change that feeling. Hunger does not feel good. You want to cease feeling bad, so you eat which removes the bad feeling. When you starve, you feel bad and when you eat, you relieve the bad feeling. Relief is a good feeling.

When it is cold, you are programed to seek warmth. Your survival instinct forces you to stay alive. Cold is a bad feeling. When you find the warmth of a fire after being cold, you feel relief. The fire feels great. You are exposed in the cold and you are safe by the fire. You will die in the cold and you will survive in the warmth.

If it is raining, you must seek shelter. It feels miserable to be in the rain for very long, so you seek cover. Coming in from the rain feels like relief. It feels better to be dry than to be wet. It feels better to be clean rather than dirty. It feels good to be satiated rather than hungry. It feels better to be rested rather than exhausted. When you feel good, you survive. When you feel bad, you could be in danger. Your very survival may be on the line.

Physical existence programs you to seek better conditions. You are wired to do just that. But when survival is not on the line, the seeking of better conditions might end up keeping you stuck where you are. Let's look at how this all works.

When you are hungry, you seek food. You are focused on eating. At first you think about what it is you would like to eat. Your hunger motivates you, so you think about what would be the most enjoyable thing to eat. You are focused on good food. As you become hungrier, you are less concerned about what you want to eat. You are now a food-seeking being and anything will do. Your desires are brushed aside when the problem becomes intense. After a while, you will be so hungry that you'll eat things you never thought you would. Anything will taste good to you.

When you are cold, you desire warmth. You will do anything to be warm. You will do things you wouldn't normally do to be warm. Your focus is on being warm when you're cold. You want to change the conditions that surround this present moment from cold to warmth. Once you find warmth, you feel relief.

This is the mechanism of survival within this environment. Survival is a good teacher. You must be aware of how you feel and the conditions around you, otherwise you'll suffer. When you relieve your suffering, you feel relief.

Your life is relatively free from the need to simply survive. You have created your environment so that you can focus on more than just survival. You have created conditions in which you are more concerned with thriving than surviving. You have enough food to eat, and you have created the technology that provides shelter wherever you are and warmth whenever you need it. You heat and cool every environment so that you are not exposed to extremely high or low temperatures. In fact, you've stabilized your environment in such a way that the temperature you experience falls within an extremely narrow range.

You have controlled your conditions to such an extent that you have become masters of your domain. The slightest inconvenience sends you seeking an improved condition. You are incredible manipulators of conditions. If something is not quite right, you seek to fix the problem as quickly as possible. Soon you are searching for problems that do not exist. You must then inform the world that there is a solution to this new problem so you can all line up to buy the next product. We applaud your ingenuity.

However, this constant focus on what is wrong has led you down a path to where you do not want to go. As you know, when you're focused on the problem, the problem gets bigger. The problem and the solution vibrate at two different frequencies. When you are focused on what you do not want and you believe it is a big problem, you can't see the solution and the problem escalates.

When you are hungry, your focus is much more on food than on hunger. It's an instinct and naturally works this way. When you are starving, you might complain about your situation, but you can't spend too much time dwelling on the problem because you must find something to eat. Pretty soon your mind becomes consumed with the solution. Your mind simply switches from the problem to the solution. You find the frequency of the solution quite rapidly. You still complain about the problem, but nature and instinct guide you to the solution. However, your desire for something good to eat is completely abandoned once the problem of starvation becomes intense. Notice how your desire evaporates when you become desperate.

Man has been programmed by the survival instinct to seek relief in order to end suffering. Suffering means death and relief means survival.

When you feel like you are suffering, you seek relief. When you are lonely, you seek companionship. When you are bored, you seek excitement. When you are angry, you seek revenge. When you are ignored, you seek attention. You seek to change the conditions in order to feel some sort of relief. But emotional suffering is unlike physical suffering. If you're physically suffering, you will be guided to the appropriate relief. If you are emotionally suffering, you will have disconnected yourself from your own guidance system because you are in a negative state of being.

As we have mentioned, your access to your guidance system is predicated on your emotional state of being. We want you to practice feeling good so you can maintain your communication with your inner self. When you find yourself in a negative state of being, such as depression, you lose access to the communication coming from your inner self. Your current vibrational stance in depression is out of tune in vibrational terms. You are resonating at a lower frequency than your inner self and therefore you have temporarily lost the connection.

All emotional suffering leaves you out of touch with your inner self and without inner guidance, so you are forced to find solutions on your own from your limited perspective. The solutions you find will not be likely to provide you with an improved situation. You might experience momentary relief, but soon you'll be right back where you started.

If you have ever felt lonely in your life, you might have desired a mate. From the low-vibrational stance of loneliness, you seek relief in the arms of another. Just as if you were starving, you did not particularly care what the food tasted like; you just wanted to relieve the suffering. When your loneliness has become unbearable, you will find comfort wherever you can.

If you have an abundance of food, you can create the meal of your heart's desire. You can spend time preparing the meal and share it with your friends and loved ones. You can elevate the meal so that it is something special and memorable. From your stance of abundance, you create something beautiful.

If you have a lack of food, you will simply eat the next thing that comes along. While you might find relief, you will not necessarily enjoy the experience.

If you have an abundance of companionship, you might take your time and consider what it is you really want in a mate. You might then gain patience and allow the universe to bring you exactly what you desire. You do not feel lack (loneliness), so you are not in any need and you have no particular problem that concerns you. Your stance is one of abundance and confidence that you will find exactly what you desire in a mate.

If you are without a mate and you suffer in loneliness, your stance is one of lack. You emanate desperation. This is not an attractive quality. When desiring a mate, you want to quite literally *be* attractive. The stance of confidence and abundance is attractive, while the stance of lack and desperation is less attractive.

Let us clarify something here. Everything is attractive. This is a universe based on the Law of Attraction. You cannot be anything but attractive. What we are emphasizing is that when your stance is confident and abundant, you become attractive to what is most wanted. When your stance is in lack or desperation, you become attractive to what is not wanted.

When you attract what you want through your feelings of confidence and abundance, you will attract the mate that is the closest match to what you desire. When you stand in a place of lack and desperation, you might also attract a mate, but the qualities of this person will be aligned with what you do not want. In this case, your new mate will cause you to feel even lonelier and more desperate.

When you attempt to change the conditions of your life simply to find relief, you do so without proper guidance from within. You are unable to leverage the powers of the universe to deliver what you truly want. Your attention is focused on something unwanted and your desire is to remove yourself from these conditions. Your uninspired action might move you out of these specific conditions, but you will be placed in another equally unwanted situation. You'll become trapped, repeating the same cycle until you make a radical change in your approach to life.

II.

You have become very good at changing the conditions. You are adept at fixing problems. If something's not working, just throw it away and get a new one. If your boss is mean to you, just quit your job and get a new one. If your spouse does something wrong, just get a divorce and find a new one. If your employee comes in late to work, just fire him and hire a new one.

It's almost too easy to alter the conditions at the slightest hint of a problem. When you face something you don't like, you resolve it simply by spending money or taking some action. However, if you created the condition, if the situation is there for your growth, what are you really missing?

You energetically create the conditions of the present moment. If you've created something you like, then everything is fine. If you have created a condition you do not like, then your first impulse is to change the condition. You change the condition by removing yourself from it or by removing something else from it. You do not bring anything to it.

The condition you do not like is there for your growth and expansion. You can only expand by observing the condition, understanding why it's the way it is, and learning from it or growing from it in some way. If you leave the condition or if you change the condition, you've missed an opportunity for growth.

Let's look at a few simple examples. Let's say you're married and you find yourself arguing with your spouse over money. You find the condition you're in to be one of lack. Your spouse does not feel this way and spends money on something you find wasteful. You confront her by making her wrong and you create an argument. She defends herself by attacking you. You've had enough; you cite irreconcilable differences and end the marriage. You've missed the point of the relationship.

If you were not a vibrational match to your spouse, you could not have come together. You might grow apart and many relationships run their course over time, but in this case, there was something for you to learn. Your feeling of lack was not shared by your spouse. You had something to learn. You were meant to expand as a result of the condition. Your spouse was there to help you grow, not just in the area of abundance, but in many areas of your life. She was the person who would most likely be able to help you expand your consciousness, but you believed you had differences that were insurmountable and rather than face your creation, you decided to change the conditions.

Learning, growing, and expanding can sometimes be painful. If you are not operating from a stance of consciousness, your ego can get in the way of your growth. If you believe you must defend your persona against perceived attacks, you'll believe it is right to change the situation.

Your ego wants your persona to remain as it is. You want to expand and become who you really are. You must change your persona quite substantially as you grow into who you really are. Your ego will be fighting this change every step of the way. As you become more conscious, you'll begin to realize that your ego is trying to keep you in your present form. It will cause you to view opportunities for growth as attacks on your very being.

The conscious thinker sees all conditions for what they are: opportunities for growth and expansion. As you become more conscious, as you allow yourself to expand into who you really are, as you learn to react neutrally to conditions, you'll reduce the power of your ego. Once your ego has been placed under your control, you will no longer desire to be right. You won't have to defend yourself anymore. You won't see arguments or differences of opinions as threatening. You'll begin to bring something to the condition.

Imagine finding yourself in a condition you do not like. Imagine dropping your judgment of the condition and observing it from a position of neutrality. Imagine what it would be like not to fight against it, not to fear it, not to worry about it, not to go into the future or the past about it, but just to be in it and see what happens. Imagine if you could go one step further and bring something to it. Imagine what you could learn from that.

There is nothing inherently right or wrong in any situation. It is your judgment of it that makes it what it is. Conditions are neutral. If you see it as wrong, you will experience it from that stance. If you see it as right, then something much different will result. If you are neutral to it and simply observe it, you will discover why it is there.

What we can say is that every event, every situation, and every condition is there for you. There is something for you to discover about yourself in each and every condition. The conditions are constantly changing, yet they all have one thing in common. They are all there for you.

If you find yourself in a condition with another person or with many other people, just know that it has been arranged this way. You are supposed to get something out of it. The others are supposed to get something out of it as well. However, you are not to concern yourself with how the others are being in this situation. They do not make a difference as far as what you are supposed to receive is concerned. You get what there is to get from the condition and they may or may not get something. That is for them to decide.

So we now know there is something in every condition that will help you grow and expand your consciousness. This is what you want - believe us. You are here to joyously expand. Expansion might feel painful at times, but it need not be. It is simply your limited perception that makes something seem painful. From the higher perspective, it need not be painful at all. All expansion can be joyous.

We want to talk more about bringing something to the condition. We have used this example in the past, but it is important to reiterate what can be done with any situation you find unpleasant. When you bring who you really are to the condition, you energetically change it so it works for you and you can experience joy in the growth process.

Let's say you feel stuck in a dead-end job. You have desires, interests, and passions, and this job is not providing any of that. You want to have fun in what you do. You want to enjoy the company of the people you work with. But this job is not fun and you do not like a lot of the people. However, you find yourself here. What do you do now?

Your first instinct is to quit this job and find another. But there are problems with that. You have this job for a reason. The reason is that you are currently a match to it. You vibrationally match the job you don't like. If you were not a vibrational match to it, you wouldn't have it. What does this mean? It means this job is the perfect match to who you're being now. If you were to quit this job without changing who you are now, you would end up with another job that vibrationally matches who you are now. You cannot escape your vibration. You must radically change your approach to life and who you are now to receive something different. This is the basic law of the universe and it cannot work otherwise.

Now, this job happens to be perfect. Can you wrap your head around that statement? The job you don't like happens to be the perfect condition to help you change so you can get the job you really want. You can't change if you leave the condition. You must learn what this condition is trying to teach you. You must allow yourself to be changed by the condition so you can attract the new condition you prefer.

What is it about this present job that you do not like? What's the number-one reason you don't like this job? Let's say it's because you are not paid enough, which you believe means you are not appreciated. This is usually one of the problems at the top of everyone's list. You might have noticed a trend that many companies are now addressing this universal issue. Employees don't feel appreciated, so employers are rewarding them with symbols of recognition rather than money. You see, they've figured out a way to soothe their employees without spending money. These people actually say they prefer the recognition over money. What does that tell you?

If you believe you are not appreciated, it's because you have an issue with your own sense of worthiness. If this issue persists, no amount of money, recognition, or appreciation from your employer will solve your problem. The condition has been set up so you can grow as a result and learn to appreciate your own undeniable worthiness.

If you think you would feel better if the condition changed, you would not. Since you haven't altered your vibration, since you haven't changed how you feel, you will still get the same feelings from the changed condition. You think that if your boss would just give you a raise, you'd feel better. You think the raise would be the acknowledgment of your fine work and that would make you feel worthy. But it doesn't work this way. If you change the condition without changing your feelings about yourself (in this case, your feelings about your own worthiness), then the new condition will show you those same feelings as manifestations, but on a more intense level.

You have the job you don't like because you feel like you're not appreciated. You hope and pray that your boss will give you a raise to show his appreciation. However, you have not changed how you feel. If, by your powerful wanting, you get a raise, you'll feel better for a little while. However, because you have not addressed your own feelings of unworthiness, you will feel even more unworthy.

Your boss will expect more from you because you're being paid more. From your stance of unworthiness, you will cause more situations to arise and you will be shown very harsh examples of exactly how you feel. At this point, you had better start looking at the situation before it becomes dire. You must now bring something to the condition. You must lean into the experience.

You can see how this would be very difficult if you were not living consciously. It is very difficult for many unconscious creators to see that their unwanted conditions are there to bring them to a new level. Most will see themselves as victims of uncontrollable situations. But all conditions are created and controlled by the individual. You just have to look at the condition from a higher perspective.

If you are able to consciously approach any condition from the stance of fascination rather than victimhood, you'll quickly grasp the message in the condition and use it for your direct benefit in this life experience. Imagine the power of having that attitude about any occurrence. Abandon your habitual reaction and lean into the experience with the intention of joyously expanding.

Let's return to the job you think you hate. You feel underappreciated, but you are not. No one is really treating you any differently. No one really thinks ill of you. If they did, they would have removed you from their condition. If you're there, you're okay. This is your experience. You feel unworthy. Accept it and work on it. That's easier said than done, we know. But let's imagine you are making your way to consciousness and you're reading this book and you've just had an "Oh, wow!" moment. You've just realized that you haven't been feeling appreciated in your job. You hadn't thought about it before, but now you realize that maybe it's true. Maybe you're feeling unappreciated and maybe you're not really feeling all that worthy. So what do you do?

On your path to consciousness, you must first identify how you are feeling and then realize that it isn't true about you. You are worthy, you are good, you are fun, you are love, and you are on your way to who you really are. Everything else is just fear. So what do you fear? Look at what you fear and then realize it is an irrational fear and isn't real.

If you're not feeling particularly appreciated in your job (or marriage, or family life, or with friends, or by your employees, or in any other situation), what are you afraid of? What is it you fear? There is always fear in the condition and that's why you want to avoid dealing with it.

In order to get the most out of the condition you find yourself in, lean into it by overcoming all fear. Be fearless. Be honest with yourself. If you have come to realize that you are not feeling worthy, you may express it to others or just keep it to yourself. But now you must start acting as if you are worthy. You must reduce fear and start being confident. You must exude confidence. It might take a little time, but start being different. Start acting differently. Start acting like who you really are, even if you're not sure who that is. When you start acting with confidence (even if it's an act), you'll start to see things change. Boy, will they change!

III.

In any condition in which you find yourself, there is always some resistance to what is. Think of the happiest moment in your life. Maybe it was your wedding day, the birth of a child, a wonderful vacation, or any other highly pleasurable event. There was always some resistance to what was happening in the moment. Even in the best of times there remains a little resistance. But the resistance is relatively small. Mostly you were enjoying the moment and having fun.

Now think of an event that was not pleasurable. Maybe it was an illness, a funeral, or being fired from a job. In these conditions, there is much resistance to what is. The more resistance to the conditions in the moment, the more difficult the situation. While you do benefit from these unpleasant events, because they help you identify what is preferred, you still have the choice to decrease the resistance.

A radical change in your approach to life will be the conscious reduction of resistance to any event or condition. While you are in the moment, whether it's pleasurable or not, you can lower your resistance and increase the fun. Instead of wishing the condition was better, you have the power to actually make it better in the moment. Just reduce your resistance, and the moment gets better.

This is the exact opposite of what you and all your fellow humans have been doing up until this point in time. If you find yourself in a condition you do not like, you resist it. If it gets worse, you resist it even more. Your resistance always makes it worse. When you can consciously ease your resistance to what is, you'll automatically improve the situation.

Let's go back to the example of the job you don't like. Never mind why you don't like it; if you're thinking of quitting, you're resisting the situation. You don't even have to discover what it is about you that makes you not like the job. If you want to quit, that's all you need to know.

We have explained that you cannot seek a better condition until you change something about you. In this case, all you have to do is change your approach to the condition. All you have to do is lower your resistance. Once you do that, everything changes. When you change your stance from resistance to allowance, you improve every situation. The radical change you are seeking is made available to you through learning to allow rather than resist.

Does this make sense to you? When you are in love, there is no resistance. When you hate, there is great resistance. You can choose love over hate. You can choose joy over sorrow. You can choose to have fun rather than to wallow in self-pity. You can choose to release fear and just allow whatever it is to happen.

When you understand that every condition presents itself for your benefit, you can begin to ease your resistance and allow the change to take place. When you know that there is a lesson in there somewhere, you can stop resisting what is there for you to learn. Even if it is a little painful, you can understand that the pain is fabricated by your ego's defense mechanisms. Nothing is really going wrong. You just have to get to another level and this is how it's going to happen.

A lot of the time you will need to shed an aspect of your persona that is not helping you to become who you really are. This is the difficult part. When you are forced to strip away part of your personality that seemed to be important to who you are, your ego will put up a fight. The negative emotion you will experience is your indicator that your ego is fighting a battle that does not serve who you really are.

You have this job where you feel underappreciated. You feel you deserve to be treated better. You want to be respected and heard. You feel you're worth more and you should be compensated better. You do not have the desire to do your best work because no one will appreciate it. You feel like finding a new job. You are resisting the conditions you are immersed in and you are not allowing the opportunity for change these conditions are offering you.

You could see that there is an underlying issue that causes this condition to manifest in your reality. You could look inside and figure out that you are not feeling worthy and so the condition has presented itself for you to grow as a result. The unconscious person would simply suffer in the condition or leave it by quitting. Or, the unconscious thinker could just wish for the condition to improve on its own. These approaches will not work.

The conscious thinker realizes there's something to this condition. She believes that there is something to be gained. She knows that she has an opportunity to be changed by the condition. All she has to do is lower her resistance and allow it to happen. She doesn't even need to figure out exactly what change needs to take place. All she has to do is go with it and allow whatever is meant to happen to happen.

So she begins to lower her resistance. She starts to observe what's really going on. She leans into the condition and decides to have fun. She consciously removes fear from the condition. She realizes that when she lowers her resistance and starts to have fun while relaxing her fears, the change will take place and the condition will resolve itself.

She goes to work with a new attitude of love, joy, and fun. She becomes present in the moment. She realizes that everything really is okay and that there's nothing to worry about. She begins to take pleasure in her work. She leans into it and brings energy to it. Then, miraculously, everything changes.

She is no longer worried about the results: she simply focuses on the process. There is nothing she needs to do, because she cannot lose. She was going to quit anyway, so what's the worst that could happen? She begins to make decisions differently and this makes a big difference.

When her stance was resistant and she felt like she was not being appreciated, she made decisions based on what was best for her. These were all fear-based decisions and were quite resistant in nature. Now that she has consciously reduced her fears, she makes decisions based on what is good for all. Her decisions are based in love. She has nothing to fear, so she does not need to protect herself. She has eased her resistance and is no longer primarily concerned with what's best for her. Rather, she's simply asking, "What's best?"

Her ego was trying to prop up her belief that she mattered, that she should be respected and that she should be heard. Because she was insecure in this regard, she believed certain things were happening that weren't really happening. She believed she wasn't being heard, respected, or appreciated. The Law of Attraction made her beliefs present themselves in her reality. But if you were to look at the situation as a casual observer, none of this really happened. It was all her interpretation of events, not actual events. The events were neutral. She just interpreted them to mean that she was not respected or appreciated.

Now that she is allowing the condition to play out with less fear and resistance, she is being shown signs that things are improving. She has lowered her defenses and now her interpretations of events are different. She now interprets the very same events as positive affirmations of her worthiness. Isn't this miraculous? Nothing has changed but her approach to this condition.

The conscious creator has changed her approach from being resistant to allowing the condition to play out. She didn't try to change the condition; she simply changed the way she was being within the condition. The condition can't change; only you can change. Unconscious thinkers fear change. Conscious creators realize they must constantly be changing.

Stop trying to fix the conditions. Instead, try changing your position. Stop resisting what is and start looking for clues in the condition. As you change your approach to the condition, you'll see improvement, But it's not the condition that's really improving - it's you.

IV.

For most of your entire life, you've been in the state of wanting to change your conditions. No matter what period of your life, you had resistance to the conditions of your life at that time. You were always resisting. You were resisting in times of struggle as well as times of joy. In the times of struggle, there was much more resistance in you than in the times of joy. But even in the good times you still worried, you still complained, you still found reasons to want to change the conditions.

Your first solution to any problem is to change the conditions. As we have already stated and will continue to state, you must get over your need to change the situation. You must make peace with what is. You must find reasons to appreciate all the good in your life. You must be in the moment and see that everything is actually good and nothing is wrong.

You cannot come to know who you really are until you start accepting the conditions as they are. You are supposed to change as a result of the conditions. The conditions are there to help you change. You are not to change the conditions, you are to appreciate them for what they are doing for you.

Change your approach to the present conditions and the conditions will improve. Remove yourself from the conditions and nothing changes.

From the higher perspective, everything is right. If you could see the conditions of your life as they exist now from our higher, broader perspective, you would feel complete joy. You would appreciate so much that's good in your life right now. You would not dwell on the past or worry about the future. You would just see how wonderful it all is. You would not want to change it; you would simply appreciate it and go with the natural flow of it.

You can reach this higher perspective now. We have a fun exercise for you. We can show you how good your life has been all along the way. So use your imagination and play with us as we bring you into a new awareness of you and your life.

Imagine you could take a one-week vacation - not to somewhere exotic on your planet, but to a week sometime in your past. Imagine if you could be you again at the age of seventeen. You will be transported back to a random week in your seventeenth year. You get to experience what your life was like then. You get to be in your body as you were when you were a younger version of you.

Think of what your life was like then. Maybe you were in high school. Maybe you lived at home. Think of your relationship with your parents. What was it like to interact with them back then? How would you do it differently? How would you be with your parents when they were also younger?

Think of your siblings and your friends. Think of your boyfriend or girlfriend. Think of school or the job you had back then. Think of your teachers or your boss. What was it like?

From your older, wiser, broader perspective, everything would be fascinating. It would be so interesting to see how you handled your life back then. You might have struggled in school, or fought your parents, or had drama with your love interest at the time. You might have had adventure and tried new things. But the younger version of you still worried about its future and obsessed about its past. Even at that wonderful age, you still resisted the conditions that existed.

You are a different person now than you were when you were seventeen. If you are younger than seventeen and are reading this book, then think of a time that was roughly half your present age. The exercise will work just as well. As you move through time, your perspective changes. This is the purpose of aging. As you grow, as you become more experienced, as you move along your path of self-discovery, you change. You grow and expand with each new experience. You become more. Your vibrational frequency increases.

Imagine now that you bring the present you back to the seventeen-year-old version of you. You can now bring something to the conditions. From your older, wiser and broader perspective, you can work inside the conditions and go with them, not against them. You can lean into the conditions and act in a way that serves who you know you'll become.

How would you be now with your parents at that age? Wouldn't it be fun to go back in time and interact with them from the perspective of your older, wiser self? What would that be like?

If your parents have made their transition to the nonphysical, most of you would relish this week with them. The seventeen-year-old version of you might have rebelled against them, but the older, wiser version of you appreciates and loves them. You see that they were just trying to do the best they could at the time. You see all the positive aspects of who they were at the time. You might spend the entire week just being with them. This is a radically different way of being than that of your seventeen-year-old self, who did not fully appreciate them and who maybe even fought against them.

You would enjoy going back to school, even though at the time you did not appreciate it. You wanted it to be different than it was. You complained about your teachers and the subjects and the system. You look back on it fondly now, but at the time, you had a lot of angst.

Imagine going back and bringing something to it. The older, wiser you would love this experience. You would participate in class, have meaningful discussions, debate your teachers, enjoy taking tests, and you'd have more fun. You now realize there was nothing you needed to learn and that your grades really did not matter as much as you thought they did. Most of what you learned you've long forgotten. So you could have just had fun with all of it.

You were self-conscious at that age. You worried about every little aspect of your persona and your physical appearance. But if you lived once again in that young, vital body, you would adore how you felt. You would appreciate your physical features. You would love how you feel in your body. You would not stress out over minor blemishes. You would appreciate everything about your physical body. You would run and jump and swim and play. You would appreciate the mix of hormones that rushed throughout your system.

Even if you chose a week that was stressful or painful during that seventeenth year, you would love every minute of it. You would bring so much more to who you were. You would see so many reasons to appreciate the conditions that surrounded you. You knew the road ahead would have a few bumps, but it would all work out. You would thoroughly enjoy your one-week vacation to your life in the past.

We ask that you now think of this next week in your present life as that one-week vacation to your past. Imagine that you are twenty years older than you are now. You have the opportunity to go back and live your life as you were twenty years before. Imagine the older, wiser version of you coming in to take over your body and your life for the next week. What would this person do?

What would the twenty-year older, wiser you do with your week in the life of the present version of you? How would he or she act? What would he or she find most interesting about your life now?

The older, wiser, expanded version of you would relish every boring minute of your present life. They would call all the people in your present life and say how much they love and appreciate them. They would spend time with parents or children if they're around at this time. They would host dinners with friends. They would appreciate your job, your co-workers, and all the people in your life.

The older version of you would bring so much to the present life you're living. They would lean into the situation and give it their best from their higher, broader perspective. They would find your life so easy and fun and would enjoy themselves immensely. They wouldn't waste time wishing the conditions were different because they would be aware of where these conditions will take you and are happy with the ultimate outcome.

But most importantly, the older version of you would enjoy the moment and have no reason to think of the future or the past. However, they would probably place some bets on the Super Bowl if they could remember who won that year.

During your vacation back to who you were, you will really notice something quite remarkable. You will notice how different you were back then. You will experience in real terms how far you've come. Your thought patterns now are so different you wouldn't recognize yourself. You might know it's you and your younger body, but the way you think, feel, and experience life has expanded. Your thoughts are more expansive, your understanding of life is more expansive, and the way you feel is easier. You react less impulsively. Your mental state is clearer.

You may simply chalk this difference up to your maturity, but it's more than this. Maturity is another term for expansion. You haven't so much learned from life experiences as you have expanded as a result of life experiences. Your vibrational frequency is quite different now.

Your exuberance as the youthful version of you caused the change that has taken place within you. Your desires were very strong and often quite focused. It was at this time in your life that the energetic aspect of who you really are began to blossom. You became who you are now as a result of much of what you wanted in your youth. Your life was cast from the standpoint of the hopeful dreamer you once were.

V.

The trajectory of your life was set forth from that time in your life. You were launched onto the path that eventually led you to the person you have become. Everything you have experienced thus far in life was created by the imagination of your younger self. You altered your course along the way, but much of that was simply fine tuning. Unless something drastic occurred to shift you to a new course, this was the path that led you to where you now stand.

The trajectory you are on feels right much of the time. You are a vibrational match to everything you experience and what is in your life now has been created by you from the vibration you emit. You are expanding as a result of your life, but the expansion lies along the boundaries of this path that was created many years ago. You are mostly comfortable in your life. It is familiar and feels right to you. It seems as though things are working out and for the most part they are.

But it is interesting to note the powerful creative abilities of your youth. What is it about that time that caused your path to be formed? Why was that time so intense? How was your entire life determined by the desires you created back then? What can you do to change the course of your life right now?

You might speculate how your life would be different had you experienced a different childhood. If you had different parents and were raised differently, what would your life be like right now? Were you destined to move along the path you're on, or would it be a completely different journey?

Here is how we would answer these questions. You must first consider your inner self and what you intended prior to your birth. You intended mostly to enjoy your time on Earth and to be happy. Most of your intentions were general in nature. You also intended one or two specific things you wanted to explore. Your inner self was and is fascinated with life on this planet and there are some things you wanted to explore during this lifetime. So you chose the time and place of your birth along with your family and this set you off on a trajectory that would best serve your intentions.

What you experienced during your childhood created the younger version of you, who at some point in your youth created desires that would determine the basis of the rest of your life. Your younger years, between fourteen and twenty-four, determined the path you would lead for the rest of your life.

Think of your life as a two-stage rocket. When you were born, the first stage created the lift-off. When you were a teenager or in your early twenties, the second stage fired. Both stages worked together to get you where you are now. You have tiny little boosters that can slightly alter your course, but basically your course was set by the second stage. However, there is now a third stage you might discover, the stage of awakening to consciousness.

Almost everyone you have ever met, including yourself, was set on a course that was determined prior to their birth and then in their youth. Most people never move very far off-course. Their path is easy and comfortable even if it doesn't really go anywhere. It is usually less than what was wanted and is often unfulfilling.

In your youth, you thought you could do anything. You felt invincible. Then somewhere along the line you lost that feeling. Maybe reality set in and you modulated your dreams. Instead of becoming what you really wanted, you became comfortable. Unless you are one of those rare individuals who is focused on a single mission, you are really just going down the same old path.

The desires you had in your youth and even as a child were created based on what your inner self wanted to explore. The essence of what you enjoyed doing as a child and what you wanted to do as a young adult are what you intended to explore prior to your birth. Those are your passions. That is your main interest in this physical experience. If you are not actively engaged in those passions now, you might not be fulfilling your life's promise.

Many of you will have difficulty remembering what you were really interested in back then. Some of you have gone to considerable lengths to alter the memories of your childhood. But if you can remember what you liked to do as a child, what you were most interested in during your youth, you can gain insight into what you want to do with the rest of your life.

We are not talking about anything that might prove your worthiness to another, especially your parents. Many of you have been influenced by the adults in your life to such an extent that you wanted very much to please them. So you might have the false desire to become famous, or to become respectable. You might want to prove yourself worthy by becoming well known and admired. Or you might have wanted to pursue a certain profession in order to gain the respect of the elders in your life. This is the false path many of you created in your youth.

We want you to think back and discover what you were really interested in as a child or young adult. Think about what you enjoyed. What was naturally interesting or fun? What would you have done if it were up to you? This is what you really want to explore. Sometimes these things that delight you are considered strange by those around you, especially your parents. Your parents wanted you to pursue something they considered good or right. They wanted you to be safe and support yourself. How you turned out reflected on them. When asked what their child is doing, they want to give an answer that will impress their friends.

But their desires were not likely to coincide with yours. In fact, it is more likely that you chose them for their differences. This would help you to be free of their influence. You would rebel against how they lived their lives, seeking something truer to who you really are instead. If you rebelled against your parents, you had a better chance of finding your true path.

Now you find yourself living your life and wanting the conditions to be different. What now? You feel you have not lived up to your potential and you are not at ease with the present conditions. You want change. You picked up this book because the word "change" was in the title. How can you alter your conditions so they better represent what you want now? You can't; you can only change you.

Your conditions in this moment are unchangeable, so we consider them perfect. We see you going around trying to fix the conditions, but nothing really changes. You might change the outer appearance, but your feelings remain the same. This constant, never-ending game of fixing what is broken is going about things backward.

You create your reality from the inside out. Your primary desires set off the trajectory of your life. You are resisting the conditions and you seek improvement. So you start messing around with what is happening on the outside, rather than tinkering with what's going on inside.

Your reality is like a film that was shot long ago, edited, and projected onto the screen. Once it's been projected, it cannot be changed. You want the movie to be different as it's playing rather than enjoying it for the film it is and then creating a new film next time. Great filmmakers are inspired to create better movies each time. They leap from one level to the next with each new film. They explore new subjects with each successive movie. They don't dwell on the past by looking at what was wrong, they are inspired to reach for something more.

Let the conditions show you what you've created, appreciate what is, and be inspired to create something better in the following moments. This is how you effectively alter the conditions of your life.

VI.

You are a master at altering your conditions. You believe that if you get angry enough, the conditions will change. You might even believe you can influence the actions of others to do what you want so that this will change the conditions and you will feel better. But this approach is ineffective and will only cause the conditions you do not like to be prevalent in your life.

When you try to change the behavior of those around you, whether they are bad drivers, rude strangers, employees, co-workers, or especially, your family, you cause conflict and inner stress. You cannot create in another's reality. You cannot change another by forcing them or wanting them to change. You do not like some aspect of the other person, so you decide to ask them to change. Since you are focused on what you do not want, all they can be is what you don't want them to be.

When you see a person doing or saying something you consider wrong and judge their behavior to be wrong, you are not seeing the person or the situation from the higher perspective. We are talking about anything you consider to be wrong. Whether it is something important or something trivial, if you judge it as wrong, you're not being neutral and you're not looking at it from the higher perspective.

When someone makes a mistake and you notice it, whether it affects you or not, and you judge the mistake to be wrong, you are resisting the conditions as they are specifically presented to you. This is important to remember. If something happens, even if it's in a distant part of the planet, and you notice it, it is a condition that is there for you. If you judge it to be wrong or bad, you are resisting the condition and you want it to change. When you resist the condition, you are not allowing what you want to flow to you. You're not being conscious, you are not expanding as you intended, and you are not gaining insight from the situation.

If something happens close to you, whether it's trivial or tragic, it's happening for you. If you feel negative emotion when you judge it to be wrong, you're not viewing it from the higher perspective and you're not benefiting from the occurrence that is happening for your growth.

In order to radically change your approach to life, you must understand that the conditions are always right and there is something for you in each condition. If you can learn and practice becoming neutral to the situation, even when it's really small or really big, you will start to get what's in each condition. You will improve your ability to expand. You will increase your vibrational frequency. You will move rapidly along your path to new levels of consciousness.

The easiest condition for you to try to change is the behavior of your children and your spouse. You believe you must teach these people to act in a way that pleases you. If you can whip them into shape, your life will be easier. You won't face as many moments that cause you to feel negative emotion. But this approach is short-sighted.

By trying to change another, especially your child, you influence them away from who they really are. When they alter their behavior in a way that allows you to keep calm, they are simply tip-toeing around your issues. They can only do this for so long before they feel the urge to fight back or leave.

When you allow others to be their genuine selves, you create an environment of conscious expansion. If your spouse does something to cause you to feel negative emotion, realize that the situation is neutral. Your spouse did nothing to purposely harm you, and you must now see the lesson or the issue that comes up for you.

Let's say that your spouse brings home a new car and you feel negative emotion. Why would this manifestation event make you feel bad? What is it about this seemingly good occurrence that causes you to judge it to be wrong? There are several issues that might come up for you. Let's say you can't believe your spouse would go out and spend money on something as big as this without consulting you. Would this upset you? If so, why?

You might be feeling that you don't have enough money and that he should not be spending it on a new car. You might be feeling that he should consult you since you are an equal partner in the relationship. You might feel bad that you weren't included in the decision. But you must see that these feelings only revolve around you and that your spouse has nothing to do with your issues. His actions, while they seem important, are actually neutral. How you react to the situation sets your course for the future.

Can you imagine the power of adjusting your perspective in the moment from an act you deem wrong and instead appreciating the moment for letting you know that your knee-jerk response to this situation will only cause you to suffer more in the future? Do you see that if you get angry at your spouse, you accomplish nothing? You can't change him, the conditions surround the event, or the event itself; you can only change you.

If you were to lash out at him for not seeking your prior approval after the fact, you seek to change the moment. The moment is already fixed in time and space. You can't change it. Oh, but you think you can change your spouse so that he never does anything like this in the future. You might change this one behavior in the short term, but it will not last and something else he does will seem worse next time.

If your spouse was the kind of adventurous and freedom-seeking person that could buy a car without letting you know, then this is an aspect of his personality you were drawn to when you first met. If you make him feel bad for being who he is, you can't continue the relationship with the person you fell in love with. He must change who he is in order to be with you. If it's not the car, it will be something else. This is your issue, not his. If you demand him to change, then something will change. He will either suffer in being who he is not for you, or he will find someone who accepts him for who he is.

But the most important aspect of this condition is not that he bought the car without consulting you, it's that you missed the opportunity for growth embedded in this event. The only reason this event happened was to bring you to a new level of awareness of your own limiting beliefs. If you could have accepted the situation, analyzed what made you feel bad, and then realized it was a limiting belief about lack of money and your feelings of worthiness, you could have altered your beliefs rather than the conditions.

Sometimes, it seems like there are so many events, situations, and conditions that cause negative emotion that you just want them to stop. It's too much. Things are happening too quickly. You feel like you can't stop and analyze every one of them. But you could if you were more practiced at neutrality. Since you've been living in duality for so long, you feel that even this aspect of your growth is wrong.

It might be difficult for you to accept that the conditions are there for your growth. You are supposed to understand each one and, in the moment, as it is happening, you are supposed to get what there is to be understood about what you're feeling. You are meant to become aware of why you feel bad, why you want to change the condition and then, instead of trying to change the condition, you change you. You were not meant to react unconsciously to every single occurrence. You intended to get good at this and to grow and expand.

All you need to do is practice. Just start with the little things and work your way up from there. When you're in a hurry and you come to a stoplight, realize that this is for your growth and expansion. Relax and try to change your perspective of lack of time. Use this as a time to reflect on the abundance that surrounds you, including the abundance of time. Think thoughts that remind you that you are an eternal being and you have all the time in the universe. Remember that there is nothing you must get done and there is nothing that can go wrong.

When you start to feel appreciation for the red light, you have made a great step forward. Now start to pay attention to the other drivers and how you interact with them. Think of the cars as robots just going about their business. You wouldn't try to change a robot, so you allow the cars to go where they will. You just move swiftly around them without giving them a care. You will soon notice that stoplights are more often green and bad drivers are becoming scarce.

When we say that there is something to be gained from every situation, every condition, and every occurrence, we are simply asking you to think about what is happening and what you're feeling. You need not remain in any uncomfortable situation and some conditions you cannot help but change. If you find yourself in a dangerous situation, simply leave. If you feel uncomfortable, you must go with that feeling. All we are asking you to do is think about your reaction to the conditions and allow that thought process to alter your perspective.

Chapter Twelve

A Radical Change in Your Approach to Children

We have talked about the topic of children before, but we feel that a subject of such importance must be addressed within the framework of this book. Your current approach to children creates an environment where they become influenced by others to such a degree that they often lose touch with who they really are and what they intended to explore prior to their birth. A change in your approach to children will allow them to realize who they really are and why they came into this physical reality.

The easiest way to look at children and understand how the system of physical reality was designed to allow them to follow their true path to becoming who they are is to imagine what would happen if they were left to grow naturally without the influence of adults. Imagine that a child was born and raised without any formal system of education or without the influence of its parents. That is quite a stretch for many of you who are parents. But what would happen to your child if they were raised by conscious people who loved them but who were not their parents?

We are not saying it would be better for children to be raised by anyone other than their parents. We simply want you to step out and imagine what the difference might be. When we look at the process of parenting, we see that the influence of the parents has a great deal to do with their fear of loss. The survival instinct has caused the parents to protect their young.

But, in these modern times, it becomes a complex job to protect children from the perceived dangers of the world.

Let's imagine you were an indigenous person living thousands of years ago. You and your tribe were nomads. You lived in simple, portable structures and primarily survived off the land. Your greatest fears revolved around the elements and predatory animals. Your fears may have been intense, but they were confined to the weather, falling, drowning, starving, and being eaten.

Today you are not too concerned with the fear of nature, as you have mostly overcome the natural dangers. However, there are many more modern dangers you believe you must protect your children from. You are worried about so many things that you are on constant alert. Overprotecting your children limits their freedom and opportunities for growth. The very things you fear most, which are highly unlikely, cause you and your children to feel insecure. When you allow fear to corrupt the natural ease of the child, you make it difficult for your child to become who they really are.

When you watch the news and see a story of an abducted child, you fear for the safety of your own child. You believe that if it can happen to one child, it can happen to any child. But you are simply unaware of the Law of Attraction and the mechanism of your vibrational frequency. You think these terrible things can happen to anyone, but they can't. The victim must be within the same vibrational frequency as the abductor. It cannot work any other way. It is a universal law.

The vast majority of children are safe from harm. Ironically, it is your fears that influence them to adopt fears they might never pick up on their own. These fears cause them to view the world differently than they otherwise would. Their version of the world they live in is now out of alignment with what they knew of the world prior to their emergence into physical reality.

The world is defined by your feelings about it. You create your world based on your beliefs about what is and what is not possible. When you add a fear to your set of beliefs, you change the fabric of your reality. When you consciously diminish the intensity of a fear, your world automatically brightens and improves. Your experience of reality is diminished by your irrational fears and is enhanced every time you release an irrational fear.

When you influence children by asking them to believe that something terrible is possible and they adopt this belief, you've caused them to alter their actual reality. When they pick up a limiting belief, their experience becomes different. The child has physically changed, and their world has also changed.

You cannot create in the reality of another. However, you can and do influence others. When you shine as a beacon of consciousness, you influence others toward finding their true path. When you caution another and that person adopts your limiting belief, you cause a shift in their reality. You did not create the shift; you simply influenced them so they would cause the change to occur.

You can influence others so that they release limiting beliefs or so that they adopt limiting beliefs. Which would you prefer? You are only in control of what you do, but by being who you are, you have substantial influence over others, especially impressionable children. When you say something unconsciously, as you were inclined to do before you learned about the universal laws, you do not support those who are seeking to find their true path.

In the natural state, when left free of the influence of others, children will learn from experience. This is an experiential world and each child has a path to follow. When left alone they will be guided by their curiosity to discover what it is that brought them here. They had intentions of exploring this reality prior to their birth. Most of those intentions were general in nature, but one or more were specific. They wanted to be launched along a trajectory toward their individual interests and passions. When you influence them away from their ability to find those passions, they will encounter more difficulty finding their true path.

Curiosity naturally leads to the discovery of passion. A child who is interested in a subject will follow that interest to the discovery of other interests and passions, which will eventually lead to the exploration of that which was intended prior to birth. The process of discovering and pursuing a passion is what we call "bliss." This is the natural state of the child and the adult.

When you are allowed to pursue your passions with abandon and are not influenced away from that which interests you, you live in a state of bliss. This is the natural state of being for humans in this physical reality. Bliss is what you would feel if you could focus solely on what you find fascinating.

Unfortunately, most of you do not allow yourselves to pursue your passions. Some of you have not yet found your true passions. Some of you deny yourself your own passion. You believe that you could not earn enough money while pursuing your passions. You give up your passions and instead choose to support yourselves in jobs or businesses you do not really enjoy.

Many of you are following what we might call "false passion." You have been influenced to such a degree by your society that you are following the dreams of your mass consciousness or the dreams your parents held for you. You might outwardly appear to be successful, yet you are not enjoying your true passion. You are pretending to be happy while following the path society deems worthy. What you really want to explore may not conform to the expectations of your society. Your parents may not approve of what you consider fascinating.

If you can see this in your own life, you must be able to understand what you are doing to your children. If your parents or the society of your youth made you feel like what you wanted to do was wrong or impractical, then you cannot allow this to occur with your own children. If you were guided away from what really interested you as a child, you must change this approach when dealing with your own children.

II.

When left free from the influence of others, children will naturally gravitate to what interests them. The Law of Attraction will match them with their natural interests. Every single being is unique and all children have their own interests. These interests, when left alone and uninfluenced, will lead them, step by step, to that which they are here to explore. They might be interested in bugs and snakes, which you might find reprehensible. Yet this interest will lead to other interests that will eventually lead them to bliss. If you influence them away from this one interest, you lead them off their path to bliss.

When a child shows an interest in something you deem worthy and you ramp up their interests by encouraging them to follow this one interest, you also lead them off their path to bliss. Your influence is very powerful. If you praise them for being interested in something you think is good, they will start to gravitate to those subjects you approve of. They will seek the good-feeling of your approval. They will no longer seek what interests them because in these early stages, they are emotionally and instinctually tied to your approval. Your display of love means their survival is assured. They will seek your approval of their interests in order to receive your display of love.

As a parent (or teacher, grandparent, babysitter, family member, or anyone else of influence) you cannot guide them away from their interests, or toward your interests, or even encourage whatever they may be interested in. You can only allow the Law of Attraction to bring what they need when they need it. This is a challenge for nearly everyone. You believe it is your duty and your right to guide your children to what you know, based on your own experience, is best for them. But you must see the situation from the higher perspective and allow us to help you understand it with the proper description of the mechanism of physical reality. Let us start.

Do you agree that everything is vibrational? This is a vibrational universe and you are translating vibration through your five senses. You are very adept at this and your world seems vibrant and real. However, everything is vibrational and you interpret these vibrations in a unique manner based on your own vibration. If something is not a vibrational match to you, it does not exist for you.

You have agreements among you as to what each vibration means. You think the color blue that you see is the same blue everyone else sees. It is not. It is unique to you, because while the color blue is a vibration, you see it from the unique perspective of your own vibration. The color blue for you is a blending of your vibration, which is unique to you, and the vibration of the color blue. Since your vibration is unique, your perception of blue is unique as well. Therefore, no one sees anything the same way you see it. Almost every person in the world assumes that everyone else is sees the same things they do.

Your experience is based on your vibration. Everyone else's experience is based on their vibration. Everyone experiences their world in a unique way. That's why we call it "their world" and not "the world." Your children experience their world in a way you cannot begin to imagine. Even if you could remember how you viewed your world at their age, it would be a completely different reality.

You were a perfect match to the Earth when you were born. The Earth was vibrating at a frequency and you matched that vibrational frequency at that time. While your vibrational frequency has raised as you have experienced life, Earth's frequency has risen at a far greater rate. The children born today are coming with higher frequencies that are an exact match to Earth as it is today. This is why it is so easy for them to adopt new technologies while you struggle with them.

Your children are vibrating at a much higher frequency than you are. They come more equipped to live in the current environment of Earth. What you see as the problems of the world, they see as the challenges and fun things they have come to experience for themselves. What your children will be interested in will not likely be of interest to you. The basis of the generation gap is simply the difference in vibrational frequency between parent and child.

Your children are more advanced than you are. They are more conscious and they naturally understand the laws of the universe unless you influence them away from those laws to man's laws. They naturally gravitate toward whatever interests them. They are born fascinated with their world. You do not need to interfere with their discovery process.

Allow children to adapt to their environment, explore their reality, and discover their interests on their own. Allow them to flow from one interest to the next. Do not be concerned if they like something one day and leave it the next. If your child likes trucks and you buy him or her toy trucks, don't worry if they give the trucks away and pick up a doll. Do not become attached to their interests. Do not judge their interests as good or bad, right or wrong.

You may encourage the discovery process carefully, but if you want to allow your child to find bliss, you cannot interfere with the process. If your child is interested in stars, you might drive him or her to the country to look at the stars on a clear night, but you must not do anything to encourage or discourage their interest. They must be allowed to freely follow this interest or to abandon it completely. If they feel that your happiness is tied to the interest, they will pursue the interest past the point of that interest. The interest was just a step in the process of discovering their passion. If they linger there a while longer than what would be natural, they might miss the next step.

We can feel that many parents reading this will have difficulty allowing their child to naturally move from one interest to the next without their guidance. It will be hard for some of you to believe that your child was born in an advanced state of evolution and does not need your guidance. You want to do all the things your parents did not do for you. You want to give your child all the love and attention you did not get. But if you lead your child in a direction other than the one they have intended to travel, you simply make life more difficult than it needs to be.

You cannot do any wrong when raising your children. There is no wrong anywhere in the universe and there's nothing you can do that we would consider wrong. If you desire for your child to find bliss, we are simply explaining a better approach to support what it is you say you want. If you want your child to experience ease and the joy of life, you will allow him or her to naturally find his or her passions.

III.

Two hundred years ago, it was considered acceptable in certain societies to own another human and to beat that individual into submission and servitude. One hundred years ago it was considered acceptable in certain societies for a husband to beat his wife. Today, in many cultures it is acceptable for parents to beat their children into submission. This practice will be considered barbaric in just a few years. If you believe it is acceptable to control the action of a child through the use of punishment, especially corporal, we want to lead you to a new perspective.

Your child is born as a being of love and worthiness. Your child expects total freedom and well-being. When these expectations are not met, your child understandably freaks out. Physical reality is a dense and intense form of existence. It takes some getting used to. It is a harsh environment compared to the complete ease and bliss of the nonphysical realm. That's why babies cry and sleep so often. Infancy is a period of adjustment.

Children are born into this existence knowing they are immortal, invincible, free beings of love. But their experience suggests otherwise. In a natural state, free from outside influence, children would experience love and joy while also experiencing some discomfort with their new reality. They would fluctuate between joy and discomfort. They would soon get their bearings and adjust to their new environment and begin to thrive within their own bodies.

Children do not understand the concept of duality. They do not know of judgment until they are taught it. They do not understand the concept of right and wrong. They do not naturally associate with anything wrong. They must learn what is wrong. Just because they do something that you or society considers wrong, they are born without the concept of wrong. To be punished for something they cannot perceive is confusing. To be punished by the ones who are supposed to care for them and love them can only diminish their impression of their own worthiness.

Your society has rules. To fit into your society you feel you must obey these rules. You want your children to fit into society, so you desperately seek to impress upon your children the importance of these rules. You mistakenly believe that without your guidance, your children would behave in such a way that they might become outcasts. This is a flawed premise. Let us explain why.

Your child was born with a set of intentions. Every child is a vibrational match to its parents, the earth, and their environment at the exact time of their birth. They all knew what they were doing before they entered this world. They were prepared. They intended to love and be loved, they intended to feel joy, and they intended to expand from the experience of life. Most of their intentions were general in nature and it is these intentions that will ensure their ability to integrate with their society. They don't need you to condition their behavior. This will all occur quite naturally.

When you seek to make another conform to your rules before they are ready, your actions might diminish their personal feelings of worthiness. As the parent, you have a tremendous responsibility for the self-esteem of your child. When you try to control their behavior, you inadvertently cause them to lose faith in their guidance system and their own understanding of their worthiness.

Now, we understand that this is another difficult subject for most parents and you might not believe us when we tell you that your child will adapt to your society and conform to its rules. It will happen naturally, just not on your timetable. They will not likely conform as fast as you want them to. There may be some embarrassing moments. But let them experience those moments (or at least some of them) so that it will not be you making them wrong. Allow others to make them wrong if they must. But you will notice that while the scene may cause you some embarrassment, your children will learn to follow the rules of society on their own. As long as you do not make your children wrong, they will stand a better chance of maintaining their worthiness.

When you punish your children, you make them wrong and you diminish their worthiness to a degree. When you allow them to learn from experience, you enhance their feelings of worthiness. When you attempt to control their behavior through the use of a physical form of punishment, you risk irreparably harming your child.

IV.

Your child came here to explore physical reality and to pursue certain interests, just as you did. You will not know what these interests are until they have evolved. They may come at an early age or much later in life. If your child is allowed to progress naturally, at their own pace, they will come to discover what it is they are here to explore. Allow the Law of Attraction and their own inner guidance system to assist them as they explore their world. Do not judge their methods or the speed at which they travel their own path. Allow them to behave as naturally as possible and they will make startling discoveries on their own.

Your current educational system will not last much longer. Soon you will discover that children have specific and individual abilities to learn. You will find that interest and desire spark learning. Experience is the only true teacher. Every child learns at his or her own pace. Your current method of grouping children by age and then expecting them all to learn and retain the same information at the same time is not effective. In fact, this practice is actually detrimental to the natural learning process.

Your children do not learn this way. Their ability to learn has more to do with their specific intentions to explore this Earth environment at this time. They are seeking new ways of living and they want to learn only that which matters to them. When you ask them to learn something that does not serve them, that they have no interest in, that they are not ready for, you ask them to do what is not natural. You often cause harm in the process.

When a child is expected to learn and cannot or does not, you influence them to believe that they are less intelligent than they should be. When you categorize a child as having one of the many learning disabilities you have created, you stigmatize the child and make it more difficult for that child to find their true path. The same is true of the child you label as exceptional. This child has the ability to retain useless information and regurgitate that knowledge in a way that makes you feel good. Yet this child you call smart is also less likely to naturally find their path.

Your dualistic judgment of smart and stupid does not serve the natural development of the child. In fact, in many, many cases, it hinders the child's ability to find their true path toward what they are here to experience. This is why your current educational system does not and cannot work. It is a flawed system.

If you could start with the following premise and build on it, you would create an educational system that would work. First you must believe that all children (all people) are equally worthy. No one is more worthy or less worthy than another. Everyone is here to explore a certain aspect of this reality. Everyone is completely and absolutely unique. Everyone is equal. Everyone is one.

Now that everyone is seen as equal, you must also come to believe that intelligence is not something that one is born with, but something that one attracts based on the specificity of their interests and desires. Most children are born with the same capacity for intelligence. The only difference is that some children are better able to attract more specific information. You must understand that thoughts and ideas are not created in the mind, they are attracted to it. When one reaches a certain vibration, one has access to ideas that seem new. The idea was always there, but the innovator accesses the idea first.

The attraction of certain information through thought comes when needed to those who are within the vibrational frequency of the information. The attraction of ideas comes when one has a desire to know more about a subject of interest. Fascination and desire cause information and ideas to come to the mind through thoughts that feel new. Intelligence is simply the ability to resonate with the vibration of these thoughts. This is why people often receive the same new idea at the same time even though they're on opposite sides of the planet. They simply reached a similar vibration at the same time.

Learning occurs when desire causes an interest in a certain subject and the student requires more information in order to explore the subject in more detail. When a child (or an adult) is interested in a certain subject, he or she wants to learn more about it. If a child lacks a certain skill, such as the ability to read, the child will then become interested in learning to read in order to more fully explore the subject. Desire and interest have caused the child to want to learn to read. It is at this point that the learning process is engaged. The age of the child does not matter. It is a matter of when the child is naturally ready.

If this child were forced to learn to read before he was ready, he would have great difficulty. There is a natural path to learning that is based on desire and interest. The child attracts the information needed when the time is right. If forced to learn before that time, the child will encounter difficulty. If the child does not learn at the expected pace, he will be labeled with a learning disability that will affect his entire life. If he is able to learn, he will be praised and this influence will also affect him for the rest of his life. Either way, the child will be influenced away from the path he is meant to follow at his own pace, naturally.

In a radically new approach to education, you would have no teachers, no structure, and no curriculum. You might have a building to shelter and feed children stocked with the tools they need to play and explore. It is through the act of play that children will come to discover what interests them. But there would be no formal structure. Children would be allowed to interact with each other and the environment. Soon they would discover something that interested them and the desire to learn would be ignited.

Once they find the subject of interest, they will be drawn to it. They will want to learn more about it. They will seek books or the internet for more information. It is at this time that they might ask for the assistance of a facilitator of some kind. This might come in the form of an older child or an adult. That person would not teach them anything, they would simply facilitate the child's own curiosity and help them find the information they seek. They would not guide them, judge them, or even praise them. They would simply be of assistance if and when it was needed.

Children would not be separated by age but allowed to interact in a way that is natural. The way children are currently segregated by age has affected the way your entire society conducts itself. Age does not need to be the great divider that it has become. When children of all ages are allowed to interact freely, you will discover that age itself has no particular meaning.

When children of all ages are allowed to interact in a communal setting, the older children learn to treat the younger ones with compassion rather than disdain. The younger ones learn to trust and respect the older children rather than to fear them. This was the natural order of life for centuries, but your educational system has disrupted it by segregating children by age.

A conscious system of education is based on neutrality. There is no judgment, and each child is considered equally intelligent. If one child seemed to be progressing and learning at a comparably high rate, that child would be treated exactly the same as a child who seems not to be learning. The conscious system understands that each child progresses naturally at their own individual rate. There's nothing you can or should do to change that rate. It is perfect the way it is. There is no reason for a child to learn to read at age three when the child may not have an interest in reading until age ten. Your judgment of what is right is not important. What is right is what happens naturally.

Your fears cloud your judgment. You believe that if a child does not learn to read by a certain age, the child may never learn to read. You believe that if the child doesn't learn to read, they won't be able to find a job or support themselves. You believe if they are not made to be intelligent, they won't be able to get into the best universities. You believe that if they don't receive a college degree, their lives will be ruined. But this is simply a matter of your limited perspective.

Remember that if you feel negative emotion, you have a belief that is limiting. The presence of the negative emotion (fear) indicates that you are looking at something from your limited perspective. If you reach for the higher perspective, you can reduce the intensity of your limiting belief.

Now let's assume the worst. You allow your child to progress naturally with no formal, structured education. You provide the tools to learn if he chooses, but you neither encourage nor discourage any interest he may have. What he chooses to do is play outside all day with the dog. He explores his environment every day with the dog and never finds the need to learn to read. In every way he is healthy, happy, and content with doing the same thing each day. He does this for several years and is now well past the age where every other child you know is reading.

As a conscious parent, you stick to your belief that the natural order of universal laws will eventually sort this all out. Other parents are asking you why your child can't read. As long as you stay focused and do not allow the opinions of others to influence you away from what you know is right, you can continue to allow your child to develop naturally. You trust that natural curiosity and fascination will necessitate the need for your child to want to learn to read.

Soon your child develops an interest in nature and wants to learn more about it. He looks at pictures on the computer but can't read what is written below each photo. His curiosity has brought him the desire and interest to learn to read. He then reaches vibrational alignment with reading and learns to read in a very short period of time.

Your child who is older learns to read much faster and more easily in comparison to a younger version of him who had no particular interest in reading. Children will learn anything when coerced into doing so. If you praise your child for learning something you deem important, the child will naturally enjoy it and seek your praise. However, they are learning at a pace that may not be the natural pace for them. They will not learn anything to the degree or speed that would occur naturally.

When you insert your fears into the process of learning, you influence your child. If you expect them to learn at a certain pace or standard and they cannot keep up, your judgment harms their sense of worthiness. When you praise your child as you compare them to other children, you may influence them toward a belief that others are less worthy than they are. It is equally unproductive for a child to believe he or she is more worthy than another child because he or she appears to be an exceptional student, athlete, or prodigy.

V.

Neutrality is the basis of conscious parenting. Judgment is at the heart of unconscious parenting. Here is the very tricky part of our message. It is so ingrained in you to praise children when they are good and punish them when they are bad that it might be very difficult for you to accept another perspective. But the fact of the matter is that if you treat your children differently based on their behavior, you upset the natural course of their personal growth.

If you are a conscious creator, you view your world from a stance of neutrality. Nothing is inherently good or bad. You are a creator and everything is your creation. When you look upon your creation from the higher perspective, you see all the good that exists and therefore you determine what is good about every condition or situation.

As an unconscious creator, you live in judgment of everything. Everything is either good or bad. You strive to change the conditions so that they are good based on your limited perspective. You fight against what is. You are only happy when something is as you think it should be and you are unhappy when something is not how you want it. Your feelings are caused by the conditions. You are a victim of the situation. Therefore, you are in a constant struggle with your conditions and you feel powerless.

The conscious parent can stand back and look at the situation from the higher perspective. She does not modify the child's behavior in order to control the conditions so that she feels good. She feels good regardless of the child's behavior. The child itself has no impact on the parent's sense of well-being. The parent can allow the child to develop naturally without becoming emotionally tied to the outcome. Instead, the conscious parent has confidence in the natural process of development.

The natural process of a child's development unfolds as universal forces guide the child in the direction of what is wanted and toward newfound interests and passions. When left free from the influence of others, the child will gravitate quite naturally to that which was intended prior to birth. The conscious parent can watch gleefully as the process moves the child from one interest to the next. The parent does not interfere with the process but shows faith that everything is working as it must. It is a universal law.

Your child comes into this reality with certain intentions and you can readily see those intentions at work in the personality of the very young child. Interests will arise at a surprisingly young age. The child will be curious about specific subjects and can even become quite passionate about certain aspects of life very early on. If left to discover what interests the child, he will be led to more specific interests. One interest will lead to others.

Along the way, the child will develop intellectually, emotionally, and physically. There will be many things for the child to learn through experience. To the parent, these events might seem painful and the parent will feel the urge to protect the child. But these events are part of the natural development process, and one way or another the child must be changed by these experiences. If you step in and clear a path, you do your child a disservice.

It is one thing to be the conscious creator of your own life. It is another thing entirely to have the courage and faith to allow your child to become a conscious creator as well. Your work includes allowing your children (and family members, friends, co-workers, and everyone else) to develop naturally and to become conscious at their own pace. You can neither protect them nor encourage them. They will work it all out on their own.

Certainly, if your child is in pain, you will come to their aid. You might soothe them and answer questions when asked. But your job as a parent is to create an environment in which they can grow and develop with as little outside influence as possible. You create the nest, but you don't need to feather it.

Imagine being a conscious parent and watching your child attempt something and fail. He comes to you to soothe his feelings of disappointment. What would you do? What would you say? This has a lot to do with your own personal feelings as you observe your child. You might feel bad for your child and want to soothe him. But what you're really doing is wanting to make yourself feel better. You are so emotionally tied to the feelings of your child that these feelings become your feelings. When your child is upset, you become upset and you want to feel better, so you attempt to make your child feel better.

Reverting to the unconsciously reacting to the conditions by trying to change them influences your child. He sees you attempting to change the conditions and comes to believe that this is the way things are done in physical reality. He loses touch with his inner guidance and looks to you to solve problems. He allows you to do the work he is meant to do.

When your child fails, you must allow the experience to cause the natural change. The event was created and played out in a way that was a necessary part of your child's development. The judgment that it was a failure is simply looking at it from a limited perspective. If you are to guide your child toward consciousness, you must allow the events to occur without judgment. They must be seen as neutral, even if your child reacts negatively.

What you can do is help your child see the event from the higher perspective. If you can help change his perspective, he will come to see that the event was simply a small step in a long journey. What we are trying to do for you in these teachings is explain how we see things from our higher perspective. You can do the same for your child.

We are unconditional lovers of life. We unconditionally love your world and everything in it. We never see the conditions as wrong or bad. No matter what happens, we see the good in all of it. As we shine a light on all that's good, we hope to illuminate it for you as well. You can do the same for your child.

Instead of consoling him and agreeing with his perspective of the situation, which is quite limited, you can help him view the event from a new angle. If you can react positively to every occurrence, he will learn to do the same. The ability to become neutral to the conditions will allow him flexibility in his growth. He will be able to stand on firmer ground and see the lessons in each event. This radical approach to parenting will create children who approach life consciously right from the start. Can you imagine the freedom and power this will give your child?

Chapter Thirteen

A Radical New Approach to World Citizenship

You are all one, living as individuals on your planet. You separate yourselves by borders, by cultures, by religion, by race, by sex, by age, by political affiliation, and by class. It is time for these separations to fall apart. You are one. You need not separate yourselves from each other.

You are traveling in a very small spaceship within an infinitely large universe. You once segregated yourselves on buses, but now you ride together. The same must be true of your planet. The good that will come from living together and supporting each other far outweighs the sum of your fears. The value of a one-world community is that it will allow everyone to live as you intended, in love rather than in fear.

You believe that since you were born in a certain place, you are deserving of all that you have. If another is born in an underdeveloped nation, he should be forced to stay there for the entirety of his life. He should not be able to gain access to your country or your standard of living. He should be doomed to his existence by the chance of his birth. This is not a conscious approach to reality.

While it is true that you choose your birthplace and your parents based on the trajectory you intended, you also intended the freedom to pursue your dreams. While you seal yourselves off behind the borders of your country, you create resentment among the less fortunate. This results in war and strife, which diminish your standard of living. As you live in fear of your neighbors, you hold yourself apart from who you really are. When you classify another human as your enemy, you create more separation, which does not serve who you say you want to be.

A conscious creator sees all as equally worthy and unique. You see value in all lives, all cultures, and all beliefs. You understand that you are all one, that there is no separation, and that borders are an unnatural manifestation of fear. All devices used to protect yourselves from others are based in fear and therefore perpetuate limiting beliefs.

The cost of these fears is astronomical. It costs you unseen expense in the limitation of your experience. As you are taught to believe that other cultures are bad and your culture is good, you create a framework of duality that becomes very difficult to dismantle. Limiting, fear-based beliefs are promoted and adopted by the masses. You build insanely expensive armies to defend yourselves from imaginary or even fabricated foes.

Your war culture must feed on an enemy to survive. When no real enemy exists, one is created to support its appetite. However, you will soon come to realize that your behemoth defense apparatus is ridiculously oversized for the job. You chase a ragtag group of terrorists with an army created to wage another world war. In doing so you enrage an entire culture and separate yourselves even further.

Through the institution of patriotism, your government convinces you that you need protection. But you do not. You are safe and without your army, you would have no enemy. Look at the countries without huge armies. Are they under constant attack from terrorists? Are they engaged in this battle? Why not?

You cannot eradicate anything in this universe. You can never defeat an enemy for your fight will always increase fear and support more limiting beliefs that will give rise to newer and more powerful enemies. When you kill one, you cause two more to take his place. Fear creates the desire and inspiration to stand up and fight. When you create an atmosphere of fear, you create your own enemies.

This is an attractive universe. You cannot push away what you do not like. You cannot lessen the intensity of anything by your attention to it. You should not feel powerless when you are so very powerful. Why do you feel the need to display your power? What is the basis of your fears?

There is no right and no wrong in regard to your continued and never-ending wars against people you fear. But what you are perpetuating with your struggle against your fellow man is an unconscious pursuit that goes against the laws of the universe. Your struggle is futile and until you change your approach, it will continue to escalate. It might move from one region to another, but it must grow. It is universal law.

A radically new approach to your enemy would be the release of all fear. As you move from unconscious to conscious, you move from fear to love. As you accept others as they are - less developed, less conscious, or less evolved - you create an environment of love and acceptance. As you shower them with love and support, you create a framework that supports who you really are.

Can you become conscious in an environment of fear? Of course. Can others also become conscious regardless of the actions of their government? Yes, certainly. But can you also realize that the old approach is not working and can never work because it violates universal law? Can you remove your attention and support from it? Can you not condemn the old approach but rather support love and appreciation for everyone?

You cannot fight against any structure and topple it. Just as we have taught you about your own life, you must seek what is wanted rather than avoid or deny what is unwanted. You don't need to make your government wrong. All you need to do is support what you want.

You are not your government, but your government is a reflection of your country's mass consciousness. When you move your attention away from fear and toward love, you radically shift the totality of that consciousness. When others decide that patriotism is a fear-based belief in one's own superiority, the consciousness of the country moves away from nationalism and toward acceptance. You can only believe what you want to believe. You cannot preach your beliefs to others, for you will simply create tension. You can shine as an example of love to which others will gravitate. You can be accepting of others and they will become accepting of you.

When thinking about another culture, try not to get caught up in propaganda. Realize that your war institution is simply trying to maintain its survival by creating despicable enemies for you to hate. You can rationalize the existence of a war machine only when you believe there is something to fear.

When there is no real enemy, the war institution will create one for you to hate. It is a matter of survival and it will fight to survive. If you can withdraw your attention from its fabrications, you can move your support to something that will benefit what it is you want, rather than what you do not want. Your war on terror is not real. You could dismantle this war and all wars with a few weeks of love and acceptance.

You have no need for protection. You have no real enemies. If you did not have a defense industry, you would have no enemies. If you used that energy for love, acceptance, and support of the worthiness and value of all others, you would attract love, rather than hate. Which would you prefer?

II.

You are in a time of awakening and millions of people all over the world are coming out of the haze of duality and embracing neutrality. When you come to know the laws of the universe and the mechanism of physical reality, the mass consciousness of your world will shift. There will be more of you living in love and less living in fear. Change will occur naturally and swiftly. Flawed institutions will crumble and human separations will fall apart. You will become as one and will live in harmony. You will allow the standards of all to rise and you will balance your own standards as well.

As you learn to base your personal decisions on love, your government will begin to do the same. You will look back on this period in your history and you will not truly believe the progress that has been made is such a short time. Here is what will happen as mass consciousness moves from fear to love.

Without fear, you have no need for armies or borders. You will have no need for many different countries and governments. You will have no need for separation because you will operate from a stance of love and acceptance. You not only tolerate your cultural differences, you appreciate those differences for the tapestry that is created. When you have a mass consciousness that has shifted from fear to love, you have no need for any institution that constricts your personal freedom.

As consciousness shifts from fear to love, you will see all as truly equal and worthy. You will not condemn someone to prison for doing something you do not approve of. In an environment of love, you will support those who are still operating out of fear and lack. You will help them rather than locking them away, out of sight.

Your attention will be on what is wanted, not fighting against what is not wanted. More of you will understand the laws of the universe and you will understand that giving your attention to anything from a stance of fear will only cause the object of that fear to grow. You will realize that anything and everything you want is attracted from a stance of love and appreciation. You will realize that the way to build the society that serves what you want is to create it out of love, not fear.

All of your decisions will be based in love. You will eliminate most of your laws, since they were created out of fear. You will come to understand that your laws only restrict the freedom of law-abiding people and do little to control the actions of those who would commit the crimes regardless of the law. You will move toward freedom when you make decisions based in love.

Much of the fear in your society is the fear of loss. You believe you are entitled to the wealth you enjoy. You fear that sharing your wealth with the poor, whether they live in your own country or in another, will cause you to lose your standard of living. But you offset this grand lifestyle by operating from a stance of fear. You must constantly be on guard, for you perceive that others may take what is yours.

In the future, you will be more aligned with abundance and less focused on lack. You will not believe that resources are scarce but that the power of creation is abundant. You will not fear losing anything because you will understand that you are the creator of your reality; when you believe in your creative abilities and understand the mechanism of physical reality, you do not worry about the possibility of loss. Loss will cease to exist as a fear.

The fear of loss can only occur in the unconscious mind. If you understand how this reality is designed, then you can never lose anything. The loss of something only makes room for a new thing to enter. If you give away everything you own, you allow new things to come. If you hold onto what you have out of fear, you prevent more from entering your reality.

When a society, as a mass consciousness, releases its fear of loss, miraculous changes can occur. By the time this happens, your government will be unrecognizable from the form of government you are so familiar with today. In the near future, you will come together as a people, understanding the laws of the universe and the mechanism of physical reality. You will no longer have separate approaches to governance. The conscious will lead the unconscious to a new awakening of reality. What will really be important is how you represent yourselves as a people.

The great shift will occur when you come to understand that you are all one. This might be the most surreal aspect of awakening. The fact is that you are all extensions of creation. You all come from the same place. You will all return to the same place. It is simply an aspect of physical reality that makes you believe you are separate. But you are all one.

Individuality seems like a preferable condition, but it is not. You have simply become accustomed to it. When in the nonphysical realm, you will flow together as one of many. You will prefer to be together. You will not see individuality as preferable.

Harmony is a blending of vibration. To live and experience harmony is to live life as who you really are. Without fear, there would be only love. You do not need to fear others, as they cannot create in your reality. You do not need to fear the poor, for they cannot take from you. But if you can share what you have out of love and abundance, you can experience a release of fear and love will grow. Out of love comes greater abundance. You have no enemies when you live in love. Everyone is your enemy when you live in fear.

Now imagine your country governed by conscious people operating from a stance of love. They do not fear loss, for they know of the abundance that is the basis of this reality. They do not argue, for they know there is no such thing as wrong, just differences of perspective. They work to see the unique perspective of others and from that view, they understand what others want. They do not judge, for their position is neutral. They accept what is and place their attention on what is wanted. They do not see problems to solve, but simply orchestrate the mechanism of government from a position of acceptance and appreciation.

III.

From your perspective, you might believe that the result of their inaction would be chaos. You might conclude that a land without laws would fall into anarchy and strife. But would it really? If the majority of citizens were consciously aware of universal laws and the mechanism of physical reality, they would realize that their lives are of their own creation. They would not fear others who operated outside of acceptable behavior, for they would be aligned with what they wanted. Others would not be able to affect their reality.

In order for this to occur for you, you have to release your fear of loss. If you did not fear another taking away your possessions, you could not be robbed of them. If you did not consider your possessions to be yours, you could not lose anything. If you allowed your possessions to come and go, you could not lose anything. Do you see that it is your approach to possession that causes the possibility that your things could be taken from you? A radical approach to possession would be to realize that you cannot own anything.

If you could not own anything, then nothing could be taken and you would lose your fear of loss. If you were without the fear of loss, nothing could be taken. It would defy universal law. You would maintain everything you wanted for exactly the time you wanted it and it could never be taken from you. It is only when you fear loss that you can lose.

Now imagine the difference between how you operate now, as you believe you own things and they can be taken from you, and who you would be if you understood that there are no things and you cannot own anything. Is this a stretch for you? Objects in physical reality are created by your thoughts. Everything you have is a manifestation of a feeling that turned into a thought that turned into a physical thing that somehow entered your experience. But the thing is no more real than the thought. Actually, it's just as real. It's just that it's really not physical. You know it's there in your presence when you interpret its existence through your physical senses. Yet it's only a vibrational representation of your thoughts. It's not real. Nothing is. This is all an elaborate illusion.

You understand that, don't you? This is a vibrational reality that represents itself physically. The same thing occurs in the nonphysical realm, yet we see through the illusion. It's all for fun. The whole thing is just another way of being. So why not make it more fun by releasing fear? That would make this experience so much more enjoyable.

Now let's imagine everything has been taken from you. As you are living your life with your set of beliefs and your current approach to life, you would judge this as a bad thing. Why? Because you would feel bad. That's right. After all is said and done, you want to feel good. This is a feeling reality. You want to avoid feeling bad and enjoy feeling good. That is why you want money. You believe money makes you feel good. It does, to an extent. But when you fear losing your money or your possessions, you feel bad. Your fear makes you feel anxious, nervous, and worried. Now, what creates your reality? Your feelings!

If you feel worried that you might lose your money or your possessions, what do you think is likely to occur? The universe is going to give you experiences in reality that match how you feel. It feels good to think about money, so the money comes. When the money arrives, you fear losing it and it goes away. It's just a mechanism of physical reality and it can be no other way.

Now imagine if you didn't need money to feel good, and you simply felt good. The universe would bring you physical representations of the way you felt. You would experience feeling good in physical terms as you practiced feeling good. You might receive money or possessions that made you feel good. Now, since your approach to possessions is different, you no longer fear loss and therefore your possessions cannot leave your experience until you want them to. It would not be physically possible.

Let's say you feared losing your possessions. What you feared was the pain of loss. What you feared was the feeling associated with loss, which is a bad feeling. But the worry you were feeling all along was also a bad feeling. Then, when you lost your possessions, the feeling of worry was released. You had nothing more to worry about, so you felt relief, which is a good feeling. The irony is that you thought your possessions made you feel good, but since you feared their loss, you actually felt bad. Once they were lost, you returned to a natural state of relief, which feels good.

If you are worried about losing something, you might as well lose it, because the feelings that stem from fear of any kind are not worth it. The fear is the bad feeling. If you fear something, you might as well give in to it or change your perspective in such a radical way that the fear dissipates. This is a feeling universe. The only thing that matters is how you feel. You must demand that you feel good. It is your right to feel good. Only fear can make you feel bad.

We have come to tell you that there is nothing to fear but fear itself. This is a very powerful message that was given to you long ago. It's completely accurate. There is nothing so serious going on here that you should fear anything, not even death, for there is no such possibility of death. Death should be a celebration just as happy an occasion as birth. It is in the nonphysical realm. You cannot die and you cannot lose anything or anyone. The only time you lose is when you succumb to your fears.

If you are afraid of loss, then lose everything or give everything away and see what happens. You'll be surprised. If you lose everything and wallow in self-pity, you might remain there for a little while, but soon your natural vibration will allow things to come to you and you will rise again. If you have gone through a devastating loss, you will notice that you come out the other side in a much better condition. Your perception changes. You see things differently. You have expanded as a result of the experience.

The longer you dwell on the wrongness of what happened, the longer it will take to rebound. But you will rise one way or the other. When you've lost your money and possessions, these things have less power over you.

After the loss, your perspective shifts. You begin to realize that the way you feel is far more important. You believed that the things made you feel good, but they were just representative of how you were feeling. They were tokens of the feeling, not the feeling itself. Change your approach to what you fear and you'll feel better.

Pretend for a moment that you're a slave owner. You own a lot of slaves and you use them to power your business. The labor is cheap. You only need to provide them with minimal food and shelter. You can't imagine how you would operate your business without them. Your products would cost too much and no one would buy them.

Soon you hear of people who think slave ownership is wrong and they want to take your slaves away and set them free. You don't believe it is right for others to take property you lawfully own. But they want to change the laws and make it so you can no longer own slaves. You fear the loss of your property and believe that losing it will ruin you.

So your slaves are set free after a long and costly struggle to keep them. Your property is gone. But what really happens? You find alternatives to their labor. You might hire free men who will be more motivated and actually produce more products for less money. You no longer need to hire people to make sure your slaves don't escape. You no longer worry that your slaves may revolt and kill you. Because you have undergone a radical change, you find better methods for doing things. You innovate out of necessity.

If you keep doing things the same way because you can't imagine how it could all work out otherwise, you can never get to a better place. It is only after a disaster that you are forced to radically change your approach to life. It is only out of necessity that you innovate. Yet, if you feel negative emotion, you must radically change your approach. If it's not working, you must change it, not fix it. Radical change always leads to the path of discovery.

IV.

You are magnificent manifestors. You have created a world where the price of fuel, food, and labor is very cheap compared to the wealth many of you enjoy. However, the low price of these commodities comes at a cost you are not considering. Soon you will have to look beyond the low prices to what these things are actually costing you.

We want you to look at the way you purchase and consume goods. You are so focused on low prices that you are not seeing what is really happening. You believe you have finally created the world you have always wanted. Your ability to travel throughout your community and the world costs less in real terms than ever before. The prices you pay for food is less than is realistic. You search the globe to find the cheapest labor and now you are finding workers in your own nation who must compete at these low wages. You think this is a good thing. You call it the free market. You believe that competition is responsible for the low cost of everything. But you're ignoring the long-term effects of your desires.

You scour the planet searching for and extracting energy. You are doing such a fine job that you are producing more fuel than ever before. This keeps the prices so low that you do not seriously consider other alternatives. You now produce vehicles and devices powered by cheap fuel and you believe you are making your lives better. But all this consumption leads to an environment that does not serve you.

You pollute your atmosphere in such a way that it harms your ability to live as you desire to in the future. The only problem with the human life span is that it is so short that you are tempted to ignore the long-term effects of your actions. You might think about your children and grandchildren, but you don't really care what happens after that. If you continue to consume fuel at your current rate, you will make life more difficult for future generations.

This is your playground. It was designed for you to experience physical reality. You have lived many lifetimes in the past and you are eager to live many more in the future. If you destroy your playground, where will you play? This is your world. It has been created for you and those who will follow. You can change your approach to your environment.

Ironically, the fuels you have discovered and made so cheaply are actually quite inefficient. There is a far greater source of power that awaits. It is so abundant that energy will basically become free for all. This will completely change how you operate. Imagine a world with limitless clean energy in inexhaustible supply. It is waiting for you to find it.

However, because you live in happy ignorance of the real costs of your current energy sources, you do not find the proper inspiration to seek this new energy source. You are content with what you have, so you keep drilling and producing. Once you've reached the point of no return, you'll be forced to find something else and you'll discover that it was there all along. It was right under your fingertips. You just never looked because you didn't have the need. But what if you're too late?

If your actions change the temperature of your planet by a few degrees, your planet will correct itself in time. But during that time you will wish you had not caused the problem in the first place. Earth is an organism much like your body. It seeks well-being and allows that well- being to flow. It will correct the problem on its own. But Earth lives in centuries while you live in days. It will seem like a slow process from your perspective.

When you factor in the actual cost of the potential damage to your way of life, the price of fuel increases exponentially. If you were to calculate the effects of temperature change in loss of life and property, the average gallon of gas would cost hundreds of times more than what you pay now. So what is the solution?

The solution lies in your awareness of the real costs of fuel. You are living cheaply today by mortgaging the future of your grandchildren. Their world will be a much different place. They will look upon you in a way you would not like. They will make it work, but they will endure unnecessary hardship and struggle. When you think about them, you might see your world from the higher perspective.

What if a gallon of gas cost $20? What would you do then? You would find alternative means of travel. You would discover alternative sources of energy. You would create new technologies. You would find new solutions. You would do things differently. You would slow the damaging effects of your current technology until you discovered a new technology. You must radically change your approach to life in order for the new solutions to manifest themselves into your physical reality.

Fuel prices will never get much higher than they are now in real terms as long as you allow those in the oil industry to freely compete and operate as they do today. Their focus is on the discovery of new technology that will enhance the production of energy through the use of fossil fuels. Their focus is steady, and through the Law of Attraction they will just get better and better at producing fuel. Your government will have to impose some constraints so that fuel prices increase dramatically. Only when the focus shifts from the production of current energy sources to the discovery of new energy sources will the Law of Attraction help you find the new energy. It's there and if you focus on it, the laws of the universe will bring it right to you.

Today it seems like gas is expensive. You couldn't imagine what you would do if gas prices were any higher. You don't know how you would make it. But just like those slave owners, you'll find that everything will work out in the end. There is always a better solution. But if you don't radically change your approach, you won't be able to align with the solution. You can't see the solution when you're consumed by the problem. But it is there waiting for you and trust us, you can find it.

V.

Just as you can readily see that your cheap fuel prices are taking a toll on your planet, you might also see that your cheap food prices are taking a toll on your bodies. For most of the history of man, food has been in short supply. You've made tremendous strides in recent years and have created an amazing mechanism of food production. You have lowered the real cost of food as you've greatly increased its supply. But much of your foods are designed to be so cheap and last so long that they provide little value to your bodies. As a conscious thinker, you are well aware of this. However, there are many in your society who believe that low cost and good taste are all that's needed and they do not see what's really happening to their own bodies.

You have designed the artificially processed hamburger to taste better than the naturally produced vegetable. You have made it cheaper as well. You have allowed others to prepare food for you and you believe that cooking your own meals is too difficult and time-consuming. You are mortgaging the long-term health and vitality of your body by eating cheap, processed foods prepared by others.

Food is the fuel of your body. Water and food energize the mechanism of your body and feed the cells. Your body requires energy and it reminds you to fuel it through the feeling of hunger. Hunger is a feeling. It's not an emotion, belief, or thought. It's a feeling. Your body guides you by the use of feelings. When you feel hungry, you must eat and the feeling of hunger is replaced by the feeling of satiation. If you overeat, you feel bloated and stuffed. This is your body's way of telling you that you've gone too far. If you eat within the guidelines of how you feel, you maintain a healthy body.

Feeling is the communication of your body. Hunger feels bad; satiation feels good; overeating feels bad. It's a simple design. When you eat food and feel bad, it's your body's way of telling you that this food is not in harmony with the health and well-being of your body. You can eat any food and receive feedback from the body. If you eat an apple and feel good as a result, the apple is good for your body. If you eat a strawberry and feel bad, the strawberry is not in alignment with the well-being of the body.

You can test any food using this method of eating and then analyze how you feel. If you eat a bag of potato chips and feel good, then the bag of chips is in alignment with the well-being of your body. If you eat a slice of bread and feel bad, then bread is not in alignment with the health and well-being of your body. This method allows you to discover what works for you. You are unique and what is good or bad for you may be quite the opposite for another. What your body requires is independent of conventional wisdom, which wants to group people into categories. Learn to identify which foods create good feelings and which ones create bad feelings.

This method really only works when one food is eaten at a time. When you combine foods, your body will respond with a mix of good and bad feelings that becomes confusing and muddled. Let's say you eat a peanut butter and grape jelly sandwich on white bread. You may have a body that feels good when eating peanut butter, bad when eating grape jelly, and good when eating white bread. The overall feeling you receive is mixed. Because most of your meals are combinations of different foods, you feel a similar mix of good and bad feelings after each one. You become numb to the feelings. It's only on the rare occasion when you eat a solitary food that you get a clear signal.

Experiment with this and you'll learn to grasp how you are feeling in response to any single item of food you eat. Eat a piece of meat by itself, without anything else. One or two bites is all you need. Notice that while it may taste delicious, you will receive a clear feeling from your body. Be honest with yourself. Pay close attention to the feeling in your stomach and throat. Feel the energy or lethargy that comes after eating the meat. Try this with all different types of meat and fish you enjoy.

If you feel good after eating something, then your body is sending a clear signal that it can readily transform this food into energy that supports the continued well-being of the system as a whole. When you eat something and feel bad in any way, it's a clear indication that the body cannot effectively convert this food into energy. When the body has difficulty with anything you consume, you put stress on the system.

You have an amazingly adaptable body that can endure stress for long periods of time. But eventually the stress becomes too much and certain key components of the system begin to break down. The vitality of the body relies on an environment that is relatively free of stress. Stress can be physical, as in the foods it receives, or emotional, as in the thoughts you think. In this case, we're discussing the physical implications caused by the types of food you ingest.

You are emotionally tied to certain foods based on your beliefs about them. Many of your beliefs are culturally influenced. The foods you ate as a child may have great sentimental value. Your mother may have prepared foods for you as her mother cooked them for her. You have a belief that this is the food of your people and you carry on ancient ways of preparing and eating foods. But these foods may not be in alignment with the well-being of your unique body. Your body may not want the food of your people. Your body might want something else.

When testing what it is that works for you, you must realize that you have certain built-in biases towards and against foods based on your inherited beliefs. You must remove the bias and analyze how you feel. You must strip away the emotion of the food and understand the feeling the food gives you from the perspective of your body. If it feels good after you've digested it, the food aligns with the well-being of your body. If not, it causes some amount of stress on your body.

When you learn to eat only that which feels good to you based solely on feedback provided by your body, you will come into alignment with the well-being that is natural and intended. Once you learn to remove unnecessary stress from the body, both physical and emotional, your body will thrive. In an environment free of physical and emotional stress, you will maintain the perfect health and weight for your unique body.

Many of you want others to lead you to what is right for you. You read books and attempt to follow programs and diets prescribed by others. You take blood tests to see what is good and bad for you. Yet this is not the design. You were meant to eat one thing and understand if that one thing makes you feel good or bad. You were meant to listen to what your own body is saying. You are unique to all the world. What works for you is different from what works for others. This is the basic design of the system. The design is diversity. If you all ate the same things, there would be no diversity.

You can eat and enjoy whatever you want and your body will adapt. There are some foods that are toxic to your body, but your body adapts. It will seem to be sending you mixed signals. It may cause cravings. If you feel cravings for something that is toxic to the body, it is a signal. A craving is intended to be an unpleasant feeling. Hunger is also intended to be an unpleasant feeling. When you're hungry, you relieve this unpleasant feeling with food. Any food will do. You could eat something of absolutely no value and you will feel relief in the eating of this food. It doesn't mean the food was good for you; it just means you ate something. How you feel *after* the eating of the food is what you are supposed to notice and pay attention to.

When you have a craving, you can only satisfy it by eating a certain food that contains the ingredient that causes the craving. How you feel *after* you've digested the food is what you're supposed to pay attention to. In most cases you feel bad after you've ingested something you crave. The craving is a very powerful signal that the object of your craving is not in line with the well-being and vitality of your body.

The most common food humans crave is sugar. Sugar, in many forms, is toxic to the body and causes stress. If you crave sugar, you are being told to pay close attention to how you feel after you've digested the food containing the sugar. If you feel good, then there's no issue. If you feel bad, then you would be wise to discontinue the consumption of that product in the future. It is causing stress on the body and hindering the natural flow of well-being your body was intended to receive.

If you eat an apple that contains sugar and you feel good, then the apple promotes the well-being of your body. If you eat a candy bar and you feel bad, then the sugar contained in the candy bar comes in a form that does not support the well-being and vitality of your specific body. You might have friends who can eat candy bars every day and feel fine. What works for them may not work for you. You are all different. Test what works for you and then adopt this information when choosing foods to eat.

You never really know what anyone else is feeling when they eat a particular food. They may not even know themselves. All you can do is pay attention to how you feel and what makes you feel good. There is no cure-all. You are unique. Don't listen to the opinions of others. Listen to the opinion of your own body and integrate that information. You will see dramatic improvements to your health and vitality as you radically change your approach to food.

Of course, the well-being that flows to you, which is supported by the foods your body appreciates, only works in an environment free from stress. If you are eating all the right foods but thinking unpleasant thoughts, you will not maintain a stress-free environment. Your thoughts must also be aligned with well-being. You can eat all the best foods for your specific body, but you will continue to hinder the flow of well-being if you continue to cause stress through the thoughts you are thinking. If you're going to worry about your weight, your health, your relationships, your finances, or your children, no amount of wheat grass juice is going to make a difference.

VI.

The products you buy are often priced low due to the exploitation of cheap labor. In time, the desires of these desperate people will cause a change in their economy and their children, grandchildren or distant ancestors will receive the benefit of their great wanting. However, you do not support what you want by gaining at the expense of underpaid laborers. It is in your best interest for people to earn enough money so they may thrive rather than simply survive.

Of course, the exploited worker has the ability, as everyone does, to create their own reality. However, like most, they are creating from the observation of their outside world. All they know is poverty and exploitation. They believe this is the course of their lives and they do not allow themselves to think very far outside the bounds of what they believe to be their lot in life. We are not talking about the beliefs or perspectives of the exploited worker, we are talking about your personal approach to cheap goods at the expense of the worker. We are talking about you.

You have a certain approach to purchasing products that is not at all consistent. One day you might buy a shirt, or a vegetable, or coffee, or a luxury sports car. You buy the shirt and the vegetable because they are extremely inexpensive. You buy the coffee and the sports car because they're extremely expensive. You are not thinking about what you're doing with your money.

We are not asking you to be concerned with the amount of money you're spending. We think it's very good to have an approach to money that allows it to freely flow in and out. That's how money works when you're allowing it into your life. You allow the flow out so the flow in may come. You do not hoard it, for you realize that it is a flow of energy and that the accumulation of money is inefficient.

In many cases, you seek the lowest possible price. In some cases, the manufacturer of the product realizes this and goes to great lengths to reduce costs. The use of low-quality ingredients and cheap labor creates the illusion of low price. When you consider what is necessary to create a low price, you might think of a better return on your money.

Low wages, whether in foreign countries or your own, make for a wider disparity between the rich and the poor. This disparity is responsible for some conflict, and while it may seem like we are promoting a certain political agenda, we're primarily concerned with your alignment with who you really are.

If you are operating unconsciously and living in duality, you see your world from a very limited perspective. You are focused on getting the best deal possible. You are trusting that the seller will work everything out. You are not concerned about the quality of the raw ingredients of the product or about the people who labored to create it. You might even be thinking that these people are lucky to have jobs at all.

The exploited laborers are forced by the conditions of their birth to survive by laboring in extremely poor conditions. They have no other choice. They were born into an environment (by choice) that set them on a path to this end. They certainly intended to experience some specific things, but they did not intend to linger in despair. They believed that they would learn to feel their way out of the condition. Many of them are doing this with the help of conscious people all over the world. The connection of people through the internet has helped many remove themselves from extreme working conditions and move on to greatly improved life experiences. But in order for this to occur on a larger scale, you must become conscious about how and where you spend your money.

If you are living consciously, you understand that your money is energy and you want to use this energy for positive purposes. You consider where the money is going and who will be benefiting. As you help to raise the conditions of the workers, those people will begin to allow for new possibilities to come into view in their own experience.

Here's how this simple system works. An impoverished person must survive through menial labor. The conditions of their life have afforded them no opportunities thus far. They believe their destiny is one of hard labor and early death. They see no future for their children other than what they've experienced. They dare not dream.

Without dreams, they do not summon universal laws to their aid. Without hope, they have little chance of awakening. These people will remain unconscious victims of what they call fate. When all they see is poverty and despair, they seek to feel better through low-vibrational actions. This might be through the use of substances, abuse, or violence, none of which works and mostly mires them in desperation for generations to come.

However, if one of them is offered the opportunity to live life differently, hope is suddenly created. Hope signals universal forces that make change possible. When one of them finds a job at a fair wage or is given a small loan to start a business, others become inspired and allow for new possibilities. This is how real change is made in a short time. As more and more find alignment with what is wanted, they begin to believe in better possibilities and those small advancements cause great shifts in vibration. Through the conscious awareness of your spending, you can make great strides toward the vibrational improvement of their lives.

Like everything else, money is vibration and has the ability to cause great vibrational change. When you think about what you are doing with your money, you make the transfer of energy purposeful and powerful. You need not unconsciously use your money to support the exploiters. Now you can think about those who may be exploited themselves and you might consider what your money does to benefit or hinder their vibrational tone.

You are all one, even though you're experiencing physical reality from the perspective of the individual. You are all equally worthy and unique.

You are meant to live and play together in harmony. You are not meant to take advantage of others who were trapped by the conditions of their birth. You are meant to think about each other, for you are all one. You can aid one another. You can support one another. When you understand that you are equally important to the continuation of the expansion of consciousness, you must realize that you need each other. Think about others from their perspective and in doing so you will change your own world for the better.

Chapter Fourteen

A Radical Change in Your Approach to Money

There is momentum in everything. Money is a product of momentum. As you allow for the possibility of more money, more money flows. It's as simple as that. So how do you get this momentum started? How do you create an environment in which money can begin to flow? Let's look at the subject of money in a radical new way.

Money itself is not the object of your desire. Sitting in a room full of money means nothing in and of itself. It's only what you can do with the money that's important. So when you take your focus off money and place it squarely on what is wanted, the money must come so that you can get what it is you want. You do not want money; you want the house, car, object, vacation, or experience of something. Money simply allows you to have what it is you want. So simply realize that money is a tool of the universe. Money is one way (but certainly not the only way) the universe can bring to you what you want.

To get whatever it is you want, take money out of the equation.

Money does not mean anything. You simply see it as the most obvious vehicle that will take you where you want to go. But this hinders you. This is a limitation because you think that the only way to get what you want is to earn more money. If you can't see a reasonable way to earn more money, you start to limit your own desires. It is this belief that you must know how the money will come that makes money difficult to come by.

Imagine a world where there was no money and the only way you could get anything was to simply ask for it and it would be given to you. You feel hungry and you think of your favorite meal. You push a few buttons on a device in your home and the meal appears within minutes. You see a new outfit in a magazine and you push a few buttons on a device and the outfit is delivered right to you. You see a destination on your planet and with a push of a few buttons on a device, your trip is all arranged for you. Anything you think of in this utopia is delivered right to you.

This is not some distant future; this is now. You can do all of these things and more right from your computer. But you don't. Why not? It's because you believe you must have money first. This is a flawed premise.

It is only in how you approach the subject of money that makes money harder to attract than is necessary. You must change the way you think about money. Don't think of it as a thing, think of it as a universal force like gravity or time. Think of it as a construct of this physical experience, because that's exactly what it is. Money, time, and space do not exist in the nonphysical realm. These are all aspects of this specific physical reality.

Think of money differently in this time in your society's history. Money has never been so abundant. There are so many who experience so much abundance. In the near future, money will be phased out. Money is evolving from a limited supply of something of great value to an unlimited supply of something with little value. Think about that. That is the evolution of this aspect of physical reality.

In the early days of your society, time and space were perceived as abundant, but money was a precious commodity. Most people had all the time in the world. Time moved very slowly. They also experienced an abundance of space. The world seemed very large. They could travel only very short distances. They knew very little of other parts of their land. They spent time listening to stories of far-off places. They had almost no money and survived on very little.

Today you are experiencing a perceived lack of time and space. Your days are moving by so quickly and your world is shrinking, but you enjoy more wealth than ever before. You live lives of opulence and grandeur that ancient kings would envy. You have technology that allows for the exploration of your interests in great detail. You have more freedom than ever before. But you find yourselves running out of time and space.

As your vibration is raised, everything moves faster. You can sit at your computer and a meal will be delivered to you within minutes. What once took hours to prepare now takes very little of your own time. You just traded money for time. It's convenient. Money buys you more time. You see an article of clothing you admire and purchase it right from your computer. What would have taken time and great expense to fabricate yourself now takes just the click of a few buttons on your computer. In a matter of days, it's delivered right to your doorstep.

So what's the problem? Oh, you say you can't have everything you want instantly? That is a problem indeed. You poor people. Yes, there is sarcasm in the nonphysical as well.

You birth a desire and you notice it doesn't come. That is the extent of your problem. You then blame this awful situation on a lack of money. If you had money, you would have this thing. Yet the money was only one way the thing could come to you. Since you believe you don't have money (which is not true), you don't allow this thing you want to be given to you.

Now let's go back to this utopia where there is no money and you get everything you want. You have a device and whatever you want is entered into the machine and, depending on what it is, it comes in moments or days. Little things come quickly and bigger things come in a few days. You get whatever you want, whenever you want it. You only have to wait a little while for it to be delivered.

You have lived this way your entire life, so you come to expect that whatever you want always comes. It is a natural aspect of this utopian environment. You don't know how it comes, just like you don't really know how the electricity or water comes. You assume there's some sort of facility that produces power and water and delivers it to you, but you have no idea how all of that works. Similarly, you don't really know how all of this stuff you ordered is produced and delivered to you. You just accept that someone's making it happen.

So you live your life contently and when you birth a desire, you enter a few keystrokes into your device and in a little while it comes to you. You order it and expect it to come. You don't find any reason that it will not come, so it always just comes. You are not worried about it not coming in the future, so you do not hoard stuff. You just allow your desires to present themselves and you enter your desire into your device.

This is exactly how it works in this reality today. You, however, limit what comes to you based on how much money you currently have. That makes no sense at all. Money comes when it's needed unless you believe it's not going to come. When you worry about money, you stop the flow. Worrying and complaining turns off the spigot. Money isn't even the best way for you to get what you want anyway. It's simply one of the many ways the universe can bring you where you want to go.

Everything you desire is a feeling. You believe you will feel a certain way in the experience of what is desired. You want adventure, so you travel to some exotic location. You want fun, so you go to an amusement park. You want drama, so you engage in gossip. You want luxury, so you buy expensive bedding. You want to feel appreciated, so you buy your spouse a gift. It is the feeling that you are looking for. Sometimes money allows you to buy the feeling and sometimes it doesn't.

Think of the feeling you are wanting and realize that there are many ways to receive that feeling. This is a feeling reality. What you feel is important. You want to feel good. You want to feel excited. You want to feel fun. You want to feel sexy. You want to feel courageous. You want to feel respected and admired. You want to feel love and appreciation. You want to feel happiness and joy. You simply want to feel. Sometimes money makes it easier to feel these things. Sometimes it is useless.

II.

Money itself is not very powerful. Money is really a crutch. It just seems like things would be better with more money, but that's not always the case. You can't see very far up the road from where you are now standing. You believe that this aspect of physical reality makes life better. You assume it would make life easier and more secure. But it has nothing to do with the money. It has only to do with you and the vibration you are offering.

Your vibration is the only thing that matters. If you are vibrating within a frequency range that aligns with what you truly desire, money may flow in so that you can be given what you've asked for. But other things may flow instead of money. If you wanted to experience something, you might be introduced to someone who can give you that experience. If you desire a physical object, someone may give you that thing you desire. The universe is open to the path of least resistance. Sometimes money is not necessary. Sometimes it gets in the way. If you believe that money is the only means by which something can come to you, then you've limited what can come. In fact, if you believe that money is needed to bring you the feeling you're looking for, and you don't have enough money, you block it from coming.

Realize that money is just one avenue of manifestation. It is the one that really gets in your way because it is so abundant. If you lived a life where there was no money, then the only way something could come to you would be from the hands of another. This is how it would work in a society without money. You would expect it to come and you would not know who was going to bring it to you, but that would not matter. You would be open to all avenues. You would not stop it from coming because you would not have a reason to doubt its delivery. You use lack of money to create doubt and therefore you stop attracting what you want. Money is just your excuse.

So what's the best approach to money? Money doesn't matter. This might be hard for you to conceptualize, as you've been living in an environment that seems based on money. Money intrudes into every aspect of your life. Money is the number-one thing you're thinking about on any given day. Yet, it is not really money you are considering, but always the lack of money.

Living as opulently as you are, living as abundantly as you are, you are constantly engaged in this observation of lack. You are not alone. There are few people who are primarily focused on abundance. You see them every once in a while. They're the ones in those yachts and mansions and private airplanes. They are not thinking about lack. They know that all the money they need is available. They don't worry about it too much. They seek more of it not because they're experiencing lack, but because they have created an environment around money that continues to build momentum. Momentum demands they receive more.

Momentum is the key to money and to everything else you want. Momentum moves slowly at first and then speeds up as it gets going. Imagine your car has run out of gas. You and a friend struggle to push it, as it is motionless. But as you get it moving, you find that it gets easier and easier to keep it going. Pretty soon you're jogging behind it as you make your way to the gas station.

While you're pushing your car that's run out of gas, you'll notice that it becomes a bit harder as you approach a small hill. You have to really push to keep it going up that hill. But once you've reached the top of the hill, your job becomes easier as you go down the other side. In fact, when you're on the downward slope of the hill, it's all you can do to keep up with it.

This is how money works as well. At first it may take some effort, but once it gets going, it's fairly easy to maintain the flow. Once in a while, as the money is flowing and momentum is continuing to maintain the flow, you'll reach a small hill and will have to work a little harder to keep the momentum going. But once you've reached the top of that particular hill, you'll notice how it becomes so much easier and the flow of money becomes faster. In these times, it might even become a little scary as the momentum moves faster than what is comfortable.

III.

The trick to money is not thinking about the it and allowing momentum to maintain the flow once you get it going. So, if you are not supposed to think about money, what are you supposed to do? Follow your interests, become consumed with your passions, don't worry about money, and the money will flow as it's needed to support your passion.

The chef who opens his own restaurant has an approach to his business that is much different than that of the millionaire who opens a restaurant. Let's see how their approaches differ.

The culmination of the chef's dream has been to open his own restaurant. His primary desires are for freedom and acknowledgment. He wants to do things his way. He wants to show the world his talents. He believes that his passion for cooking should be shared with the world. He has been constrained by the demands and desires of his former employers. Now he can do things as he feels they should be done. However, being a chef as opposed to a millionaire, he has a tenuous relationship with money.

The chef has either saved money over a long period of time so that he can now open his own restaurant or he has borrowed the money from family members or investors. Either way, he has great concern for the money that will be owed. He considered the costs of building and opening the restaurant. He worries about operating expenses and chooses a location based on its rental amount. He chooses interior furnishings and fixtures that meet the limitations of his budget. He hires employees he feels will mesh with his personality. He chooses products that will allow him to make the best dishes possible, even though they may be very expensive. He is more concerned with the functionality and size of the kitchen than the ambiance of the dining room.

The chef is motivated by factors other than money. He wants the feeling of being in control of his own destiny. He believes he will enjoy the freedom of owning his own restaurant. He wants to cook dishes he loves to cook. He doesn't want to be told what to do. He discounts the operational expertise of his former employers and believes he can do it all himself. Maybe he can.

If the chef is truly passionate about every aspect of his new business, from the paperwork to the decor, he might be vibrationally aligned with success. If he is not worried about losing his investor's money or about his own reputation, he is likely to be quite financially successful. But this approach is like pushing the car uphill. It is more difficult than it needs to be.

Now let's examine the millionaire's approach to opening a restaurant. The millionaire sees this new venture as a puzzle to be put together. Once all the pieces are in place, the puzzle will transform into a money-making machine. The whole idea of the new venture is to make more money. For the millionaire, making money is her passion, not cooking. Every decision revolves around the return on investment. She wants to put money into the creation of the business and earn a return on that investment for years to come. She doesn't primarily care about the quality of the food, the location of the restaurant, the satisfaction of the employees and customers, or her own reputation. She doesn't even care that much about the money that's going in. All she wants to do is assemble the pieces so that the business itself is successful and earns money.

This seems like she's primarily focused on money, which we have just said you should not do. But here's the big distinction. When *you* focus on money, *you* are really focused on the lack of money. When the millionaire is focused on money, she is focused on the abundance side of the discussion. She is focused on creating more money. That's her passion.

If this was your passion, you'd be a millionaire or on your way to becoming a one. But that is not really of interest to most people. You have your own interests and passions. You have your own ideas. You can focus on your idea without worrying about the money, and your focus away from money and onto what you love will allow money to flow as it's needed.

You are influenced by your society to believe that money is the cure for your problems. It never is. Money is the result of passion. Some people are passionate about money and are able to generate it at a very high rate. Some people are passionate about art, or computers, or music, or beauty and these people, when they're not thinking about their lack of money, can generate it just as easily as the millionaires.

If you are passionate about business, if you enjoy risking it all on the chance that your idea will be successful, then that's where you'll be led. But if you're not a risk-taker, if you can't imagine having dozens of employees and lots of investors relying on you, then you need not follow this path to money. Your path to money comes through following the interests and passions that are unique to you and not worrying about the money side of the equation. If you would just have a little faith in the powers of universal forces, you would attract all the money you wanted as it was needed to allow you to continue the pursuit of your passion.

Will you become a millionaire by following your passion? Who cares? The best possible life experience is one in which the individual is happily consumed by something of great interest. The pursuit and immersion into one's passion is bliss. Bliss is the highest form of living. When you find bliss in what interests you, money will flow to you in the amount required to continue that pursuit. It is only when you worry about money that you start climbing that hill. Focus on what interests you and you'll be going downhill more of the time.

IV.

There is abundance and lack and everything in between. You are either moving up the hill toward lack or down the hill toward abundance. When you are primarily focused on something of interest and that interest takes most of your attention, you are more tuned to abundance than lack. In those times when you feel stuck, like nothing is working out as you think it should, you are more focused on lack. Abundance feels fun and exciting, while lack feels depressing and sad.

You feel your way to abundance and you feel your way to lack. Abundance feels good. It feels like success, joy, happiness, fun, excitement, enjoyment, etc. Lack feels like worry, conservation, protection, hoarding, insecurity, fear, etc. This is a feeling environment and you either feel your way toward abundance and prosperity or you feel your way toward lack and loss. You can choose how you feel and what you think. You can choose to observe abundance and feel good or you can choose to observe abundance and feel bad. You determine what anything means.

So what are you constantly saying to yourself? What are the thoughts you are choosing? Are you able to see that everything is working out or are you consumed by worry and fear? Do you bring meaning to the current condition or does the condition make you feel a certain way? It really is up to you.

Those who live in abundance have figured out that it is what they say to themselves that makes the greatest difference. In good times, they praise themselves for their ability to attract abundance. In bad times, they remind themselves that things will improve. They are forward-looking people who are able to keep their thoughts in line with what they truly want. They understand that they create their own reality even if they are unfamiliar with the laws of the universe and the mechanism of physical reality.

Those who are best at attracting abundance use the laws of the universe to their advantage, even if they don't really know how it all works. Their habits of thought have guided them instinctually to their successes. Their perceived failures are often grand, yet they are able to rise again to even greater success. How is this done by so many successful people? It is simply a habit of thought they have stumbled on that causes them to achieve great things.

You are aware of the laws of the universe and you know how all of this really works. You have all the tools you need to create an environment that will lead you to the abundance you seek. If you have not achieved what you desire, it is simply because your old habit of fear-based thinking has created an environment of lack.

We can't really use the word "lack," since you do live an extremely abundant life when compared to the lives of so many others on your planet. You must admit to yourself that you are simply seeking a higher degree of abundance. Your sense of lack comes from observing others who seem to have more. It is your comparison to those you deem more successful that causes any sense of lack. Your comparison is also what keeps you from reaching this new level of abundance you so desire.

If you could live without comparing yourself to those more abundant, you would feel extremely abundant as you now are. Without your attention to the lives of others you perceive to have more, you could only compare yourself with others you perceive to have less. This would make you appreciate what you had and you would feel amazingly abundant.

If you could only observe the lives of those who have less than you, you would feel more abundant and this would feel good as long as you did not feel sorry for the less fortunate. In your abundance you would want others to feel your sense of accomplishment. You would hope for others to achieve your level of success. You would want to inspire others to your heightened level of attraction. You would truly feel abundant, since you would not be observing others who you felt were more abundant.

It is only your comparison that causes you to feel more or less abundant than you really are. It is the observation of what you want that causes you to feel lack. When you see a certain luxury car on the road, you wonder how you could ever own such a car. You might imagine that one day you will be driving that car. You might even think that dream is not really a possibility. But it is only how you think that will cause the dream to manifest or not.

You allow yourself to rise to a certain level of abundance and after that you usually find yourself stuck. You believe you should be doing better than certain people but not as well as others. You expect to live in a certain manner and no less than that is acceptable. But you set the bar. You decide how opulent your life will be. You control every aspect of your life with your own thoughts.

If it was really important to you, you could begin the path to the life of your dreams today. You could begin the manifestation process that would allow you to have that life. If you really, really wanted it, it would come to you. But you don't really want it. You really want what you already have. If you look around at your life and what it's like, it is made of the stuff you really, really want. If something is missing in your life, you don't want it enough to sacrifice what you believe is necessary to sacrifice in order to get it. This is a flawed approach to abundance.

You believe that in order to get what you really want, you must do this and this and this. But you don't really want to do all of that, so you believe you'll never get what you really want. And for the most part, you are right. For this is the process by which almost every human approaches the manifestation process. If you want a good job, you must go to college. If you want a nice house, you must make enough money. If you don't want to do these things in order to get these things, you can't expect to have them. You believe that if you're willing to sacrifice now, you can get the things you want later.

You have seen people who operate this way and sometimes it works. If they put in enough effort, they get what they want. You observe someone efforting their way to what they say they want and in time they get it. Yet the effort only causes the specific manifestation to occur. It only causes what they imagine in their minds to come to life. But, for the most part, this image of what they want isn't really what they want. It's only what they thought would make them feel better. For many people, the accomplishment of the dream doesn't feel the way they thought it would. This is why the manifestation is never really satisfying for very long.

You are focused on abundance and you think that the accumulation of money will solve your problems. You believe that if you could just get a few more dollars, everything would be better. Life would be easier. You wouldn't have to worry. But this flawed approach to money is precisely why you don't feel you have enough money. So we're going to let you in on a little secret. Are you ready?

The security you seek is not in the accumulation of money, it is in understanding and having complete trust in the powers of universal laws and the mechanism of physical reality. Once you learn to trust that you are always provided for as long as you allow it, you'll have nothing to worry about.

You must retrain your brain. You must realize that the illusion of your outer world causes you to react with fear, when nothing can ever harm you. You are secure as you are. Let's see if we can convince you.

First of all, as you look back on your life, you have constantly worried about some sort of lack. But was this lack ever real? Weren't you really always taken care of? Didn't it actually work out? You are now standing here and you have a certain life. Though you may have had more money in the past, you never really stopped worrying, even in those good times. You worried when you had money and when you didn't. But the worrying never helped and really there was nothing to worry about. It all worked out to bring you here.

If you had eliminated the worry in your past, we assure you that you would have enjoyed your life more. The worry never helped and actually it held you back. But that's okay because you're here now and without the worry, who knows where you would be? We just want to emphasize that all the worrying was not necessary. So why not give it up now?

If you can give up worry, you can accept that things are always working out for you. You are the center of your world. This was all designed for you. You are the main attraction in your universe. Everyone else plays a supporting role. You get to decide how it turns out. So why not make the most of it?

There is a simple premise in the Law of Attraction: what you want is given to you. It is the basis of all reality. You create a desire and then allow the manifestation of that desire to enter into your reality. You cannot fight it. It is working out, whether you know it or not. All you can do is interrupt the process with thoughts of doubt, fear, and worry. If you had no doubt, it would come. You can see this in your life now. Whatever is there in your life right now made its way to you because you suspended doubt long enough to allow it to come to you. Most of what you have, you expect to have.

None of what you have came to you out of the blue, even if you think it did. If you were surprised when you got something, it's only because you were unaware of the work you did to allow that thing to come. You talked yourself into an environment of allowing and then it appeared. You did what was necessary to align with the feeling and then it came. This is the process of all manifestation.

There are certain things in your life you just expect. If you believe you deserve a nice car then the car you drive is the best car you think you deserve. It's as simple as that. If you do not believe a nice car is necessary, then what you drive reflects this habit of thought. The same is true about the home you live in, the mate you're with (or not with), and the interests you pursue. If you think you're worthy of more, more will come. If you no longer think you're worthy of what you have, it will go.

Worthiness is a large aspect of physical existence. You are influenced by your society, your family, your friends, your lovers, your peers, your employers and your subordinates. Your relationships with others cause you to form an opinion of your own worthiness. As a child, you were born knowing your undeniable and absolute worthiness. Then your parents informed you that you were not as worthy as you thought. Others reminded you of this as well and by the time you became a teenager, you were convinced that your inadequacies confirmed your unworthiness. The rest of your life was devoted to reclaiming your worthiness. This is what causes you to want much of what you want.

Your desires fall into one of two categories: true desires and false desires. Your true desires spring forth out of your knowing that the desire aligns with who you really are. Your desires for love, fun, happiness, passion, interests, etc. are true desires. When a desire is formed from the pursuit of passion, it is a true desire. False desires spring forth in order to justify your own worthiness.

When you want to prove something to the world, this is a false desire based on your feelings of unworthiness. When you want to become a success to prove others were wrong about you, you are following a false desire. You can achieve a false desire just as you can achieve a true desire. The only difference is that the false desire will not be satisfying when it manifests. If you want something to make you feel more worthy, then this is a false desire, because you are already worthy.

Many people who desire money do so to prove their worthiness. If you felt worthy, you would not need to prove it by displaying wealth. You would not need to justify your existence with money or success. You might become wealthy, but this would not ease your insecurities. You would have all this success, yet the one thing you really wanted was to know your own worthiness and your successes did nothing to improve your own sense of worthiness. It was a false desire.

True desires arise from your awareness and understanding of your own worthiness. You are as worthy as anyone who has ever or will ever exist. There is no difference in worthiness among you. You are all equally worthy. So trying to prove it by manifesting a false desire does nothing. You are already worthy and your work is to recognize that fact.

True desires come out of passion and interest. The side effect of following one's passion is abundance, happiness, bliss, security, harmony, appreciation, etc. What you really want is to be found in the pursuit of passionate interests. Fascination will lead you to everything you really want. That is the key.

If you desire wealth because it is part of something you're passionate about, then wealth will come and you will feel great satisfaction. If, however, you believe the accumulation of money will make you feel a certain way, if you think it will relieve feelings of uneasiness or insecurity, you are following a false desire and your feelings will not be eased.

You already know whether money itself is something you're passionate about. If money is your passion, you already understand that money is energy and you love manipulating that energy. You know how money works and you find yourself involved with money out of fascination. Accumulating money does not make you feel more worthy; you simply enjoy the dynamic aspects of it.

If you are not passionate about money, you must drop the subject and find your true passions. If money was not part of this discussion, if you didn't believe you needed money, what would you want to do with your time? What is your fascination? What are you curious about? What do you really love to do more than anything else? Why are you not doing that right now?

V.

There are many things you can be naturally passionate about in this physical reality. There are many possibilities for exploration. Money is only one of them. It happens to be a prominent aspect of your society at this time and it is easy to be influenced by others to think that the pursuit of money as a passion is respectable. Your parents may want you to enter into a profession that will allow for the accumulation of money. They see only certain routes to the attraction of money and they want you to follow these paths. They may want you to become a doctor, or a lawyer, or a businessman, because they think that this will insure your accumulation of wealth and security. But it has nothing to do with it.

You came here to explore certain aspects of physical reality and this you cannot deny. You will be naturally drawn to certain subjects. If these subjects align with what society judges as good, then you will have an easier time of it. However, if you are drawn to something your society judges as wrong, or strange, or unsafe, or not respected, you will have to pursue your passions in opposition to their desires. You might be influenced toward another path, but you cannot deny what it is that fascinates you. Your pursuit of anything else will lead to the creation of many false desires.

If you have an interest but don't think you can earn money in the pursuit of your fascination, then you will struggle down a path of regret. You cannot pretend to be interested in something just because there is a way to make money. If money is not your passion, you will endure hardship and sacrifice that is not necessary.

A radical approach to money is to realize that it is always the side effect of your true passion. When you are involved in doing something you truly love, the Law of Attraction will bring you all the money you need to support that passion. This is how money works. When you feel the lack of money in your life, physical reality will reinforce those feelings. When you are not thinking about the money, it will flow in exactly as you need it to. When you take your mind off the money, you allow it to come. By being completely absorbed in what you're doing, you don't have time to worry about money and you create an environment of allowing so that the money comes to you.

Everyone takes one of two approaches to money. They either feel that there is a lack of money in their life or they feel that there is an abundance of it. The poor person thinks of lack, while the rich person thinks of abundance. The pauper doesn't know where the money will come from and the millionaire knows that it could come from any number of sources.

Money is energy. You don't really know where energy comes from. If you think of electricity as energy, you believe that it comes from a power plant or a battery. If you think of sunlight as energy, you know it comes from the sun. But if you think of life force as energy, you probably don't really understand where it comes from. There are many sources of energy and they are flowing to you to provide you with all the energy you need.

Most of you feel energized and do not consider where the energy is coming from. This is your natural state. It's only when you feel a lack of energy, such as when you are ill or tired, that you question the source of energy.

The same is true of money. Money is another form of energy and it can come from many various sources. However, when you start to define the source of money, you actually remove all the other sources. When you believe that money can only come to you through a paycheck, you limit the natural flow of money. When you believe that money can only come as a result of effort, you limit the flow of money. It is always you who limits what is unlimited. You do it through your thoughts and beliefs. Alter your beliefs and you increase the flow of money. Change the way you think and you create an environment of allowing.

A radical change to your approach to money is created by altering your perspective on the subject. Unless it's your passion, remove your attention from it. Understand that you will naturally attract money by removing your attention from it, because unless money is your passion, your attention to it is based in lack. Removing your attention removes the lack and allows the money to flow.

The best way to remove your attention from money is to follow your true passions. When you are absorbed in doing what you love, you create an environment where money must flow to support your passion. Don't worry that the flow is not enough or that it will cease; simply focus on what you love and know that the money must come as you need it. If you want more money to come, you must increase the size of your passion. As you get more involved in your passion, the flow of money must grow as well.

You may see examples of individuals who have followed their passions and attained great wealth. For most of these people, it was not money at the heart of their interests, it was just that the money followed as they pursued their true passions. As those passions became bigger and they explored their passions more fully, the money increased as well. But it was not the accumulation of wealth they were interested in, it was whatever their passion was at the time. The wealth was simply a natural side effect.

VI.

You are a determined people living in your fast-paced, modern society. You have created many desires and you have also created preferences. This is the game of life. You are here to create and seek that which is preferred. But you also have a cognitive brain that helps you plan out your path to your desire or away from what is unwanted. You are going about all this in a way that is inefficient. It is due to your limited perspective and your lack of trust in the laws of the universe. Your old approach to life has become a habit and now you must adopt a new approach to manifesting your desires.

You want something, so you try to explain to yourself and to others how you will achieve your goal. You plan it out and then take action. You can see what it is you want. You think it will make you feel better when you get it. Until then, you choose not to feel good. It is this thing that you want that will make you feel good. You are used to observing the conditions and feeling a certain way based on what you've observed. If the conditions are right, you feel good. If they are wrong, you feel bad. So you'd better create conditions that are right, otherwise you risk feeling bad.

Your reality is simply a reflection of how you predominantly feel. If you are feeling good, conditions will come together to show you examples of your good feelings. If you are in a good mood, people will smile at you. You will enter into nice conversations. People will hold the elevator for you. You'll get the first parking spot.

But you've created the habitual response to what you observe. You react either positively or negatively to the event. You judge it as either right or wrong, good or bad and you believe that money is the easiest way to change the conditions.

If you hate your job, you believe you could start your own business if only you had the money. If you hate your home, you believe you could buy a new home if only you had the money. If only you had the money, you could leave this relationship that you do not like. If only you had the money, things would be better.

This is not how the laws of the universe work. If only gravity were not so strong, I would weigh less. But gravity is a law and there are other laws which you must come to understand and utilize for your benefit. You project a feeling and it manifests into your specific, individual reality. You might never have thought about your feelings before. But this is simply how the universe works.

Money cannot change anything. It is neutral and comes as it is required for the manifestation of what it is you feel. This is neither a good nor a bad thing, it just is. If you are feeling good as you are pursuing your passion, money comes as it is required to fulfill whatever manifestation is part of this feeling energy you are emanating from within. In passion, the feeling is good and you are enjoying yourself, so the money that comes reflects that. Sometimes, as you are pursuing a passion, you encounter a challenge and the money is blocked because you believe you must overcome the challenge. But once you start feeling good again and enjoying yourself, the money begins to flow again.

If you are miserable in a condition, you might be able to generate money so you can alter the condition. But you do so from a negative position and nothing will change. The conditions might appear different, but the feeling remains the same and you will be faced with the exact same issues. They will just be wrapped in a different package. If you are feeling neglected in a relationship, you might leave that one only to feel neglected in the next relationship. You've done nothing to change the feelings, so the conditions remain the same. You might feel powerless in your job, so you borrow money to start a business. You've changed the conditions, but you haven't changed the feeling, so the new business will reflect back on you in a way that makes you feel powerless once again.

In this reality, you cannot escape the way you feel. Your world is always a match to how you're feeling. If you feel bad, physical conditions will present themselves to match how you feel. These conditions may present themselves to you in the form of unwanted bodily conditions or unwanted environmental conditions. Until you change how you feel, you will continue to encounter physical manifestations of these feelings.

Your work is to practice feeling the way you would like to feel and then to watch how the world forms to match those feelings. You want to feel good. You want to be interested, loving, happy, joyous, patient, caring, empathetic, fun, etc. Practice these feelings often. This is your only work. This is all you have to do. Be interested, loving, happy, joyous, patient, caring, empathetic, fun, etc. and observe how these feelings manifest into your personal reality. If money is a part of the manifestation, great. If not, it is not necessary.

You don't need money. Money is just a construct of your present society. In the future, it will not be necessary. It is not necessary now. You simply need to practice the feelings of what you prefer and allow the universe to show you evidence of how you feel. Remove money from your attention and it will come exactly as necessary for you to feel the way you want to feel. Think about what it is you want, not how you'll get there. Money is not the means to what you want, it is simply one of the many tools the universe uses to bring you a physical representation of how you are feeling.

Chapter Fifteen

A Radical New Approach to Action

There are two types of action: inspired and uninspired. There are two states of being: positive and negative. Action is inspired from your state of being. If you are in a positive state of being, such as happiness, action inspired from this stance aligns with what you truly want. When you are in the state of being of rage, action inspired from this stance does not align with what you really want or who you really are.

Your quest is to become who you really are. This is your true desire. It is a process of evolving to higher and higher levels of consciousness. What is right for you may not be right for another. What is right for another may not be right for you. Your only concern is what is right for you. Do not involve or concern yourself with the opinions of others.

When you are inspired to take some action from a place of bliss, the action will always lead to what you truly want. This action has the leverage of the universe and a little action goes a long way. This is also true of inspired action that comes from a state of being you would consider to be negative. Action inspired from a negative stance has tremendous power as well, but this is the power to bring you what you truly do not want. It takes you further from who you really are.

When you are in a rage, you will be inspired to do something you will regret later. This is the natural process of manifestation. When you are angry, you will attract thoughts that are a match to how you feel. You will be inspired to action that matches those thoughts. You will be inspired to fight against something and these actions will have consequences you do not want.

However, you can control your actions. You have the ability to stop and think about what is happening. It's not easy, but with practice it can be done. As you approach higher levels of consciousness, this practice will become easier. Before taking any action, you must analyze your state of being. If you're feeling good, the inspired action aligns with who you really are. If you're feeling bad, the inspired action aligns with who you are not. You can stop and consider another course of action once you realize you're in a negative emotional state of being.

When you are passionate about something and you want more, you will increase your vibrational frequency so that you reach higher-level thoughts. These thoughts have never come to you before because you have never been at this level of vibrational frequency. These are new thoughts. The thoughts inspire you to new action. These actions produce new, more effective results. The result of your actions raises you to an even higher vibration. These are highly leveraged actions that produce unprecedented results.

However, you often do not allow your state of being to raise high enough to bring you new thoughts and inspire you to powerful action. You are doers, not thinkers. You believe you know what action must be taken to produce the results you want. But your limited perspective does not allow you to see what actually must happen for you to receive the results you desire. You try to get there on your own and you take action that is not inspired. These actions may produce some results, but they do not have the leverage of the universe and are therefore meager in and of themselves.

Action taken without the inspiration necessary to leverage universal powers is most often unproductive. This is why many people who have achieved great things went through great struggle to do them. You believe that you must endure pain to experience gain. It is a core belief of your society. You must work hard to get the results you so desire. Yet, this is counter to universal law. It is not this way at all. Let us explain.

As you create a desire, you set forth a motion within the structure of physical reality. At the moment you decide you want something, the path to that desire is plotted and universal forces go to work to create the physical manifestation of that desire. This is a complicated process involving lots of moving parts and precise timing. When you interfere with the natural process needed to bring you where you want to go, you delay the manifestation of your desire. You make it harder for all concerned.

The universe never stops working to bring you what it is you want. You can interfere as much as you like, but know that your interference delays the process of manifestation. When you take uninspired action because you believe this action will lead to the manifestation of your desire, you cause the universe to take a detour. You get in the way of its natural course.

Imagine you want a mate. You have had many relationships in the past and these have forged within you the concept of the perfect mate for you. You need not write it down, for the universe knows exactly what you want and the minute you decide you want this person in your life, the universe starts the manifestation process. By birthing your desire, you engage the mechanism of physical reality. Your perfect person is on their way to you and you are on your way to them. You will rendezvous together at the absolute perfect time.

There's a lot of work that needs to be done prior to your rendezvous. You must be altered in such a way that you are ready for the meeting once it occurs. You need to be transformed from who you are now to the version of you that will be ready to recognize this perfect mate when he or she arrives. If you met this person today, you would not be vibrationally ready and would not understand that this is the one. You wouldn't want to mess this up, would you?

So what do you do in the meantime? You take only inspired action. You take no action until you are inspired to do so. You do not listen to your friends who say you must do this and this and this. You do not listen to your mother who says you should not do this or that. You listen to your inner self, for it will guide you.

Does this suggest you should not date in the meantime? It depends on what you are inspired to do. Maybe you do not date. Maybe you wait for this person. Maybe you do go on a few dates. Maybe an interim relationship will lead you to the person of your dreams. How many people do you know who have met their spouse because they dated their spouse's friend first? It happens all the time.

The only thing you need to do is become aware of your emotional state of being and then only take inspired action from a positive state. You will be inspired to take action from a negative state as well. But this action will lead you away from what you want. If you are feeling lonely, you may be inspired to go to a bar and meet someone new. But the feeling of loneliness is a negative emotional state and the action inspired from this stance will create manifestations of unwanted things. It will stall the process of attracting what you truly want.

You might be feeling good and in a high emotional state of being when a friend asks you to come to a party so you can find the person you're looking for. You must stop and think about this offer before accepting. Are you inspired to go? Does this sound like a great idea? Does it sound like fun? Or are you just going out of desperation? The party might be a step in the manifestation process. Or it might not. You will know by what you feel. If you are excited to go while in a positive emotional state, then this is inspired action and you must go. This party is leading you to your rendezvous.

II.

In your old approach to life, you chose actions based on what you thought was appropriate given your specific set of goals. If you wanted a job, you searched the want ads. If you wanted a mate, you went to places where a mate could be found. If you wanted anything, you planned a course of action. You may even have made a checklist. A lot of the action was not enjoyable, yet you plowed your way through it believing it was necessary to achieve your goals. It was not. In fact, it often took you away from what you wanted or created a situation that brought you what you thought you wanted before you were ready.

The manifestation process is simple. You create a desire and the universe goes to work to bring the manifested version of that desire into your personal reality. The fulfillment of the desire is always more elegant and satisfying than you can imagine. When left alone, without your interference, the universe always brings about your creation in the most pleasing and perfect manner. You just have to get out of your own way.

You are doers. You do not like to sit around and allow things to happen. You want to make things happen. You want to get the ball rolling. You prepare by taking action. When the action fails to produce the results you want, you often continue doing the same things hoping for different results. This never works. So you shift your actions until something does work.

This may seem like success, but you are only comparing it to what was, not what could have been. And often the success comes at the wrong time in the wrong manner. It could have been so much grander had you allowed the universe to work it all out for you. All you have to do is create an environment where the universe can make the changes in you that are necessary to bring you the manifestation of that which you desire.

So what action do you take and when do you take it? This is the key question in the process of creation. If you are not doing something, how are you creating?

All desires stem from a feeling you would like to experience. It is the feeling you want expressed in your personal reality. You want to feel a certain way. The feeling could be love, freedom, success, accomplishment, joy, or any number of other good-feeling feelings. It is the feeling you want. That feeling is what will be manifested in physical reality.

Let's imagine you want to feel attractive. In order to accomplish this, you believe you must get your hair done, buy a new wardrobe, and lose twenty pounds. We will also imagine that you do not have any ulterior motives, such as ending loneliness or leaving a relationship you don't like. You just want to feel good by looking good and being attractive.

The feeling of being attractive has nothing to do with how you judge your own body. It only has to do with the energy or vibration you are emitting. Your judgment of your own body is beside the point. To become attractive, you must feel attractive as you are now and everything will line up to make you more attractive. You do not have to do anything other than feel attractive.

What stalls your progress is your belief that you are not attractive as you are in this moment. If you don't believe you are already attractive, you cannot become more attractive. So the first step is to realize that you are already the person who has what you want. This is the toughest part of your journey because you see yourself lacking that which you desire.

If you want to be attractive, you must understand that you are attractive. If you want to be in love with someone, you must understand that you are already in love with yourself. If you want to be wealthy, you must know that you are already wealthy. If you focus on the lack of what you want, you only attract more lack. This is the trick of manifestation. You must realize you are already that which you want to be and you already have that which you desire.

The universe brings you more of what you already have. If you want something you don't think you already have, you must act as if you already have it so that the universe can bring you more of it. That's all there is to it.

This is such a radical departure from what you have believed your entire life that it will be the most difficult thing for you to comprehend. You must be that which you want in order for what you want to manifest into your reality.

You believe you are attractive to a degree. If you buy new clothes, change your hairstyle, or lose a few pounds, this might make you feel more attractive. If it makes you feel more attractive, you will be more attractive to a degree. That degree is based on your judgment of the success of these cosmetic changes. If you don't feel better in the new clothes, you won't be any more attractive. If you think you need to lose even more weight, you won't feel any more attractive. If you judge your new hairstyle as unflattering, you won't exude the vibration you want. But it never has anything to do with these cosmetic, physical changes. It was always how you felt that created the environment that would allow for the manifestations to occur.

You have the choice to feel good or not. You can control your feelings with practice. The best way to do this is to realize that you create your own reality by the way you feel. Your feelings create an environment where thoughts come to you. You can change your feelings and thereby alter the quality of thought which comes to you. You can feel good or bad. When you feel good, good-feeling thoughts are the natural manifestation of your feelings. When you feel bad, bad-feeling thoughts are the natural manifestations of your feelings. You can change how you feel so that you naturally attract thoughts that feel better.

If you feel good, you will be naturally attractive. If you are having fun, enjoying your life, being in a good mood, appreciating everything around you, being happy, you will be attractive no matter what you look like. If you use the way you look as your excuse to feel bad, you will not be attractive no matter how good looking you are. Nothing else has anything to do with your attractiveness other than the way you feel.

If you want to be rich, you must feel rich. If you feel abundant, you will be shown the physical manifestation of that feeling in your personal reality. If you do things to feel more abundant, you will increase the levels of abundance that will be represented in your personal reality. If you use your lack of money as your excuse to feel bad, you cannot improve. It's as simple as that.

Change your perspective and you release feelings of lack. Focus your attention on what is going well and you raise your vibration. It is your vibration that allows what you want to manifest in your personal reality. Nothing else matters.

If you want something, you must acquiesce to the universe. You must not get in your own way. You do not have to state what it is you want because you could not adequately describe the feeling you want into words if you tried. You describe it with your vibration. Now, how do you change your vibration so that it aligns with what you want? You do nothing until you are inspired to do so.

|||.

In the future, you will be blended with your inner self. When you transition to the nonphysical realm, you will rejoin your inner self. You can rejoin your inner self now and this will allow you to do only the action that is perfectly aligned with your desires. Your inner self can see the road ahead where you cannot. Your inner self has a broader, higher perspective when your own perspective is limited. Your inner self will guide you if you allow the guidance from within.

When you become fully blended with your inner self, you will realize that the thoughts that come to you are communications from your inner self. You will trust that communication fully and do what you are inspired to do at the precise moment. You will not doubt the communication because you will know that everything is done with your personal best interests in mind. Even if the result of the action does not offer immediate results, you will know that the action was a step in the direction of your desires. Mostly inspired action will be incredibly productive and enjoyable.

When something goes the way you think it should, you will feel elation. When action results in something that doesn't seem the way you imagined it, you will know that it is a step in the direction of what is wanted. You will no longer feel frustrated because you will become aware that you cannot see the path to your desire. Anytime something appears to go wrong, you will realize that it is only your limited perspective that creates the illusion of wrongness. You will realize that everything is working out as it should.

With this understanding that you are being guided straight to whatever it is you want, you will end feelings of frustration, disenchantment, failure, and fear. You will be able to maintain your positive emotional state of being and from this stance you will receive the communication from within. But most importantly, you will end the unnecessary and unproductive habit of taking action without the proper inspiration.

You will learn to trust the process. You will understand that the journey to that which you desire is a personal one and that while you cannot see the road ahead, your inner self can. You'll realize that your limited perspective will not allow you to see the path to your desire and you will not seek help from others who claim to know your path. You realize that your path is unique and that no one has ever or will ever travel the same path to your desire. You might seek advice when inspired to do so, but you will ignore unsolicited advice from others, including your parents and peers.

What others may think of the way you travel your path will have no effect on your journey. You will block out their opinions and instead turn inward and listen to the communication from within. When you are inspired to an action, you will do it gleefully. You will not observe the results and judge them; instead you will trust the process and continue to maintain your positive emotional state of being.

So, we return to our question. If you are not inspired to take a particular action, what are you to do? You are to practice feeling good. Everything you want is already known by the universe and you are in the process of rendezvousing with it. Any time action is required, you will be inspired to take it. Until you feel inspiration, don't do anything other than what makes you feel good. You needn't worry that it's not coming, for as long as you're allowing it to come, it's coming. As long as you're not getting in the way, it's making its way to you.

Do nothing? How odd. You're not accustomed to that, are you? You are like a shark who never sleeps, always moving, always doing. Now you must relax and take no action until you feel inspired to. When an idea arrives that sounds interesting or exciting and you want to do it, then do it. This is the action that is part of the process. This is the action that is needed to move you to the next step. No matter the result, if you were inspired to take the action, it was a part of the process and it was the right action.

When you feel the inspiration to act, you are receiving communication from within. You get the idea for the action. Notice how the thought of the action is associated with a feeling. This feeling is the same feeling as the basis of your desire. This is the common base feeling of that desire. This is how you will know that this feeling that comes from this idea that you are inspired to follow matches the feeling of your desire.

As you receive the idea and are inspired to take the action, your mind plays a movie that projects the action into physical form in your mind. You see yourself taking action. You see what you expect is the result of that action. Sometimes what you see in your mind prior to taking action will be the result and sometimes it will not. But the result you see is what inspires you to take the action. When you take the action and it does not turn out as you imagined, you might react to it negatively. You might see the action as a failure because it was different from what you expected. But you must not worry. This result is an integral component of the process. It's just that you cannot see where this is now taking you.

Imagine you want a job. You prepare yourself for the process of attracting the job you want. You do not search the want ads or take uninspired action. You simply maintain a positive emotional state of being, knowing that you will be inspired to take the right action when necessary. The universe knows the perfect job for you. It may not be quite ready for you and you may not be ready for it. A certain timing is key to providing you with this job that matches what you want. So you wait and you maintain your positive attitude.

Suddenly the phone rings and someone tells you of a job that's become available in their company. The idea to act on this information comes to you and you feel the same feelings you hold for the job you really want. You are very excited and set up an interview. As you drive to the interview, you maintain your positive state of being and rehearse the interview in your mind. You see yourself getting the job you want. You meet with those responsible for hiring you and present yourself as an excellent candidate for the position. Everything goes well, but you do not get the job.

If you did not trust that this inspired action would lead to the perfect job, you might feel frustrated or angered by the results of your action. You might question the intentions of the universe. You might believe that this whole Law of Attraction thing is a fantasy. But if you did believe in the laws of the universe, if you did believe in guidance from within, if you were true to who you really are, you would understand that this interview was simply a necessary step in the process. If you had patience and saw the event from the higher perspective, you would understand that everything is working out for you and that this particular job was not the right one. The right job is coming. This was just part of the process.

So you maintain your positive attitude. The next day, the phone rings; the person on the line was given your name by someone you met yesterday. It appears you made an impression on that person and that while he could not hire you, he referred you to someone he knew would have a position that was right for you. This was the only way you could have gotten your perfect job. This was the process and it unfolded elegantly. All you had to do was maintain the proper emotional environment and trust that you were being taken care of by universal forces.

IV.

There are times when you feel you should do something you would rather not. You have created agreements among yourselves and you abide by standards of behavior. Yet it is when you do what you do not want to that you cause more problems than solutions. Forced action does not align with what you truly want.

When you do something based on an agenda but you are not inspired to do it, you cause manifestations to occur that do not support where you want to go. You can and do make things happen. But these things are not going to get you where you want to go, because the timing will be off. You will be moving, but you'll be arriving before you're ready.

We'll go back to the example of finding a mate. You decide you would like to enter into a relationship. The universe already knows what you're looking for and the process is started in that instant. You have had relationships in the past and you've observed the relationships of others. You have synthesized all of this data into the perfect mate for you. However, you are not ready for this person to arrive. Nor is this person ready for you. Things must happen in order for you two to meet. It must be the right time and the right place. If you meet too soon, you won't recognize each other.

There is a timing that will be organized by the universe. You must modify certain beliefs and thought patterns before you can understand that this person is the one for you. You will undergo certain specific changes that will not only allow you to recognize this person, but also to notice their positive aspects right away. This will forge a bond between you that will be strong enough to endure the early hardships of a relationship so that the seed of your love can grow its roots and take hold. Without all the right things done in the right order at the right time, you'll miss your opportunity. Don't worry though, because a new opportunity will begin and the process will start all over.

But why mess it up when you can allow it to happen naturally? Because you're impatient. You want to make it happen rather than allow it to happen. Now that you are aware of your habits of action, you can take a new approach to doing and simply start allowing.

You can't make what you truly want happen; you can only allow it to happen. The desire starts with a feeling. "What would it feel like to...?" "I think it would be fun to..." "I think I would like to feel..." It's always the feeling first. Then the plan is set in motion instantly.

You want to feel what it's like to be in a loving relationship with someone who understands and appreciates you. Wouldn't that be nice? Wouldn't it feel good to have a partner in this life to share everything with and to experience life together? That's why you want what you want. It's always the feeling.

But you don't have that feeling now. That feeling is missing. Once you decide you want that feeling, you think you need to take action for it to materialize in your reality. It will materialize, but you don't have to do anything you don't want to. You only have to do what you are inspired to do. You only have to do the things that are exciting, fun, and interesting. Do you see how this is a perfect system?

The design of physical reality is easy to understand when you look at it as the playground it is. There are universal laws at work regardless of the type of reality you find yourself immersed in. Whether it is nonphysical reality or physical reality, these laws are absolute. This is simply the design and basis of the universe. Once you understand this, you can see how it all works.

For instance: you have a guidance system that's built into your body in the form of emotions. When you experience a positive emotion, such as exhilaration, you know you're on the right track. Your thoughts are in line with what you want. When you feel a negative emotion, such as frustration, you know your thoughts are out of alignment with what you want. You're off track. One emotion feels good and the other feels bad. You are meant to gravitate toward feeling good and away from feeling bad. It is a simple design.

The same is true of action. You must take some action for your desires to manifest. Action is the most powerful tool of creation. When you want to do something, you're taking inspired action that will lead to the manifestation of your desire. When you don't want to do something, you are not taking action because you understand that it will not lead to your desire. The good feeling you have when taking inspired action is your clue that this is what is needed in the process of creation. When you do not want to do something, this is your indication that this action is not part of the creation process.

When you take inspired action, regardless of the result, it is part of the process of creation and is therefore necessary. When you refrain from taking action that you are not inspired to take, you keep the process moving. However, when you take action when not inspired to do so, you create a rift in the process and the universe must work out all of the variables that have changed as a result of the uninspired action. This action has changed the course of events to some degree. It is likely that the action has delayed or changed the process in some way.

Often you do things because you are impatient or you believe you should always be doing something. This results from the unnatural influence of your society. Your beliefs surrounding the attainment of goals must be radically altered. Whenever you do something you would rather not do, you make things harder on yourself than they need to be.

Your impatience leads you to take action that causes manifestations that on the surface may seem like success. Yet if you are not ready for the manifestation, it will not be satisfying. Remember that it is you who has to change in order for the realization of your desire to be fully realized. If you do not change, you can't receive the fullness of that which you want. This is one of the reasons so many successful people feel unfulfilled.

You do not have to do anything you do not want to, even if your peers think you should be doing it. If it doesn't feel right, don't do it. If it doesn't sound fun, interesting, exciting, or fascinating, don't do it. If you are consciously aware of who you're being and where you're going, you can feel whether the action is inspired or uninspired. But in order to be fully aware of the inspiration to take action, you must be conscious. You must release your habit of fear.

V.

Sometimes you will be inspired to take action but will refrain out of a sense of fear. This is a valid reason for not doing something. You should always listen to how you feel. Just understand that if the fear is irrational, you have some work to do on yourself before you can achieve whatever you desire. Fear has the power to keep you from performing inspired action. You can make up stories about any action. However, you must be true to who you really are and think about the logical outcomes.

If you want a mate, you must meet your mate somehow. If you're afraid to meet people, you are going to make it harder on yourself than necessary. If you have this desire yet resist it out of fear, you will cause yourself to experience great pain and suffering. Once you've birthed a desire, you have set in motion a series of events that must unfold. When you resist the desire through fear, you cause inner conflict and stress on the body. You must work to diminish the intensity of limiting beliefs, which will reduce fear.

If you are fearful of action that will bring you what you want, you will be torn in two. On the one hand, you will be inspired to do certain things, yet you will be afraid to do them. If the thing you're inspired to do isn't likely to kill you, then the fear that surrounds it is irrational and you can release your fears and do it anyway. If you make up excuses why you can't perform this action you're inspired to, then it's simply fear that's blocking your path. You need not fear any action in which you feel excitement, interest, or fun. Just do it and see what happens.

In most cases when you take action that is inspired and you move through your fears, you will feel exhilaration. It will be exciting and fun. Even if the action does not turn out as you thought it would, you'll still have the sense that it was worth it. Since you don't know the true implications of your inspired action, you can trust that it was all part of the grand scheme to bring you what you desire.

Fear keeps you from most of the action that comes as inspiration. When you receive an idea, you analyze it and come up with reasons why you cannot proceed. You tend to think about the negative ramifications of your actions. It is all well and good to analyze your actions, for if they are not inspired, they may be forgone. However, when it comes to inspired action, you must move through your fears and take the action at that time.

Inspired action feels different. It feels like something you really want to do. It feels like the action itself will be fun regardless of the outcome. When you are more focused on the action than the result, you know the action is inspired. When you remove your attention from your desired result and instead place it on the action or the process, you can rest assured that the action is part of the plan regardless of the outcome.

We want to emphasize that you cannot really imagine the intended outcome in all situations. This is what gets you stuck. When you have a predetermined notion of the outcome and the results do not match up to your expectations, you immediately fall into victimhood and failure consciousness. However, it is only your limited perspective that creates the illusion of failure.

You cannot fail. There is nothing you have to do. You are on an endless journey of self-discovery and expansion. You are becoming who you really are. Along that journey, you must encounter certain very specific lessons. These will move you to a new level of consciousness. It might seem like a setback, but rather it is a step in the right direction. But until you've reached a certain level of conscious awareness about the process of growth, you will continue to be confused by the results.

Remove your attention from the results and keep it on the process. Be aware of how you feel. Take note of your present state of being and listen to the guidance from within. The most important aspect of taking inspired action is knowing what you want. If you want something because you think it will feel good and you're in a positive emotional state of being, the inspired action will always lead to what you want.

However, if you are trying to change the conditions by taking action, you will not be moving toward what you want. If you want to feel better by removing something unwanted from your life, it simply won't work. The conditions might change and you might be briefly distracted, but you won't relieve the condition you don't like. When you take action to change something you do not like, you cause more of it to enter. The action stirs up the energy. When you are wanting something, this stirring up of energy through action is purposeful and efficient. When taking action to alter a condition, the action creates more of the same condition.

If you hate your job and want a new one, you will encounter all kinds of coincidences. You will see ads for other jobs. You will hear about other opportunities. You will see signs pointing you to a new job. It will feel a little like inspiration or divine intervention. But when you are trying to find a new job because you hate your current job, you will simply move to new conditions that emphasize the aspect you did not like about your old job.

This is an attraction-based reality. You can't move away from what you don't want, only toward what you do want. When you are trying to stop something from coming to you, you attract it. You attract everything wanted and unwanted by your attention to it. If you feel lack, you'll attract more lack. If you feel good, you'll attract more physical representations of that good feeling.

You can want a new job because you hate your old job. This is a valid desire in the eyes of the universe. It is as valid to the universe as any other desire. And the universe will deliver to you that new job you want. But the universe also knows that there was an aspect of your old job that you paid a lot of attention to. This is the aspect of that job that you hated. The universe only knows that you thought a lot about this aspect of the job and it believes that you must really like it otherwise you would not think about it so much. So the universe makes sure this aspect is an even larger part of the new job. See how simple all this is?

The universe will line you up with the job it believes is perfect for you based on what you are thinking about most. If you are thinking how much you love your co-workers, the universe will find you a job where there are even more co-workers to love. If you hate your boss because he doesn't respect you and this is what you've been wanting to get away from, the universe will find you a new job with a boss who makes you feel even more disrespected.

You will be inspired to take action when you want a new job because you hate your current job. The inspiration will feel like something you want to do. The action will result in a new job. But the conditions of the new job will be the same as the old job, just more intense. So before you take action, you must understand whether the action is leading you to something you want or away from something you don't want. You need to know the motivation behind the action. You must be aware of the stance you are taking, either toward what you truly want or away from what you do not want.

Many people will birth a desire to get some new conditions because they hate their current conditions. When they get what they want and they find that the conditions haven't really changed, they become confused. This is especially true of those of you who are becoming conscious. When you are new to the journey to discovering who you really are and you learn that you create your own reality, you see that you keep creating the same things you don't want.

You then become confused and wonder why it's not working out as you planned. This is simply because you are not trying to create something you truly want, but are trying to change the conditions you don't like. Place your attention on what is wanted without condemning what is and you will slowly move in that direction. Before any real change can occur, you must make peace with what is. If things never changed, you would accept the conditions as they are and appreciate them in their current state.

Your habit is to try to change the conditions and this is a very hard habit to break. Before taking any action, even if it is inspired, you must accept the conditions that surround you; only then can you focus on what you really want.

You may not even know what you really want. You have been so busy trying to change the conditions that you haven't really thought about what it is you truly want. You've been focused on what you don't want for so long that you've lost any notion of what you wanted in the first place.

If you feel bad, you want to feel good. You see the conditions that surround you and think, "If only I could remove this from my current situation, then I'd feel better." So you blame this aspect of your current situation and remove it. You might feel a sense of relief for a little while, but then your habit of thought will manifest something just like it into your experience. You've been thinking about this thing you don't want for so long that it has to re-enter your experience in a new form. That's just the mechanism of physical reality at work. It works every time.

When you radically change your approach to life, you start appreciating what is, thanking everything for being there, and then you focus on what you really want. You don't want something so that you remove yourself from the condition, you want it because you want to explore a new feeling.

You can't want money so that you can get away from the feeling of poverty or lack. You have to love how things are now, even if you consider your conditions horrendous. Until you appreciate the current conditions, you can't really discover what it is you want. And if you don't know what you truly want, you can't change the current conditions.

If this is the case for you, then a little action can stir things up and allow you to clarify what you really want. When you first start dating as a teenager, you don't really know what you want in a mate. So you date many people and as a result of these relationships - some good, others bad - you learn what you really want. Now you can move forward and seek what is wanted. You have gained clarity from your past relationships. Since you are not seeking to remove yourself from anything unwanted and you're in a positive emotional state of being, the inspiration to act will lead you to your next mate, who will represent everything you think you want at this point in time.

If you're not sure what you want, you must take action to explore various new possibilities. It is from this fearless exploration that you will discover what it is you want. The action may result in what looks like failure, but pay attention to what you were feeling when you were involved in the action. This is the only important factor. The result doesn't matter, it's the feeling you had while participating in the action. Did the action feel good? Did you enjoy yourself? Was it fun? Was it interesting? Was it exhilarating? If so, you're onto something. Don't judge the result. Don't give up it if doesn't work out the first time (or the tenth time, or the hundredth). Don't give up if you're not the best. If the action was enjoyable, you'll improve.

Many people will do something they find enjoyable and start comparing themselves to others. If they feel they are not as good as the others, they will quit out of a fear of failure or embarrassment. Don't worry about this. You can't fail when the action is fun. If you like what you're doing, it will lead to more good feelings. This is what you're looking for. This is your path. The feeling you're receiving from the action you're taking is your indication of alignment. If it feels good, it's worth pursuing.

The same is true of action you do not enjoy. Something may look like fun, such as sailing. But once you get out there, you may not enjoy it. It seemed like fun from the shore, but now that you're immersed in it, you know it's not for you. You tried it and you just don't like it, regardless of its popularity among your peers. Now you can move on to whatever truly interests you.

VI.

There is a distinction to be made between motivation and inspiration. Inspiration calls you to take action that is enjoyable and that will lead to that which you desire. Motivation causes you to take action that is not enjoyable in an attempt to create a certain result. Can you see how inspiration works perfectly within the laws of the universe and the mechanism of physical reality while motivation is counter to those laws?

We agree that action will create manifestation. But action without inspiration does not leverage the power of universal forces. Uninspired action is also likely to cause manifestations that do not quite align with what you really want. And action without inspiration is just not as much fun.

Your procedure of creating goals that are then used to motivate action doesn't always get you what you really want. While you can achieve any goal, if the action needed to attain the goal is a struggle or is painful, then what's the point of pursuing the goal in the first place?

Here's how we would approach a goal. We would start with the feeling we think would be nice to experience in physical reality. We would then make sure that whatever action we take would be fun, interesting, and enjoyable. The action would be more important than the goal. If we weren't having any fun in the action, we would alter the goal. We would also be very general about the goal itself and wouldn't stick to any specific time period. Our goals would be loose by your standards.

Let's say you had a goal to lose ten pounds by summer. You wanted to fit into a flattering swimsuit you could wear to the beach and feel attractive in. So you decide you will eat healthier than normal and exercise more than usual over the next few weeks. This is the start of a goal that could work very nicely. However, the action side of it must be fun, interesting, and enjoyable.

You decide to make a chart that chronicles all the meals you eat and the exercise you perform each day of the week. This may or may not work depending on your approach. It will work as long as you keep your vibration as high as possible throughout the process. The feeling you are seeking is feeling attractive. You must believe that you are already attractive and that it will be fun to push this feeling a little further. So, since you already feel attractive, the attainment of this goal is not such a big subject. You can have fun with it.

You decide that you will run three miles each day. The first day you run, you remember how much you hate running. It doesn't feel good. It's painful. When you're running, you can't wait for it to be over. This is a sign that running is not the way to achieve your goal. You feel bad while running. In order to use running to achieve your goal, you must enjoy the overall action of running. If not, scrap it and move on to something you do enjoy.

You think you will enjoy swimming, so you find a pool and go swimming. You do enjoy this activity and as long as the pool isn't too crowded, you really like swimming. So you pencil this in as one of the exercises you will do over the next few weeks. You also try biking, hiking, walking, and a few other sports that you add into the mix. You have now assembled a variety of actions that are enjoyable and align perfectly with your goal.

The minute you begin to feel dread at the thought of performing one of these exercises, you must put it on hold until you're inspired to pick it up at a later date. You must not do anything you don't want to in the attainment of a goal. This is always counter-productive to what you really want. You must enjoy what you're doing. Do not do anything you don't like simply for the sake of the goal.

The other side of this goal is the food you will eat during the next few weeks before summer. You decide that you will keep a log in which you will detail every item of food that you eat. Will this work? Maybe it will and maybe it won't. It depends on your approach.

You decide to modify your diet so that you will lose one pound each week for the next ten weeks. You believe that the exercise will greatly help and you're not too concerned about your diet. So you decide to eliminate red meat for the next few weeks. Everything else will remain the same. As you fill in your food log, you feel happy with whatever you have written, since you haven't eaten any red meat. However, on the fourth day you realize that you had spaghetti bolognese and that it contained some red meat. Now you feel bad that you've gone off your diet and you attempt to rectify the situation by punishing yourself. You remove dessert from your approved item list for the next five days to make up for your error.

Do you see the flaw here? When you feel bad that you ate the item that was banned from your list, you are receiving an indication that you are going off track. Your plan is no longer fun. The bad feeling is telling you to lighten up. It was no big deal. When you punish yourself for your transgression, you ruin the entire purpose of the goal. All goals are designed to make you feel good as a result. But if you feel bad while pursuing the goal, what's the point of it?

The only reason you wanted to feel attractive was that you thought it would feel good. Since feeling good is your goal, you must feel good in the attainment of the goal, otherwise why even bother? Do you see the importance here? Do you realize that no matter what you want, you always start with a feeling you would like to feel? You always want the attainment of any goal so that you can experience what it is like to feel good. Why would you think it would be acceptable to feel bad in the pursuit of feeling good? This makes no sense.

Any time you begin to feel bad in the attainment of any goal, stop and think about what's happening. Take a breath and analyze the situation. Realize that all you want to do is feel good and that the action needed to attain the goal is only something to do on your way to feeling good. So make sure you feel good along the way.

You might be thinking that this is all too basic. You want to save $100 a week so that in three years you can buy a house. You think that owning a house will make you feel good. But if you have to suffer in order to save that $100, what's the point? You must come to understand that if you cannot get to your goal while simultaneously feeling good, you must reimagine your goal. You must make the path to the goal as fun as or even more fun than the attainment of the goal itself.

Now, having said all that, you can make the path to the goal fun, interesting, and enjoyable if you decide that it is important to do so. You can make anything fun, enjoyable, and interesting. You only need to want it and to think about it.

Let's return to the goal to lose ten pounds by summer. The goal is a good one because it's general and aligns with a wanted feeling rather than an escape from an unwanted condition. You've discovered ways to exercise that are enjoyable. But now you've created an arbitrary rule that you cannot stick to and when broken, you cause yourself to suffer. So, how could you redefine your diet in order to achieve your goal? It's very simple: make it fun, interesting, and enjoyable.

This is rather easy to do, but it does take some thought. For you to achieve your goal, you must eat food that aligns with your existing set of beliefs. You don't believe you can achieve your goal eating hamburgers and chocolate ice cream. You believe that pizza and fries will cause you to gain weight. So you establish a cuisine based on your preexisting beliefs. You believe that fried foods, red meat, and desserts will not conform to your idea of a healthy, low-fat diet. But you also realize that if you eliminate them from your diet, you'll break your own rules and you'll feel bad in doing so.

Whatever you do, it must be fun, interesting, and enjoyable. You hatch a perfect plan. You decide that over the next ten weeks you'll explore the cuisines of the world and you'll do so in a way that is healthy. Each day of the week will represent a region of the world. You'll explore new recipes. You'll pay attention to the cooking process. You'll look for unique and fresh ingredients. The idea is to keep it fun and interesting every day. As long as you're inspired and having fun, you'll reach your goal easily.

Now let's take a look at the way most people approach the same goal. They want to lose ten pounds because they feel fat and unattractive and they believe that the attainment of this goal will help them escape the present conditions they do not like. Their desire is to move away from the unwanted. This approach just doesn't work. Their goal is flawed from the beginning.

However, not understanding this, they press on. They do not consider that the action must be enjoyable for the goal to manifest in a way that will cause lasting change. They take the action they believe will produce the best results. So they run and run and run, and nothing ever changes. They starve themselves and while they might lose the weight, it comes right back and they're perplexed. Then they beat themselves up even more and the problem simply escalates.

What's worse is that they announce their goal to the world and when nothing changes they receive negative feedback from the world around them. "Why haven't you been able to lose the weight?" they ask. "You must have some sort of problem." "What's wrong with you?"

You say you have this goal and you can't achieve it, so the problem must have something to do with you. Maybe you're not working hard enough. Maybe you have a thyroid condition.

The only problem is that you've chosen a goal you believe will remove you from an unwanted condition. Turn the goal around and start heading in the direction of what is wanted. Make the action enjoyable, fun, and interesting. Don't be specific regarding the outcome; be general. And don't ever tell anyone else about your goals.

Chapter Sixteen

A Radical Change to Your Perception of Change

Everything is in a constant, continual state of change. Nothing stays the same. Everything is evolving, expanding, moving, forming, becoming. Every blade of grass and every person on the planet and even every single grain of sand is in a state of change. Since there is no wrong anywhere in the universe, all change is good. Your perception of a consistent environment is an illusion.

You are here to change, to transform, to expand, to be more. Your vibration rises as you experience life. Change is what you want and it's what you intended before you came to this physical reality. You wanted to experience and to expand as a result of that experience. You did not want to remain the same and you knew that this was not possible anyway.

Everything in this book has led to this final chapter. This book is about change and here's the bombshell: we are going to teach you how you can radically change. The more you change, the more you expand. You hold yourselves in a state that is resistant to change, yet you are changing and this resistance does not serve who you really are. There is a way to change that is enjoyable and fulfilling. Let's see if we can explore the subject and alter your perspective.

Everything has a unique vibration and that vibration is constantly changing in ways that may appear subtle. When one vibration interacts with another vibration or action, the result is change. The change itself can be measured and repeated and the results will be relatively consistent. However, every vibration is viewed uniquely by each individual.

Here's a basic explanation of this process. Take the vibration of a cup of water. When you apply cold to the water, you can expect to produce ice. The vibration of water is combined with the vibration or action of cold and the water freezes. This process is consistent and these two vibrations will transform into the new vibration every time. But the specific vibration of that water is always unique because the molecules that formed that cup of water were never combined in that way before. The cup of water was unique and the process of cooling the water so that it froze produced ice that was also unique.

When we take the ice and warm it, it returns to a liquid state. This new state has produced a new vibration and the water is quite different than it was before the process. The vibration of the water once it has gone through the process of freezing and melting is now different. However, you cannot easily observe the difference. This is a little easier to explain with fish. When a fish is fresh, it will taste a little different than after it has been frozen and thawed. The fresh fish has one vibration, the frozen fish has another, and the thawed fish has yet another very different vibration. It is the process of freezing, thawing, and cooking that changes the vibration of the fish.

The process itself is what changes the vibration of anything. The process can be consistently applied to produce very consistent results. You can start with the vibration of something, apply a process in a consistent manner, and expect a consistent result.

When you cook a piece of chicken, you apply a process. When you add salt to the chicken before cooking it, you alter the vibration of the chicken so that it tastes better. The combination of the chicken and the salt produce a new vibration. This new vibration is consistent. However, it is also unique because the chicken is unique and the salt is unique. But it is close enough for you not to notice the difference between one dish and the next. Therefore, you consider the recipe to be the same in vibrational terms.

You can change the vibration of something by combining it with another vibration, by transforming it through a process, or both. When the process and the combinations with other ingredients are similar, you'll produce a new vibration that appears to be what you would expect. You can combine water, flour, and yeast to make a dough. The process you use will determine what kind of dough you will create. However, you might make pizza dough many times, but each dough will be unique. You might form the dough into a round shape, add toppings, and apply heat, and your result will meet your expectations. But no two pizzas are ever the same.

Change is made to any vibration by adding another vibration and going through a process. The results will produce a vibration that can be expected but one that is always unique.

II.

Now, how does this concept of change apply to you? You are a vibration in this moment. Your vibration changes slightly from moment to moment. What causes the change? Everything. In one moment you are a certain age, and in the next moment you are older. In one moment you are thinking a certain thought, and in the next moment you are thinking a different thought. In one moment you are here, and in the next moment you're over there. In one moment you are alone, and in the next moment you're with others. Your vibration changes with every moment.

You have a set of beliefs that have been formed as you have lived your life. Each experience transforms your beliefs. You have limiting beliefs and you have beneficial ones. Your beliefs create the illusion of constancy. Your world is projected onto the screen of physical reality based on your specific set of beliefs. This tends to reinforce those beliefs and causes you to believe in the illusion that everything stays the same.

You will accept that things do change over time, but you believe that change is a rather slow process and that for the most part things really do remain unchanged. You walk down your street and the houses all look the same as they did yesterday. Once in a while a house is painted or a tree is cut down. You believe that this constant, unchanging state of your life produces security. It does not.

Why are you resistant to change? Why do you fear change? It has a lot to do with your survival instinct which, tells you that if you're alive now, you're doing something right. Don't change course and don't rock the boat.

When you think about change, you can think of it in one of two ways: will you feel better after the change, or will you feel worse? The answer depends on your point of view and your current set of beliefs. Beliefs are at the heart of your acceptance of or resistance to change. Having learned this fact, the process needed to create change is experience. Experience always alters perspective and a change in perspective automatically causes a change in belief.

In order to change water into ice, you apply the process of freezing. The cooling process will produce measurable and reliable changes in the vibration of water. The result is the expectation of ice. To change a belief, you must simply apply a process of experience that will alter your perspective and thus change your belief.

When someone enters the army and goes through basic training, it's their beliefs that are transformed. A soldier is a set of standardized beliefs, not a standardized body. In order to perform in a way that is effective, the raw person with their random set of beliefs is transformed, through experience, into a soldier with a completely new set of beliefs. The process is applied in a uniform manner and consistent results can be expected. Yet the resulting soldier is still quite unique.

The soldier could be transformed back into a member of society by going through a new training process if this was important to the military. However, the military is focused on its mission and therefore is unable to apply another process that would allow the soldier to more easily return to society. Even if there was a training program that transformed the soldier back into a citizen, the process would result in a different person from the one that was there prior to entering the military.

Experience changes perspective and that new perspective automatically alters previously held beliefs.

If you have ever heard a story in which a man goes through a near-death experience, then you are aware of the process of change. Prior to the experience, the man had a certain set of beliefs. The experience shifted his perspective on life itself and thus his beliefs were radically altered, which completely changed his approach to life. His life was one thing prior to the experience and something quite different after. It was the experience that caused a shift in perspective that resulted in the altering of beliefs.

Change your perspective and you automatically change your beliefs. Change your beliefs and you automatically change your experience of life.

III.

The previous section implies that all one has to do to change is have experiences. This is absolutely true. Have an experience and you will alter your perspective and thus your beliefs will be changed. However, most of your experiences fall in line with your current set of beliefs and they only alter your beliefs in a way that makes them even more rigid. This is due to the Law of Attraction.

So, does one change by having experiences that are not in line with their belief system? Sometimes they do change and sometimes they do not. It all depends on their ability to view the experience from a new perspective. This is the purpose of manifestation events. Let us explain further.

You birth a desire, yet the manifestation of that desire is not in your reality. You currently hold a set of beliefs that is in opposition to your desire. If you believed that you could have what you wanted, it would manifest immediately. So, in this sense, the universe must alter your set of beliefs in such a way that you will allow what you want to enter your reality.

This first step is to provide you with an experience that will alter your perspective in such a way that your beliefs will change. As soon as your beliefs have changed enough, what you want will enter your reality. Until your beliefs change, however, you will keep yourself from getting what you want. You allow what you want to come to you by keeping your beliefs malleable. You resist what you want by maintaining a rigid set of beliefs.

When you are faced with an experience that is meant to alter your perspective, you have two choices. You can see the event for what it is and receive its lesson or message, or you can resist the event and hold firm to your beliefs. If you accept that the experience is there for your personal growth and are able to see the new perspective, your beliefs will be altered in such a manner that you'll be ready for the next step, which will be another experiential event. The universe will guide you step by step through experiences to mold your set of beliefs so that you'll be able to recognize your desire when it arrives.

If you resist the events as they happen and do not allow yourself to see beyond what seems to be happening, you'll cause yourself to suffer needlessly. You'll take the experiences as random events that sometimes cause you pain. You'll see yourself as a victim. You'll believe that things are happening to you rather than for you. You will not enjoy the process of change. You will become frustrated and your set of beliefs will hold you bound to your station in life. You will become more solidified and resistant to change.

Why does one fixate on their personal set of beliefs? Why do those who are wrapped so tightly in their ideology resist change to such a degree? What is the benefit of being inflexible? Why do they believe they are right?

Those who stand firm in their beliefs and resist change fear the unknown. They hold their set of beliefs as they might a security blanket. Their beliefs comfort them. They feel safer inside the walls of their belief system. But this is an illusion propagated by the ego. There is no purpose to holding onto limiting beliefs. There is no safety behind beliefs that do not serve who you really are.

You are meant to achieve all that you desire. As soon as a desire is born within you, the universe moves to bring that desire into your physical reality. But you must change to allow the desire to come to you. You must be different. Change is the vehicle that delivers your desire.

If you understand the mechanism of physical reality and the laws of the universe, you can allow these experiential events to change your point of view and thus your beliefs. We call these experiences that change your perspective manifestation events." As soon as you create a desire for something, the universe charts a course of events that will mold your belief system so that you will allow what you want to come to you. The universe does not care what you want. It does not know whether the subject of your desire aligns with who you really are or not. It will bring events that will shape your belief system so that you will be ready to receive whatever it is you want.

You could birth a desire to build a temple or destroy one and the universe would support either desire equally. Your desire is up to you and since there is no wrong anywhere in the universe, all desires are equally valid. It is your work to understand whether the desire you hold aligns with who you really are or not. You must come to understand whether you are seeking something you truly want or whether you only want that thing to escape some condition you do not like.

You could seek to prove that others were wrong about you and become a huge success. However, this desire to prove your worthiness is a desire that has been influenced by the people around you. It is not a true desire. You have wanted desperately to become successful so you could prove your worthiness, but your success does nothing to change the opinions of others who may have viewed you as unworthy. When you discover this, you feel even more unworthy. When you realize that all this energy and effort spent pursuing a false desire produced nothing but dissatisfaction, you must rethink your entire approach to life.

Imagine you lived in a tiny village with your extended family. One day someone comes along and kills your family. You are left alone. You feel rage that someone has taken something so precious from you and your only desire is to avenge the death of the ones you loved. The universe answers your request immediately and you are set along the path of vengeance. You will now be molded into a completely new person with a wholly new set of beliefs. You will be transformed from the person you were before the death of your family into a new person who is able to seek revenge. It is not the conditions that changed you, it was your desire.

Had you been a conscious person at the time of the death of your family, you might have been able to see the tragedy from another perspective. If you were aware of the laws of the universe, you might have understood that the event happened for certain vibrational reasons that may or may not have had anything to do with you. Had you known that there is no death, only eternal existence, you might have been able to view this from a higher perspective. But unfortunately, you believed that this happened to you and your desire is in line with your current set of beliefs, many of which are based in fear.

Now, this is an extreme example we have created so that you may see how people become that which does not match who they really are. If we are love, why are there so many people who seem to be successfully creating out of fear? Why would somebody become a terrorist if any desire they have could be manifested just as easily? The terrorist could become a peace activist just as easily if that was their desire.

You have been given free will and you may achieve anything you desire. The universe, through the Law of Attraction, answers all calls. However, many do not allow the manifestation of their desires because their beliefs remain rigid.

There are many more who might become terrorists if not for their rigid set of beliefs. Beneficial beliefs (those beliefs that are aligned with who you really are) are even more powerful than limiting beliefs. Those who desire revenge might never be changed enough to actually do any harm. Their beneficial beliefs might hold them in a state of resistance from allowing the change they have asked for. They may desire revenge, yet they believe they are good and cannot harm others, especially innocent people. Since it is unlikely they will ever meet those who killed their family, their only resort is to harm those who had nothing to do with it. This goes against their belief system and they will not change.

Because their beliefs do not change, they will still struggle with conflicting feelings and will still suffer because they cannot allow themselves to receive that which they want. They will not become terrorists, murderers, or anything along those lines. They will have tremendous difficulty for the remainder of their lives as they hold on to this unfulfilled desire. Yet, they will never become that version of themselves that could hurt another innocent person.

So we see from this example that the universe does not care what you want, it only cares that you have focused on something and now you must undergo the change necessary so that the wanted feeling will materialize into your personal reality. If you do not allow the change to occur due to the rigidity of your beliefs, you will not allow your desire to manifest.

IV.

You can only change you. You cannot change the conditions that surround you or another person in the present moment. No matter how hard you try, your reality is simply a reflection of who you're being right now in this moment. If you look in the mirror, the reflection you see will not change until you change. Nothing will move until you move. Your reality is a reflection of you - that's it. You would not look at your reflection and wish it was smiling back at you. You must smile first. You must be who you want to be.

If you want something, you must transform into the version of you who will be that person. Your reality will shift when you alter your being. You become what you want and the conditions surrounding your life will come together in such a way that you will see the results of your change. Change something about yourself and you'll notice a change in your reality. Your reality must support who you are being. If you don't like what's going on in your life, make some sort of change and your new reality will be different.

Don't change the conditions; change yourself.

Let's work through this idea. Let's experiment with some change you could make right now and then we'll see if we can illustrate the result. Let's imagine you feel lonely. You don't have a lot of friends and you don't have a mate right now; you have many acquaintances, but no one is asking you out on Friday night. You want to change so that your reality changes.

You decide you will experiment with a change in who you are being and you will pay attention to what happens. You adopt a new stance of interest in other people. That's all. From now on you are going to find out as much as you can about the people in your life. You are going to become fascinated with those around you. You really don't know much about the people you work with, you don't know anything about the customers you talk to on the phone every day, you don't really know your neighbors, and you haven't talked to your family lately. But now you're going to start to find out more about everyone.

Your interest in others will be subtle. You will ask very general questions and see what answers are given. You won't pry, you'll just be interested. When someone begins a story about themselves, you'll simply listen. You will never talk about yourself unless asked. You will be interested in them.

You have no agenda. This change in your approach to the others in your life is not meant to improve your life. This is simply an experiment. You are being different than you've been before and you want to see what happens as a result.

As you become interested in others and listen to their stories, you find yourself gaining a new perspective on those around you. You find that they are happy to talk to you and they appreciate your interest. They see you in a new light and become interested in you as well. This new perspective alters some of your long-held limiting beliefs. Since your beliefs have been altered, your reality now changes. This is the mechanism of physical reality. You are different, so your reality must reflect the new you.

As a result of your new approach to others in your life, your popularity grows. Suddenly, you are invited to parties and other social events. The people you once considered boring and standoffish are now friendly and interesting. You have introduced something different into your life and this experiment has resulted in a new you. The conditions that surrounded the old you have been replaced by conditions that reflect the new you.

This experiment works in reverse as well. If you are a very social person interested in the lives of those around you, you'll experience a reality that reflects this approach to life. You have lots of friends and you're always on the go, doing something with others. You're involved in their lives and they are involved in yours as well.

Now, if you change who you're being for the sake of an experiment in reality, you'll face a new reality. Let's say you decide to stop talking to all the people in your life just to see what happens. You will not call or communicate with another person unless they call you first. Your new approach will be that if others care about you, they'll continue to call. You're the popular one, you're the interesting one, and they will want to keep in contact with you.

At first, people do call and your reality isn't much different. You talk to those who call and you participate in social events when invited. But you do not call others or invite others to social events. You simply sit by the phone waiting for it to ring.

In a very short amount of time, the phone stops ringing and you develop new, limiting beliefs. You become bitter as you realize you're not as important as you thought you were. You feel betrayed, even though it was you who stopped being who you were. Your reality reflects who you are being now.

You decide that this reality is not one you prefer and you return to the social person you once were. You realize that it is you who must establish a connection. It is you who must create the environment in which you can get what it is you want. It is you who must be the person you want to be and the conditions will reflect it. Be the change you want to see projected onto your reality.

V.

So how do you become the person you want to be if you're not that person now? What steps do you take? How long is the process? Where do you start?

You could be whoever you wanted to be right now in this moment if you let go of who you're being now. This moment is all there is. The change takes place in the moment. But since you are going to hold onto who you think you are, you're going to have to undergo the change you desire gradually. It doesn't have to be this way, but because you're stubborn, it will take some sort of process.

This is the process of manifestation. You will change as quickly or as slowly as you allow the change to occur. Remember, anyone can change instantly and many do change very quickly. It depends on only one thing: the rigidity of your belief system. If you hold on tightly to your limiting beliefs, you will not change. If you are flexible in your beliefs, you can change easily. So, are you personally flexible in your beliefs or not?

This is a question you must ask yourself and you should really look at your answer. If you can drop limiting beliefs easily, you'll change quickly. If you consider what you believe to be true, no matter how limiting the belief, you won't be able to change very much. It's all up to you.

Do you analyze your beliefs or not? If not, why not? Someone who is flexible in their beliefs is constantly thinking about why they believe something and whether that belief is limiting or beneficial. This is how you must approach your beliefs. Beliefs are mostly adopted without much thought. Many of your beliefs have come through the influence of others and you have no experiential proof to support them. You are simply a lazy believer.

It is tremendously helpful to start doubting your limiting beliefs. It is good to be skeptical of any belief that does not support what it is that you want. Conversely, it is extremely beneficial to believe in anything that supports what you want. All beneficial beliefs help you become who you really are.

If a limiting belief is true, don't believe it, for it does not support you. Just because it's true doesn't mean it's true for you. If this belief holds you back, if it keeps you from getting what you truly want, if it does not serve who you really are, then it cannot be true and you do not have to believe it.

If a beneficial belief has no evidence that it is true, it does not matter, for it is always true. If it supports what you truly want, if it makes you feel good, if it keeps you moving toward who you really are, then it is absolutely true regardless of evidence to the contrary.

In order for you to be who you want to be, you will have to adopt a set of beliefs that are different from the beliefs you now hold so dear. You must allow your beliefs to shift. If not, you won't change. Until you adopt the beliefs of the person you want to be, your reality will not reflect the new you. The new you is to be the one with the new belief system.

You cannot be attractive if you believe you're ugly. You cannot be fit if you believe you're unfit. You cannot become wealthy until you stop believing you're poor. You cannot become happy until you stop believing you're miserable. You cannot have fun until you stop believing you're boring. You cannot change until you release your limiting beliefs. It's as simple as that.

Will you now believe that you are truly, undeniably, ultimately, and completely worthy?

Will you believe that you are totally unique and that your uniqueness is your proof that you are worthy?

Will you believe that you are an eternal being and as such you have nothing to fear?

Will you believe that you are here on purpose and for a purpose?

Will you believe once and for all that this is your playground, the universe revolves around you, and this is your world to live in as you prefer?

Will you believe that all the people in your life are a gift to you so that you can grow and expand as you intended prior to your birth?

Will you believe that we are all one and we are all together, even if we sometimes appear separate?

Will you believe that you have everything you need to go from who you are now to who you want to be?

Will you believe that in this moment you have the power to alter your perspective?

Will you believe that everything you have lived, even if you judge it to be wrong, has led you to this point in your life, where you are clearer than you've ever been?

Will you believe that from here you can progress at speeds you once considered unreachable?

Will you believe that everything we have told you is true and for the purpose of helping you become who you really are?

Will you finally stop doubting what you really know inside?

Will you start listening to your inner self and realize that life can be lived on your terms if you just allow it?

If so, we salute you and we send you on your way. We are excited to see what life brings to you and we feel joy in the knowing that you will create the life you truly desire.

With all our love and our joy.

Joshua.

Special Section

Questions and Answers

Martina's Question

Dear Joshua,

For many years, 20 plus, I have experienced nearly constant lower back pain and neck pain. (I think the lower back pain may have been a result of a pulled muscle). I never let this slow me down or prevent me from doing any activities. I am a personal trainer and I work out almost every day. I have had countless chiropractic visits over the years, with varying degrees of relief. None of which has corrected the problem. This leads me to believe the pain must be from a vibrational misalignment.

Recently, I have experienced bouts of almost unbearable neck pain which radiates into my shoulder. It will resolve to a "manageable" level after a day or two but never goes away. I would like guidance as to how I can resolve the problem and correct my vibrational stance so the pain goes away.

Thanks,

Martina

Dear Martina,

Thank you for your important question. Our answer will help you tremendously, as well as many others who have similar issues with pain and other chronic bodily conditions. We appreciate that you are understanding that this is a vibrational issue, not a physical issue. You will resolve this issue by working on your vibration, not by fixing your body.

We will start by acknowledging that nothing with your body is wrong. Everything you have experienced is simply the manifestation of your habit of being over an extended period of time. Once you change the way you view your life, your conditions, and the people in your life, your pain will fade away. However, as with any condition, which has persisted over time, the condition has become a part of who you are. Therefore, you must change who you have been and become who you really are.

There is the version of you that has been living and there is a higher version of you. You will need to seek that higher version. This has been your objective your entire life, but you have been resisting the work that must be done to bring you to this version. You hold onto the pain as an excuse not to live up to who you really are. This is a very common situation.

In order for you to receive the benefit of our answer, you must release your stubborn attachment to what you think is true or not true. For you to move forward, you must allow us to enter the realm of your possibility. You must have faith that what we are telling you is for your benefit and is the absolute truth. You must release your limiting beliefs about who you are, for they hold you apart from who you are meant to be.

All unwanted bodily conditions stem from inner conflict. You want something, but you hold yourself apart from what is wanted. If you just went with the flow of life and allowed ease into your life, you would not have any unwanted bodily conditions. But for you, it is like you've been rowing upstream most of your life. You are paddling against the current of what is. You have been fighting the conditions of your life.

You are constantly thinking that this should not be as it is and that should be different and "Why isn't this working?" and "Why are these people acting this way?" This is fighting against the current of life and that is the cause of your pain. If you find yourself annoyed with someone or something, that is your pain. If you find yourself complaining about something, that is the basis of your pain.

We are not going to fix you, because nothing is wrong. The pain is just an indication of your pattern of thought, your chronic view of life, and your belief that things need to be fixed in order for you to be happy. You can't have things fixed and then be happy. That is the reverse of how it works. You can't relieve your pain and then go on to be who you want to be. You must become who you want to be and then your pain will ease and fade. You can't change who you are in order to relieve the pain. You must be content with the pain, acknowledging that it is the pain that brought you to us, that gave you this answer, and that it was the pain that finally led you to become who you have always wanted to be. You change and then the conditions will change.

It is interesting to see how you first started to notice the pain but did not change. The pain was a message, but its message was ignored. You went to healers for a cure, but they could not initiate the change that needed to take place. The only cure is for you to start living as you intended prior to your birth. Once you stop holding back, you will start to flourish and will feel better than you have felt since childhood.

If we were to tell you that there is a treatment for your pain, would you try it? If we told you there was a healer who used herbs, physical manipulation, and acupuncture that could cure you, would you visit her? If the treatment took two visits per day, consisting of two hours per visit and cost $200 per treatment, would you endure it. If the treatment lasted two years but you were cured forever, would you still endure the treatment? If you would, then what we will ask of you will seem easy by comparison. If you would not, then you have already decided to live with your condition.

Here is our recommendation. This will be very difficult for you because you have lived a certain way for a very long time and what we are going to ask of you will be extreme given who you have been up to this moment in time. But had you not been this strong-willed, this stubborn, you would never have been brought to this important moment in your life. Everything you have lived up to this moment has been perfect so that you have been brought to this place where you now stand. Are you prepared for your treatment?

You must undergo a radical, all-encompassing change in the way you have been living life up to this point. At first you will find the change difficult, but as time goes by you will begin to enjoy it. In less than a year you will look back at this moment and not even recognize the person you were just a year before. In this change, you are not required to quit your job, move to a mountain, or abandon your friends and family. The change we are asking for all takes place inside. You must decide to change your mind.

We are asking you to create a balance between what you experience in your outer world and what you experience in the inner world of your thoughts, beliefs, feelings, attitudes, moods, etc. Start seeing everything as right and good. Start viewing every person as loving and kind. Allow the conditions around you to be as they are and start to appreciate the beauty and loveliness of everything in your life. Start appreciating yourself and start loving yourself.

Pay attention to your mood and seek to feel good regardless of the pain. Make it a priority to be in a good mood and do not let the conditions you observe take you out of your good mood. Allow the conditions to improve over time, but never strive to attack the conditions as they exist in the moment. Allow everything to be as it is and start believing that it is all good.

Start to meditate for fifteen minutes each and every day of your life. Don't make excuses or give reasons why you cannot meditate. Make it your first priority every day. You have lived too long in the outer world and now it is time to reconnect with your inner world. Be patient and allow yourself time to move toward inner peace.

Stop being right, for being right is a self-defense mechanism. You are worthy and you do not need to prove yourself to anyone. Allow others to have their opinions and allow them to be wrong. It is not your place to create in the lives of others.

Start thinking of yourself as the person you really are. Start thinking bigger. Start being bolder. Start caring more about yourself and about others. Start living the life you want to live, regardless of the pain, the doubt, and the fear. Stop making excuses. Start doing only that which excites you. Stop worrying, for there is nothing to worry about. Start having fun every single day. Make your passions and interests the focus of your daily activities. Stop caring what others think.

But most important of all, start appreciating your pain rather than condemning it. It is the pain that has brought you to this place on the edge of becoming who you really are. We know who that person is and we think you're magnificent.

You are loved so much more than you can imagine by so many who are cheering you on.

Joshua

Debra Jo's Question

Good Morning Joshua,

First I want to thank you for the way you have changed my life as a result of reading your words transmitted through Gary. What fun it is to be in on this amazing transformation and clarification!!

Yesterday afternoon I was struck by a horrendous case of sinusitis. My head was throbbing, huge sneezing, couldn't breathe. I was really SICK! I kept saying to Frank - I don't get this! I am high-flying, healthy and happy. What is this all about??? I am seeing masterpieces in weeds on the side of the road!! I should not be sick.

Frank said maybe I was sick because something worse would have happened to me (I had been planning to paint the top of my giant furniture) and I was in a better situation than I might have been.

And then this morning I opened my eyes and I was completely well. I know in most people's reality, a sinus infection takes about a week to get over. So I was surprised and delighted to see I had NO symptoms and was happy and healthy again.

So my questions is: could getting sick and then getting well be more about getting well than getting sick? And how do I eliminate the getting sick at all??!!

Thank you in advance for your wonderful words!

All The Best,

Debra Jo

Dear Debra Jo,

This is a wonderfully powerful question. We are so glad you asked it, especially in your present high-flying state of being. There are many reasons you get sick and they all have to do with either the desire to be sick, an inner conflict, or a lack of balance. Let's look at each of these in order.

Why would anyone have a desire to be sick? Just think of your childhood to find the answer to this one. Being sick allowed you to stay home from school and escape whatever it was that was going on that day. You got to stay in bed, maybe you were coddled by a parent, maybe you read books or watched TV. While you may not have felt good in your condition, it was better than going to school that day. So now, in your adulthood, you bring on colds (or accidents) to escape certain things you do not want to do.

Many, many illnesses arise from conflict within. If you think of yourself one way but judge yourself another way, you have inner conflict. Your illness is a result of this conflict. It is a sign that you are not aligning with who you really are. This is always a good thing and it is always small and inconsequential. If you align with who you really are, the illness fades. If you remain in conflict about anything, the illness comes back, often worse, until you understand the message the illness is sending you.

The third way an illness or accident can come to you is when you are out of balance in your life. Being out of balance can happen when you are focused on one aspect of your life with a lack of attention to other areas you also deem important. In this case, it is your opinion of balance and your desire to correct that imbalance that leads to the illness or accident. Once the illness has come, you slow down and regain your balance.

You also come out of balance when your vibration rises too quickly for your system to catch up. This is primarily what is happening to you. It only lasts a short while because you are able to regain your balance and catch up to your rising vibration very quickly.

But we would very much like to talk about Frank's thoughts for a moment. Frank suggested that the condition arose to prevent something unwanted from happening. We do not disagree with this, but we want to applaud Frank for looking at this unwanted thing in a very positive way.

When you are faced with a condition that is unwanted, whether it is a cold, a pain in your body, or socks on the floor, it is helpful to view the present condition in the most positive way possible. When you change your perspective in the moment, you change a limiting belief. In this case, your limiting belief is that illness is bad. We know you are trying to show us that your perspective on this subject has already changed, and it has, but in the broader sense you still see some conditions as negative.

When you believe that something is negative, you have uncovered a limiting belief. This is okay for it is quite natural. As you ascend to higher vibrations, however, you will want to practice softening your limiting beliefs in all areas. If you believe that something should be this way or that way, and you are annoyed by the present condition, you have uncovered a limiting belief with regard to that subject. When you change your perspective to see only the positive aspects, you automatically diminish the intensity of your limiting beliefs. This takes practice and patience.

More than anyone else you know, you want to live a limitless existence. The practice of seeing the positive in all things you once considered negative is your tool to limitlessness. We see that you are progressing extremely well as you discover the masterpieces in the weeds.

Love,

Joshua

Jennifer's Questions

Dear Joshua,

1) Are there different levels of consciousness in nonphysical, like there are in a physical experience? In other words, when a person reemerges into nonphysical, do they have the same knowledge base as the group of beings in Joshua, or do they have to aspire to that level and go through stages of learning like we do here?

There are no levels as you would define them from your frame of reference. One is not higher than another, one does not aspire to a certain level of consciousness, one is not judged for how far one has progressed - one just expands. And as the one expands, the consciousness of all expands. You might have lived as a butterfly, but now the life of a butterfly would not be interesting because you have expanded beyond that.

In the nonphysical, you simply do what you want because it's interesting and you move in these directions with others who are also interested, so the group moves as and is as one. Since you have no resistance in the nonphysical, you possess the infinite knowledge of the universe and you allow that intelligence to flow through you. You have the same abilities here on earth in your physical form if you are interested in something and if you allow the intelligence to flow.

2) Is there ever confusion when you've made the transition to the non-physical? In other words, does anyone not realize they are dead (like the popular belief to explain ghost activity).

Some are prepared for the death experience and their transition is joyous and easy. Some of those who have been particularly grounded in physical reality have some confusion, but it does not last long. The transition for most is peaceful and easy and the memory you have of what the nonphysical realm is comes back quickly.

Ghosts can be many different things depending on the circumstances. They can be thought forms resonating with the observer, they can be images coming from a parallel universe or time, they can be nonphysical entities projecting form to initiate communication, and they can be the imaginations of those who fear that sort of phenomenon. It depends on the emotional state of the observer and their vibrational frequency.

The observer is always a match to the occurrence and thus they have attracted it. However, it is not what you describe, as someone who does not accept they are dead. Those who have trouble transitioning are simply adjusting to the environment they have forgotten. They will come to remember the nonphysical environment, because it is their home. It is similar to waking up from an intense dream and not knowing where you are. As soon as you look around, the knowledge of where you are comes back to you.

3) *When death is imminent, do we leave our bodies before experiencing the physical pain of the death experience?*

If you have ever seen a gazelle caught in the jaws of a lion, you have seen it relax. When death is imminent, most simply relax and allow the process to take its natural course. There is always the initial struggle, but once the outcome is known there is a release of tension and there is no pain. Pain is caused by the non-acceptance of the conditions. You only feel pain when you fight against what is.

4) *When we reincarnate, do we have to start all over again, or do we keep any of our spiritual "knowledge"? For example, if I reach a high level of connectedness in this lifetime, when I start my next life do I lose that knowing? If so, what is the point, and if not, how soon can I get back up to speed? Does it get easier each time and will I find alignment at a younger and younger age? Or is this a silly question since time is an illusion and all our lives are simultaneous? If that is the case, does each incarnated version of us benefit when one excels in alignment?*

Once you have expanded, you never go back. Once you have reached a certain state of expansion and beingness, you expand more. There is no regression. You move forward, never backward. Whether it is in this life, the nonphysical life, or in the next life, you are always moving forward.

You are a master of the laws of the universe. There are very few who have reached your level. We are telling you this because you can handle what we are saying. We are not saying that your life should be easy, perfect, and without challenges. We are not saying you have all the answers, for that would lead you to believe you should be more than you are. You have a knowledge of the mechanism of the universe that few possess. But having that knowledge and applying it are two different things. You will never feel that you are applying your knowledge to the best of your abilities. This is a trap that all who have such knowledge fall into. You think, "If I know so much more than the average human, why do I still experience mundane human problems? Why am I not creating my life as I desire in every detail and in every moment?"

Here is our answer. In another life you may have been a monk living in a monastery and meditating all day. You came to a certain level of spiritual expansion, but there was not much going on. Your access to your inner self and to universal intelligence was open, but your vibration was lower and life was slower. This is the easy way to this whole thing of knowing what you know.

So you wanted more experience and more expansion. You came to this life, to this time, to your parents, to this fast-moving environment, and also to coming to know the laws of the universe in a time when most were ignorant of these laws. Imagine the difference between the life of a monk and this life. Now you have expanded so much more as a result of everything you've been able to do in this life. You are now more than you have ever been and you will expand more from here.

5) When something happens in life and I recognize just escaping a "near miss", like avoiding an accident for example, or acknowledging something could have been a LOT worse... I always express gratitude for my safety and I'm left feeling like maybe it really didn't go so well but I got a chance to do it over and have a better outcome. Almost like I was given a "do-over" and my memory of it not going well is erased. Am I crazy or is this sometimes what happens when it's not our choice to transition yet?

There are two things we would like to express here. First, near misses are sometimes just that. The near miss made you feel like you got lucky and the car just missed you. But whether it was an inch or a mile, you were missed. If a bird flew at you and turned at the last second, it would seem like a near miss. But if you were looking the other way and never noticed the bird, it would not seem so incredible. You would not even notice the near miss.

The universe is working to get everything everyone wants and there is a lot going on that you are completely unaware of. Sometimes stuff happens that seems like it was meant for you, but it wasn't. You were just in the vicinity, but you were never the object of the manifestation event, which was meant for someone else.

Second, you have a choice in all of experience and you can choose when to transition and when to stay here. However, if you choose to transition, you do so far before your day of transition. When the moment comes, you will be ready.

Sometimes it seems like you were meant to transition and something intervened to save your life. If you did not want to make your transition, you were not saved; this was simply a powerful manifestation event that was created to help you alter a limiting belief. Usually the limiting belief is that you are not safe. Sometimes near-death experiences help people realize what they need to know to move forward.

6) *Are some physical lifetimes in another environment – like on other planets, or even different dimensions here on earth? And they are happening simultaneously since time and space are illusions, correct?*

Yes, all of your lives are happening simultaneously and that is hard to understand in your linear experience of life and time. When we say you expand in each life, you believe that one life follows another and that you ascend this staircase, expanding to a new level with each step. However, think of the universe and how you know it's expanding despite time. You can use your telescopes to see the birth of stars that were born eons ago. Just think of your life in these terms, where you are expanding outwards continuously.

7) *Since it's been documented that some people are able to recall memories from past lives, can some also recall nonphysical experiences from before birth?*

You can recall what it feels like to be in the nonphysical and as a child this is much easier for you because you have not yet tuned your five physical senses to this physical reality. However, once you've spent time in this physical environment, you cannot relate to what the nonphysical is. It is too different.

It is much easier to recall past lives, because you have the same references. You know what it is like to live in physical reality so you can relate to it in another time. By slowing down your vibration (through a process such as hypnosis) you might be able to connect to the vibration of a past life. Notice though how most people who recall past lives recall the past and not the future.

If all lives are happening simultaneously, then it would make sense that you could recall a future life just as easily as a past life? However, since you have no point of reference for the future, you find it more difficult to believe you can recall it. Since you have to believe something for it to exist in your reality, you can't recall the future. If you believed you could, you would.

8) *Since we are all truly connected, all of our "inner selves" are focused in groups and we exist in the nonphysical at the same time, why is having a physical experience, in which we do not remember past lives, beneficial?*

If you remembered your past life, you would be bogged down by the lower vibrational frequency of that life. Once you have raised your frequency to a level that allows you to be born in this time, you cannot exist at a lower frequency. This life would seem overwhelming. It already seems overwhelming at times. Imagine what your monk would feel like if he were brought into your life. He couldn't handle it.

You can see the older people of your society having tremendous difficulty with new technology. This is not because they are not intelligent, it's because they resonate at a lower frequency. There are things your children can do with technology that your parents cannot. It's not intelligence; it's vibration. The memory of a past life could only exist if you vibrated at that frequency. Since you are at a new, higher frequency, the past life (or future life) does not exist in your memory.

9) *Children are born at a higher vibrational frequency. How does a young person (or child) compare vibrationally to a much older person who is spiritually connected?*

You are talking about two different vibrations. A vibration that is aligned with the earth and physical reality at this time is high. The young person is ready for this environment, the other young people of this environment, and the technology that's being created today. This is a different vibration than older people have access to, no matter what their level of spiritual connection.

Spiritual connection has another vibration. You connect to your inner self, to us, to unlimited intelligence, by reaching a higher vibration on the spiritual plane rather than on the earth plane. So there are many planes of vibration. In this case we are talking about the earth (or physical) plane and the spiritual (or nonphysical) plane.

You were a match to the earth plane the day you were born and hence you were born. Generally, you do not keep up to speed with the rising vibration of the earth plane. This is why older people are nostalgic and believe that life was better in "their day." Those born today are up to speed with the earth plane of today. But they too will fall behind and new ones will come to renew the planet. This is how the earth plane was designed.

Reaching a higher vibration on the spiritual plane can be done at any time in life and this plane is more static. While the earth plane is rapidly increasing in vibrational frequency, the spiritual plane is more fixed. Once you reach resonance with the spiritual plane while existing in physical reality, you have access to infinite intelligence and communication with us and with your inner self. It is much easier for you to reach our level on the spiritual plane than it is to keep up with the earth plane.

10) *Is having communication with nonphysical intelligence, like Joshua or Abraham, really talking with "God"?*

God is a reference to All That Is, which is hard to define in language you would understand. Everyone has been influenced by religion and society to have a certain image of God. Many believe they will be judged or that God will declare whether they are worthy to receive what they want. Many "fear" God, and so we do not use the term God. We use the term All That Is.

We understand that we are God only in the way that you understand that you are God too. We are part of All That Is just as you are part of All That Is. When you talk to us and think we are God, we talk to you and think you are God. We have access to infinite intelligence, just as you do.

We are speaking from a broader perspective and we teach you to see your world from our perspective.

    Joshua

For more information or
to ask Joshua your own question
please visit

www.theteachingsofjoshua.com

Made in the USA
San Bernardino, CA
29 September 2016